The Essential Public Manager

Public Policy and Management

Series Editor: Professor R.A.W. Rhodes, Department of Politics, University of Newcastle.

The effectiveness of public policies is a matter of public concern and the efficiency with which policies are put into practice is a continuing problem for governments of all political persuasions. This series contributes to these debates by publishing informed, in-depth and contemporary analyses of public administration, public policy and public management.

The intention is to go beyond the usual textbook approach to the analysis of public policy and management and to encourage authors to move debate about their issue forward. In this sense, each book describes current thinking and research and explores future policy directions. Accessibility is a key feature and, as a result, the series will appeal to academics and their students as well as to the informed practitioner.

Current titles:

Governing in the Information Age
Christine Bellamy and John A. Taylor

Delivering Welfare (2nd Edn)
Tony Butcher

Policy Transfer and British Social Policy
David P. Dolowitz *et al.*

Whose Utility?
John Ernst

Providing Quality in the Public Sector
Lucy Gaster, Amanda Squires *et al.*

Quality in Public Services
Lucy Gaster

Enabling or Disabling Local Government
Steve Leach *et al.*

Comparing Policy Networks
David Marsh (ed.)

The Essential Public Manager
Christopher Pollitt

The Changing World of Top Officials
R.A.W. Rhodes and P. Weller (eds)

Decentralizing the Civil Service
R.A.W. Rhodes *et al.*

Understanding Governance
R.A.W. Rhodes

The Appointed State
Chris Skelcher

Social Care Markets
Gerald Wistow *et al.*

New Managerialism
Spencer Zifcak

The Essential Public Manager

Christopher Pollitt

Open University Press

Open University Press
McGraw-Hill Education
McGraw-Hill House
Shoppenhangers Road
Maidenhead
Berkshire
SL6 2QL
United Kingdom

email: enquiries@openup.co.uk
world wide web: www.openup.co.uk

and Two Penn Plaza, New York, NY 10121–2289, USA

First Published 2003
Reprinted 2004, 2006

A catalogue record of this book is available from the British Library.

ISBN 0 335 21232 8 (pb)   0 335 21233 6 (hb)

Library of Congress Cataloging-in-Publication Data
Pollitt, Christopher.
      The essential public manager/Christopher Pollitt.
         p.   cm. – (Public policy and management)
      Includes bibliographical references and index.
      ISBN 0-335-21233-6 – ISBN 0-335-21232-8 (pbk.)
      1. Public administration. I. Title. II. Series.
JF1315. P658 2003
351–dc21
                                             2002035537

Typeset by RefineCatch Limited, Bungay, Suffolk
Printed in Great Britain by Bell and Bain Ltd, Glasgow

FOR HILKKA

Always essential, occasionally (thank goodness),
my manager

Contents

Preface

This book is a hybrid. I have taken the risk of trying to combine two apparently conflicting ingredients: a serious subject matter and a conversational style. Hybrids can be very fruitful (or at least useful – the mule comes to mind) or, on the other hand, they may turn out to be barren.

The serious subject – public management and public administration – is weighty because it affects us all. Good public management is an essential part of any civilized modern society. Attempts, in various countries, by various politicians (UK Prime Minister Margaret Thatcher and US President Ronald Reagan among them) to 'roll back the state' did not, in fact, transform the 'big picture' that much. Public spending remains a substantial percentage of the gross national product in every Western European and North American country (indeed, after 20 years of cuts and 'wars on waste' in a number of states this fraction is *higher* than it was at the beginning). Governments continue to carry responsibility for a vast range of services, which touch their citizens at almost every point in their lives. *Public* administration continues to affect the purity of our water and foodstuffs, the adequacy of our health care, the quality of our education, the financial stability of our old age, the extent of gender and ethnic discrimination, the readiness of our armed forces and the effectiveness of our systems of justice and law enforcement. It also strongly influences the sustainability of our natural environment, the attractiveness of particular localities for economic development, the cleanliness of our streets and the safety of our various means of transport. When terrorist attacks demolished the twin towers of the World Trade Center in New York, President George W. Bush, in his attempt to rally a shocked nation, stood in the ruins with his arm around the shoulders of a firefighter – a memorable image – and declared the staff of the emergency services to be true American heroes. (However, within a few months of their heroism, the New York City fire and police services found themselves facing heavy staff and expenditure cuts as the new Mayor wrestled with a cash crisis (Usborne 2002).)

In most European states the public sector still accounts for a considerable percentage of the total workforce, and a large percentage of the job destinations of the most highly educated. In some the public sector remains the main location for professional jobs for women. Despite periodic cuts and downsizings in many countries, President Clinton was just plain wrong when, in 1996, he announced that 'the era of big government is over'.

Nevertheless, much *has* changed. In many countries there have been intensive and unrelenting efforts to manage public organizations and public programmes in new ways. Privatization, contracting out, public–private partnerships, decentralization, internal markets, re-engineering, citizens charters, citizens' panels, citizens' juries, codes of public service ethics, one-stop shops, performance audit, evaluation – the list of new initiatives is endless. The boundaries between the public sector, the voluntary sector and the commercial sector seem to have become considerably more complex and ambiguous. The literature on these changes is enormous, the rhetoric – from politicians, public managers and academics – incessant. *The Essential Public Manager* is an attempt to make some sense of this mass of material.

Thus I wanted to find a (moderately) novel way of presenting what we know (and don't know) about the enduringly vast range of public activities. My ambition for the book is that it will speak both to students in universities and colleges and to those practising public managers who are occasionally drawn to read a book about their work. The hope, therefore, is that it will draw in those who are beginning to study the subject seriously, and also provoke some reflection from those who are already practising the craft. Further, I would like to think that teachers and lecturers in public administration and public management will enjoy using the book – it contains a good deal of material that I have found useful in teaching, and there is undoubtedly more 'mileage' and more 'angles' in the material presented between these covers than I have been able to see or exploit in my own classes.

Despite my continuing and occasionally passionate interest in the subject, I have been reluctantly obliged to recognize that many public management/public administration texts (very much including my own) are actually rather boring to many of their readers. From decades of discussion with students, both young and 'mature', I gain the impression that only a few find much of the published material particularly memorable or stimulating. (I have taught in the UK, two other European countries, and the USA, and I had this impression confirmed, in slightly different ways, in each case.) Indeed, the whole subject suffers from an 'image problem'. Mentioning that one is studying 'public management' (or, even more, 'public administration') seldom evokes the same *frisson* of interest from the casual listener as, say, psychology, anthropology or even fashionable concoctions such as environmental studies or theatre science. Nor does it tend to generate the initial respect which follows from the announcement that one is studying econometrics or pure mathematics.

This dull image is a pity, because – I would energetically maintain – the subject of public management has many attractive qualities. It is complex, rapidly changing, socially 'relevant', intellectually challenging (and so on). And beyond (or alongside) academic study there exist many managerial roles within the public sector which are subtle, complex, fascinating, spiritually rewarding and quite indispensable – at least according to my vision of a civilized society of the twenty-first century. Thus, after many years either practising or studying public management,

I formed the ambition of writing a book on my subject that would be engaging and sometimes even amusing or intriguing. You will judge soon enough how sensible – or misguided – was that aspiration.

What I have done is to take a limited number of core issues in public management and use conversations and *vignettes* as the vehicles for rehearsing different points and perspectives. Thus, each chapter takes one particular issue or theme – the differences between the public and the private sectors, let us say – and makes it the subject of an interaction between two or more characters representing different styles or points of view. Alternatively, it tells a story of some case – either a real one or a compendium of several such cases – and/or it records the voices or writings of real public managers.

Each issue has been chosen on the basis of two criteria. First, it has to be a topic which has featured prominently in the academic literature on public administration and public management – usually for some time. In other words it is in some sense a 'classic' or 'hardy perennial', not just a passing fashion. Second, it also has to be a topic which is well-represented in contemporary public administration and public management curricula at universities. This is because I want the book to be directly useful to students.

While there is bound to be some element of artificiality about these mini-dramas, there is also, I hope, a strong dose of realism. Much of the discourse is taken, word-for-word (or almost so) from conversations I have taken part in or overheard – as a civil servant myself, as a teacher of students in public management, as a researcher debating points with my peers, as a consultant advising various public sector organizations, nationally and internationally, or simply as someone who consumes his share of newspapers, periodicals and television programmes. The text is also laced with extracts from actual documents, from official speeches and debates, and from research interview records from the various projects I have been involved in over the years.

Of course, there is a danger that a book which aims to treat serious, scholarly matters in an informal way will end up as merely self-indulgent. The reviewers will surely give their opinions on that score, but the views of the ordinary readers will matter most. If enough of them (you) find the book interesting, my experiment will have been worthwhile.

The text will by no means, however, be lacking in scholarly and scientific references. While the conversations and cases themselves remain largely unencumbered in this respect, most chapters conclude with several more 'academic' sections. First, there may be an analytical commentary on the conversation or case. Second, there are one or more subsections outlining the background to the topic and offering some key concepts and ideas. Finally, there is a guide to further reading, in which I have tried to select the most enjoyable, stimulating or important works in the field. Thus most of the chapters include the following elements (not always in the same sequence):

- Conversation, quotations or case.
- Analytical commentary on the conversation/case.

- Academic background – key ideas and research findings.
- Guide to further reading.

Of course, the list of things which this book is *not* is endless. In particular, it is not a handbook of management skills, and neither is it at all a guide to the institutions of the public sector (no organization charts of the National Health Service – I have lost count of the number of books in which they have been published, only to be embarrassed by a rapidly-following re-organization, sometimes before the book reaches the shops). Neither is theory given a prominent role. While I will yield to no-one in my conviction that theory is fundamental to academic endeavour (and, for that matter, to everyday life) its place in this book is in the basement rather than the front parlour. By that I mean that the academic findings which are reported here are, of course, theory-saturated, but that it is not a main purpose of this text to excavate, clarify and compare different theories. They will be dealt with as and when they arise in the course of treating substantive issues (and they are extensively referenced in the guidance sections) but they are not to the forefront of this particular project. Finally, this is not a history of the subject; a teasing out of intellectual threads and ever-shifting academic boundaries. That task has already been successfully accomplished by others (for example, at least for the USA – where most public administration scholars are – Larry Lynn's interesting 1996 book *Public Management as Art, Science and Profession*).

There is one other limitation that must be mentioned. This book – while I hope reasonably cosmopolitan and international – is not comparative, at least not in the full sense of carrying out a disciplined and systematic comparison between similar institutions or processes within different national or regional jurisdictions. As I am a comparativist, this absence is a matter of considerable regret, but, after some cogitation, I decided that it would be a bridge too far. The book's scope is ambitious enough. Nevertheless, I do make use of examples and references from many countries, and I certainly refer to European Union and intergovernmental issues. Thus, although the balance of examples used are from the UK, most of the issues and principles discussed are thoroughly international, and readers from at least Western Europe, North America and Australasia should have no difficulty in recognizing items from their own national agendas in these pages.

To sum up, I have tried to write a text which, first, addresses some of the core substantive issues of public management; second, does so in an inviting and accessible way and, third, offers the reader a sense of what academic research and thinking can contribute to our understanding of the field. This last point is perhaps the most important. The world of the public manager has become more and more heavily populated with organizations and individuals selling 'quick fixes'. Fashions (Zero-Based Budgeting, TQM, re-engineering, PPPs, e-governance) come and go. 'Skills training' is delivered in short bursts, often fairly disconnected from the rest of the manager's activities. 'Research' comes to mean an afternoon browsing through a keyword search on the internet. Public managers are sent on MBAs or other generic management training courses, in which issues specific and peculiar to the public sector are scarcely mentioned (but, on the other hand, social work child protection officers may solemnly be taught marketing). The impression is perhaps created that management is little more than a 'skills module' that can be 'picked up' in a few weeks.

This book stands directly against that kind of generic, superficially 'globalized' thinking. It asserts that there are enduring and distinctive issues – indeed, dilemmas – in the public sector, even if there are also many points of commonality between public sector management and management in the commercial or voluntary sectors. It allies itself with the view that management (in both public and private sectors) is a significantly context-dependent craft – that individual techniques and processes which work well in one context may fail miserably in another. So it is vital to think about *both* the instrument or practice, *and* the context into which it is to be placed. The study of public management as a partly distinct field is therefore founded on the proposition that the contexts in which public managers find themselves practising are often unique, or rare, or at least sufficiently *dissimilar* from those faced by managers in private firms or voluntary associations to make straightforward transfers of practice very doubtful.

This work is also founded on a second assumption: that independent academic research (with all its occasionally tiresome conceptual, methodological and theoretical baggage) provides a different and extremely valuable kind of understanding. At its best – painstaking, sceptical, methodologically thorough, alive to context and history – academic research provides a deep and deeply warranted understanding which it is only very rarely possible to achieve in any other way. This is, therefore, a book which stands on the shoulders of many others. In it I seek to render what must be literally millions of hours of serious research and thinking (some thousands of them my own) into something more satisfying than a snack but less of a challenge to the digestive system than a heavy academic banquet.

Christopher Pollitt
Järventaka, Finland

Acknowledgements

This book has a long list of references, which is one kind of acknowledgement. In addition, however, I must thank a number of people who helped and encouraged me with this project (though of course they bear no responsibility for it, and in some cases would certainly disagree with some line or other which I have taken). This large group includes Anne Marie Berg, Johnston Birchall, Richard Chapman, Jack Dowie, Barbara Goodwin, Ian Hawkesby, Chris Huxham, John Leach, Tom Pollitt, Peter Roberts, Chris Skelcher, Amanda Smullen, Bram Steijn, Hilkka Summa, Colin Talbot, Sandra van Thiel and Rob van Tulder.

1

Public sector, private sector – where would we be without a few good stereotypes?

Introduction

First of all, we will look at some assorted opinions, framed within a commentary from me. After that there is an argument in a pub. These two opening sections are simply intended to start some ideas running about public/private similarities and differences. Subsequently, in the later parts of the chapter, there will be an attempt to summarize what (some) academics have proposed concerning the public/private distinction, and to see what relevant evidence has been turned up. Is there really a distinct species of *public* managers, or are there just managers?

Some opinions

> . . . the best management is a true science, resting upon clearly defined laws, rules and principles . . . the fundamental principles of scientific management are applicable to all kinds of human activities, from our simplest individual acts to the work of our greatest corporations.
>
> (Frederick Winslow Taylor, founder of the 'scientific management' movement, in his famous *The Principles of Scientific Management*, 1913: 5–7)

Well, this is a clear start. Management is management is management, says Taylor. There is no suggestion here that *public* sector management should or would be any different from *private* sector management. Notice also that Taylor claims that management is (or should be) a *science*. It will have immutable laws and principles. This evidently appealed to Lenin, who was a noted admirer of 'scientific management'.

There are many points which could be made about Taylor's formulation. One is that it is not clear what for him is the scope or domain of management. For example, where does management end and policy-making or strategy-making begin – did he even recognize such a distinction? In fact much of Taylor's work was done at what would now be regarded as fairly low levels of management – the supervision of manual and manual/mechanized tasks. So it is an open question how far such 'principles' as could be derived from these studies could be stretched to apply to other situations. Would they, for example, translate from the manufacturing settings in which Taylor carried out his research to service contexts? Would they apply in the public sector as well as the private sector – to the management of a team of social workers for example, or the management of an export promotion unit? Certainly Taylor seemed to think so – 'applicable to all human activities' he wrote – and so did many other people who subsequently tried to apply Taylorian principles to government.

A second question is what Taylor meant by 'science'. It sounds as though he had what we would now regard as rather an old-fashioned view of its nature. Most philosophers of science nowadays would not think of it as an activity principally concerned with generating unchanging laws which could be applied in every situation.

We move on to our second opinion:

> While the similarities between governmental and non-governmental organisations are greater than is generally supposed, some differences never-theless exist. Most often these are differences in degree rather than kind.
> (Simon, Smithburg and Thompson 1950: 10. Nobel prize-winning Herbert Simon was probably the single best-known organization theorist of the twentieth century. This quote comes from an early, classic work on public administration.)

Simon *et al.* say that there *are* differences between government and non-governmental organizations, but from his perspective these are not fundamental. This sounds different from Taylor, although it should be noted that Simon is talking about *organizations* and Taylor is talking about *management* – not quite the same thing.

> Public and private management: are they fundamentally alike in all unimportant respects?
> (Allison 1983. Graham Allison was a prominent American decision theorist and policy analyst.)

Allison shifted the balance of his assessment further towards the 'different' pole than Simon. In the article from which this quotation comes he acknowledged that managers in large private corporations and in government departments shared common tasks, such as objective-setting, staffing and so on, but argued that the *content* of these activities, and the *circumstances* in which they were performed, were fundamentally different. He considered it unlikely that many private sector management skills or practices could be directly transferred into the public sector.

> Experience has indicated that a wide range of essential services can be pro-vided better by government than by any private business arrangement thus far invented, or, as in the case of basic research, will be undersupplied because of public goods aspects, if left to competitive markets.
> We do not need to reinvent government. Governmental organizations are needed, as they have always been needed, to enforce the rules of the game (including the rules of market contracting), to facilitate coordination

of private organizations, and to perform services that are unlikely to be performed effectively by the private sector.

(Simon 2000)

This was the same Herbert Simon as in the earlier quotation. I was there to hear him speak, with marvellous clarity and authority, 50 years after the publication of *Public Administration*, and 65 years after he first began to study public administration. But here the emphasis is different from the first quote. The argument here is that government is indispensable because it does some things better than the private sector (including enforcing the rules of the game that make modern commercial life possible, and providing services which would be undersupplied or unequally supplied if left to market firms). So this is not to say that all public sector management is completely different from private sector management, but it is to say that there are certain roles and functions which government performs better.

> The government is not GB Ltd. It does not have a strategic 'core' business . . .
> It comprises a whole range of activities, many of which have no connection
> with each other . . . Nor is there normally the test of profitability or the
> concept of profit control. There is no systematic way, other than the general
> philosophy of the party in power, whereby the benefits from resources for,
> say defence, health or motorways can be compared and evaluated.
>   (Hunt 1983: 1–2. Sir John Hunt was the Secretary to the (UK) Cabinet
>   in the late 1970s and early 1980s – under Mr Callaghan's Labour
>   administration and Mrs Thatcher's Conservative one.)

Here is a practitioner – a top civil servant – whose experience leads him to believe that government organizations are fundamentally different from private sector corporations. Notice, though that he is talking about the whole of government, and he is taking a view from near the summit. Even if he is correct, it would still be possible that, at a lower level, general management principles could be applied to specific tasks – the purchase of office supplies, for example, or the issue of licences.

> . . . the capacity to distinguish clearly between politics and administration;
> between public and private; and between national and international, is
> fundamental to territorial, representative democracy. If voters are deprived of
> that capacity, political accountability is bound to fade away.
>   (Jørgensen 1999: 566)

Jørgensen – a Danish academic – here goes wider and deeper than Sir John Hunt. He argues that the very concept of liberal democracy, as it has developed in Western Europe over the past century or so, is founded on a distinction between public and private sectors (and, note, upon two further distinctions – between politics and administration and between national and international). As we will see throughout the remainder of this book, over the past couple of decades there have been significant changes along all three borderlines. But if we cannot distinguish a public sector, says Jørgensen, then we cannot apply to it the special procedures of democratic accountability that are part of the very definition of democratic government.

> It makes a big difference whether President Carter kisses the Empress Farah Dibah in private or in public.
>
> (van Gunsteren 1979: 258)

This neatly makes the point that identical actions can carry different meanings according to the location or sector in which they take place. The public sector is a very particular place, with some special characteristics (or, at least, so it will be argued later in this book). Imagine, for example, that a businesswoman representing a big company buys a lavish lunch for a businessman from another company who she is hoping to persuade to leave his firm and join hers. Nothing unusual about this. But now suppose that she buys the same meal for a civil servant in the ministry which regulates her sector of business. This raises an ethical issue – should the civil servant accept this kind of thing? (See Chapter 6 for more on public service ethics.)

> People in the public sector are more rooted in the concept that if its always been done in this way it must always be done in this way than any other group of people I've ever come across . . . It's not that there aren't wonderful people now with a tremendous commitment to public service, but you try getting change in the public sector and public services – I bear the scars on my back after two years of government.
>
> (Prime Minister Tony Blair, speaking to a group of 'venture capitalists' on 7 July 1999)

At the time, this speech received a lot of publicity. Not surprisingly, it rankled with many public service union leaders. Equally unsurprisingly, it seemed to go down fairly well with the immediate audience of venture capitalists. To thousands of teachers, doctors, nurses and social workers, exhausted from more than a decade of constant re-organizations and innovations and 'initiatives', the accusation that they were slow to change may have seemed a trifle bizarre, but one thing that can certainly be said for Blair's rhetoric was that it was tapping into a well-established stereotype – that of 'the bureaucracy' as stubborn and slow-moving. One or another version of this stereotype has proved a popular instrument for politicians of various persuasions over a very long period of time. We will have something to say about stereotypes of bureaucracy in Chapter 2.

> Surveys show that public managers often hold stereotypes about business managers and business organizations, and vice versa.
>
> (Rainey 1997: 60. Hal G. Rainey is an American academic who has probably written more – and more influentially – on public/private similarities and differences than any other author of the past quarter century.)

Stereotypes again – this last quotation takes us neatly into the argument in the pub.

The scene

[*'The Cricketers', a suburban pub in north-east England, 'themed' as a cricket pavilion. The decoration includes rather dusty sets of ancient bats and stumps mounted round the bar and faux-old prints of bewhiskered cricketers hanging on the wall. Three neighbours are 'having a quiet pint', though 'quiet' is something of an exaggeration, given the noise coming from the fruit machine and the overhead large-screen television, which is currently showing Gaelic football. Giles is a local social worker, Dave is the salesman at the Nissan car dealership on the main road. Jeremy is a recently retired primary headteacher. They are talking about their jobs.*]

Giles: Well, it's obvious that they are different, isn't it? The bottom line for you is profit, but for us it's public service.

Dave: Which makes us sound like the baddies and you the goodies. But are you really goodies, or just do-gooders? And even if you *are* doing good, shouldn't you do it efficiently? We *have* to be efficient, whereas if you and your mates operate inefficiently nothing happens except the taxpayers' money trickles quietly down the drain.

Giles: Huh! Your garage is so efficient that your beloved customers sometimes have to wait two months for the colour and model they want. You forget, my friend, that Kath tried to buy that midnight blue Micra from you last year. And anyway, if we *are* a bit shambolic occasionally, it is probably because we are being re-organized every couple of months. I wish they'd just leave me alone to get on with my job.

Dave: Yeh, but what *is* your job? People want cars – and they pay good money for them, but who actually wants your lot? Hardly a month goes by without something on the news about social workers messing up a child protection case or finding an old lady who's been lying dead at home for three weeks. I mean, what is it you are really trying to do? Why interfere with people's lives if you can't offer them a real alternative?

Giles: It's OK for you to say that. Because you only deal with people who have money. If they don't have the money you send them away. We deal with the people who have no money, and not much else besides. Yes – don't look at me like that – society shuns them, so we end up having to take care of them. Then we get abused by people like you for doing so. What would you prefer – to let fathers beat up their children and old people starve in their hovels? There are actually millions of these folk, in one way or another – in fact I bet someone in your family gets help from us. But you are basing your whole view on a handful of extreme cases which creep into the media. Where, of course, they get exaggerated and misreported. Maybe I should judge the car trade on the basis of the three worst cases each year – they sometimes reach the newspapers as well?

Dave: Since it's your round, I'll accept that last point as fair comment. But, all the same, you do have a bit of an image problem, don't you? I mean, a lot of you social workers don't even look efficient – jeans and sweaters aren't exactly *à la mode* you know.

Giles: Oh, come off it! You all have to wear suits – it's just the uniform, isn't it? As if you can read off efficiency from the clothes people wear – like Robert Maxwell always wore expensive suits, so his business was fine, was it?

Jeremy: I worked in state schools and private schools, and I didn't notice any glaring differences in efficiency. If anything the state schools had to be more efficient, because they were more strapped for resources. The big difference isn't so much the one between public and private. It's between those jobs where you sell things and those where you provide a service. And anyway, schools aren't mainly about being efficient – they are about teaching kids. Efficiency is desirable, yes, but in the end it is not the top priority. It's really about achieving a good education.

Dave: OK, but this service versus selling idea doesn't really fit, does it Jeremy? The first thing they teach us on the salesmen's training course is that we aren't just selling cars, we are providing a service. Customer loyalty is the big thing, and if we are going to get that then we have to provide an integrated service – sales, after-sales service, maintenance, spares – a continuing relationship for years and years.

Giles: Salesmen's training course? Don't you have any women in your team then? That's another thing – I can't scratch my ear at work without thinking of the equal opportunities implications, whereas your lot sound as though they all go home to their caves in the evening dragging a dead dinosaur over their shoulders for the little woman.

Dave: Stand by your beds! Here comes our daily dose of political correctness! Thank God the private sector is free of that nonsense.

Jeremy: Well, it isn't *that* free – the women's refuge in Arlington Street is part of the private sector too, and I don't think you would survive very long down there with that kind of attitude.

Dave: No, the women's refuge is public sector, surely? Actually, our Therese helps down there sometimes.

Jeremy: It's private sector, but non-profit. It gets a grant from the local authority, but it was set up privately, as a voluntary organization.

Dave: OK, OK. But let's get back to my main point. Giles says he just wants to get on with his job. But what is that job? I know mine – I have to shift X cars each month, and keep 'em coming. I can easily see whether I have been successful or not. And if I'm not successful, sooner or later I will be out on my ear – probably sooner, since that shark Giddens took over as general manager. But Giles' Department seems to want to reform the world – to interfere in anything and everything. I'm quite willing to admit that occasionally they do good things – yes, Therese's gran gets meals on wheels and couldn't do without them. But how on earth do they know whether they are efficient and effective when they have such a vague mixture of this and that to do?

Giles: It sounds as though we are all of us in the infantry here tonight. You do what you are told to do by Giddens and I do what I'm told to do by the Director of Social Services. And she does what she's told to do by the politicians and the law. That's how I know what I'm supposed to do. Anyway, you may be surprised to know that efficiency *is* measured down at the Town Hall. In fact, we are smothered in performance indicators. And they are always comparing us with other local authorities. How would you like it if your car sales performance was printed up in the newspapers every year – alongside all the other salesrooms in the country? That's what happens to us. And we have the Audit Commission and the Social Services Inspectorate sitting on our shoulders.

Jeremy: Yeh, it was getting like that in schools too – it's one of the reasons I'm glad I'm out of it now. I went into education to teach kids, not to fill in forms for the Ministry and undergo ritual humiliation by government inspectors.

Dave: You still haven't answered my point. What is your business? What are your targets? Filling in forms sounds like just more bureaucracy to me, not real performance. We have things called competitors, and if we don't perform they take the business away from us and we go bust. That's efficiency. But the Town Hall goes on for ever.

Giles: Not true, not true. Our jobs are on the line too. We were downsized 15 per cent just 18 months ago. Everyone had to reapply for their own jobs. And back in the mid-1990s all sorts of stuff was contracted out and closed down. Most of our residential homes have gone, the vehicle fleet was rationalized – the pressures are endless.

Jeremy: And in education the government can contract out a whole local education authority if they don't like what you're doing. Headteachers are replaced: it happens every week.

Dave: But the Town Hall still goes on, doesn't it? You may replace people and fiddle about with organizations, but the Education Department and the Social Services Department are still there, aren't they?

Giles: Nissan isn't about to disappear either, is it? Nor Ford, nor VW. Your garage may get the chop but the big organizations usually survive, don't they? It's like I said – we are the infantry. We are replaceable, but big business and big government go on down the road.

Dave: You're right there. By the way, will someone do me a favour by shooting that kid on the fruit machine – those flashing lights are driving me mad.

Giles: Don't knock it – the fruit machine is probably more profitable to this pub than you or me. It's a very efficient way of doing business – what the customers want. Who are you to question the laws of the market?

Dave: Like I said, your round.

Comment

Dave's argument contains the following suggestions:

A   The public sector (or, at least, Giles' Social Services Department) is less efficient than the private sector (or, at least, the local Nissan dealership).

B   The roles of public sector bodies sometimes entail 'interfering' – controlling and punishing people, against their will, whereas the private sector supplies consumers with things that they want.

C   Public servants have to kow-tow to fashionable (but often ephemeral) notions of political correctness.

D   The roles of public sector organizations sometimes seem very broad/ mixed/poorly defined. Where this is the case it must be hard to know how to measure success/failure.

E   The private sector has competitors which keep it efficient, the public sector does not.

Let us consider each of these suggestions in turn.

Suggestion A is very widely made, and probably very widely believed, especially in the USA and the UK. (The image of government as essentially inefficient and partly unnecessary has tended to be more widely accepted in the USA and the UK than in countries like Sweden or France, despite the fact that the continental European countries actually have considerably bigger public sectors, by most of the usual measures, than the UK or, especially, the USA.) However, it is remarkably difficult to prove this alleged efficiency deficit in a strictly scientific way. There is no weighty and widely-accepted body of scientific literature demonstrating that this is so. The difficulty is partly that one would have to find identical or very similar functions in the public and private sectors, and that is not so easy. Even with schools (the example used by Jeremy in the debate) comparison is difficult. Private schools usually have more scope to select their pupils than state schools, and they may well start off with higher per capita resources – both of which would need to be allowed for in efficiency comparisons. On the other hand the state schools may gain from being members of a wider local authority network of schools which can benefit from economies of scale (for example, by establishing shared expert units for educational psychology or teaching skills). One academic who has studied public–private differences for more than a quarter of a century summarizes the state of research as follows:

> Ideally . . . studies would have huge, well-defined samples of organizations and employees, representing many functions and controlling for many variables. No one has had the resources or inclination to conduct such studies.
>
> (Rainey 1997: 71)

One test might be whether activities which were privatized (that is, where ownership was changed from public to private) demonstrated efficiency improvements – as people of Dave's opinions would expect them to. Surveying the literature, one public sector economist recently put the matter thus:

> Empirical studies of the impact of privatization upon economic performance do not give much support to the proposition that privatized companies perform significantly better than nationalized utilities. [Jackson then gives a series of references to such studies, and says they] . . . could find no significant improvements in efficiency following privatization. Changes in ownership are not the key to efficiency improvements.
>
> (P. Jackson 2001: 13–14)

A final point is that efficiency is not the same as effectiveness. Efficiency concerns the ratio between inputs and outputs – how many lessons are produced for every million euros spent on teachers, or how many benefit claims are processed per member of staff per week. Effectiveness, however, is usually defined as the extent to which an organization achieves its objectives – do the schoolchildren learn to read and write and do their sums, do benefits claimants receive enough help fast enough to live a decent life? It is perfectly possible to be efficient without being effective, and effective without being particularly efficient (a point that will be returned to in the next chapter). Interestingly Herbert Simon, in the second of his two quotations at the start of this chapter, asserted that there were some important tasks at which the government was more *effective* than the private sector.

The criteria the public sector is supposed to pay attention to extend beyond efficiency and effectiveness. For example, there are at least two more important 'E's – economy and equity. Economy is simply the minimization of inputs – spending as little as possible. Governments frequently believe that they have to make economies – although cutting inputs *may* damage either efficiency or effectiveness or both. Equity is the principle of treating similar cases in the same way. Citizens expect to receive the same services and benefits as other citizens in similar circumstances: they do not expect public servants to show favouritism to particular individuals or groups, either intentionally or by accident. Even if we stop at these four 'E's (one could go on to add other criteria) it is already plain to see that judging a public programme can be a complicated business, with 'success' on certain criteria existing alongside 'failure' on others. The issue of evaluation is dealt with at greater length in Chapter 6.

So – to return to efficiency – the truth seems to be that we don't yet know enough to make a firm generalization about public sector efficiency, one way or the other. Indeed, perhaps there *is* no generalization to be made. Public sector organizations sometimes show very considerable measured efficiency improvements (Giles' point a bit later in the discussion), and we can all think of some occasions when private sector, for-profit firms are inefficient (the totally unreliable garage which used to service my car for instance). So it may be that it all depends on circumstances – that public or private *ownership* by itself tells us little about what level of efficiency to expect. We need to know about many other things before we can predict the level of efficiency – things such as the amount of competition or *potential* competition ('contestability'), the quality of the leadership, the specificity of the task, the measurability of its main outputs and outcomes, the level of understanding of its consumers/users and so on. A number of interesting studies suggests that these other factors are more important than ownership alone (for example, Dunsire *et al.* (1988)).

Suggestion B is, in part at least, both true and important. It is *public* bodies which get left with most of the 'social ordering' functions – such as controlling weights and measures, protecting children from abuse, fighting drugs, preventing and detecting crime, imprisoning or otherwise supervising convicted criminals, and so on. These tasks have a definite 'control' element – one which is seldom part of the activities of private, for-profit firms. The 'customer' for such regulatory and safeguarding roles is often the community as a whole rather than just a few identifiable individuals. Nearly all of us benefit from an efficient police force, not just those whose stolen property is recovered but also those whose property isn't stolen in the first place, because of good preventive policing. If the Clean Air Inspectorate discover that a factory chimney is exceeding emission standards for pollutants, and insists that the firm installs better control equipment, then everyone in the area benefits. Indeed, in some cases emission reduction programmes in one country actually or potentially benefit other countries or the entire world – hence the fuss over the high levels of 'dirty' energy use in the USA, and its effects on global climatic change.

The question is: what conclusions or implications does one draw from this particular feature of many (but by no means all) public services? As Giles tries to argue, *someone* in society has to undertake these sometimes thankless and often unpleasant tasks – unless, that is, we are prepared to accept a much more liberal – and more lawless – society, in which citizens are allowed to abuse and cheat and rob each other without any controls. If we are *not* prepared to accept the consequences of such a control-free approach, then it is illogical to criticize those (mainly public) organizations whose job it is to control for carrying out controlling actions. Of course, we may think that a particular organization or official is *too* interfering or harsh, but the remedy for that would seem to be proper appeals and grievance procedures, not the abolition of the control framework itself.

The point about 'political correctness' (suggestion C) is partly just a jibe thrown in by Dave to irritate Giles. Behind it, however, stands a more general and important issue: namely, that there is a widespread expectation that *public* organizations will set high standards in respect of whatever ethical standards happen to be accepted in the society at the time. So if equal opportunities for women, the disabled and ethnic minorities is an official policy and objective, then it is to be expected that public sector employers will set a good example in this regard (see the spring 1989 issue of *Public Administration*, vol. 67(1), for a collection of articles about equal opportunities and public administration).

Again, as with the point about social control, there may certainly be individual instances where there is an excessive or extreme interpretation of what is required, but the answer to that is not to remove the obligation to behave according to high ethical standards but rather a twofold approach that has been increasingly characteristic of the public sector. First, ensure that there is an independent inspection or audit or monitoring process. Second, provide opportunities for citizens (and staff) to complain and criticize if and when excesses seem to have occurred.

The deeper problem, one might say, is where *private* sector organizations believe they have the right to avoid such ethical duties – where corporations display little or no 'social conscience'. In such cases, where 'profits come before principles', private companies may bribe government officials or employ child labour in developing countries, or knowingly sell inappropriate products to unsuspecting or underinformed consumers. We do not normally think of the Netherlands as a corrupt country, but it was there, during the 1970s and 1980s, that a public bank with almost 3000 employees and 90 offices had 'offered customers the chance to launder large amounts of black money by means of false name accounts, numbered accounts, safe deposit credits, and the so-called "envelope trick" ' (see Bovens 1998: 80–85, for a summary of the case of the Slavenburg Bank). Or, if we look at the trade in high technology military weapons, large bribes seem to have been routine, not only in Third World states but also in Europe and Japan (Sampson, 1977). And, lest British readers are beginning to feel smug, we should remember the long sequence of deliberately illegal or fraudulent activities by profit-thirsty companies in the UK. Giles' ironic reference to Robert Maxwell's suits was to remind Dave that Maxwell illegally manipulated the accounts of his companies and, *inter alia*, took large sums from his own employees' pension fund in order to invest them (and lose them) in risky business ventures (Bower 1995). As this book was being completed the papers were full of the accounting malpractices at the giant US companies Enron and Worldcom, which appeared, through their effects on investor confidence, to be having a serious negative impact of world stock markets.

Argument D is that public sector organizations have very unfocused, vague mandates, and that that is why they are inefficient. This is an interesting idea, but needs some further analysis before it can be more accurately formulated. First, it seems clear that *some* public organizations have very well-specified tasks. The Driving and Vehicle Licensing Agency issues licences. It is not that hard to measure how well it does this – the speed and cost of its service to licence-seekers. So, even if Dave is right about Social Services Departments, we should not assume that all or even most public sector organizations share that particular characteristic. *Some* public sector organizations do, however, have pretty broad missions. When the UK Chancellor of the Exchequer formally stated that 'The Government will deliver a world class education service, offering opportunity for all to reach their full potential' (Chancellor of the Exchequer 1998: 42) one may imagine that the civil servants in the then Department for Education and Employment cringed slightly. How were they – or anyone else – supposed to discover and measure the 'full potential' of every schoolchild in the country? What is a 'world class education service' anyway, since different individuals, groups and cultures disagree about what the style, content and even purpose of education should be?

Sometimes, therefore, public sector organizations are given huge, multi-dimensional roles to perform. This could well lead to confusion inside such organizations about how their tasks should be approached, and which aspects should be given top priority. It is worth pausing, however, to reflect on why this state of affairs does sometimes come about. These grandiose missions often reflect the equally heroic aspirations of politicians. It remains the case that politicians come to power by promising to do things – or undo things. They compete to do more to address public concerns (as shaped by the mass media) than the other parties. They not infrequently end up promising more than they could ever be sure they could deliver. One outcome of this process is that public organizations get left holding highly ambitious sets of political objectives. However, from a management perspective, things may not be as impossible as they seem. A strong trend of the past 15 years or so has been to supplement the grand mission or policy statement with a set of key performance indicators. Thus, for example, the vision of a 'world class education service' referred to in the previous paragraph was backed up by a whole array of specific targets and measures. At one point the Labour Government's Secretary of State for Education even prescribed how many minutes per evening children throughout the country were to spend on homework (despite 'weak, mixed or conflicting evidence as to the efficacy of such prescriptions' (Fitzgibbon 2000: 83–4). So even if the politicians have proclaimed a very broad and vague mission, staff working in the organization may be guided by a much more detailed and specific set of targets (though not by any means necessarily one that exactly matches the mission).

Before leaving argument D it should be noted that the assumption that all private sector organizations are very tightly focused can also be questioned. Although it is often said that firms are focused only on 'the bottom line', that is profit, it seems unlikely that this simple view is entirely accurate. To begin with, it can be shown that, over time, the ways in which the performance of for-profit companies has been measured has changed significantly (Meyer and Gupta 1994). At one time the key measure is the percentage return on investment, at another it is the earnings per share. Analysts also juggle with net present value, shareholder value, various quality measures and other indicators. In practice there is 'massive disagreement as to what performance is, and weak to degenerate correlations among performance measures' (Meyer and Gupta 1994: 319). Furthermore, the business literature shows that there is considerable theoretical discussion about what for-profit companies are really trying to maximize. Are they after short-term profits, or long-term profits, or growth, or customer loyalty or shareholder value? Each of these may pull in a slightly different direction.

Finally, it is as well to remember that (as Jeremy points out in the discussion) the 'private sector' consists of much more than just privately-owned, for-profit companies, selling products. Most Western European and North American societies contain large and diverse 'third sectors' (or 'voluntary' sectors) made up of 'private' organizations such as charities, social and sports clubs, religious organizations, trade unions and so on. These organizations are not principally there to make profits. They may be small, but some are quite large. They are economically as well as culturally significant – it has been estimated that the non-profit sector provides an average of about 7 per cent of jobs in Western Europe (with interesting variations, for example 6.2 per cent in the UK and 12.4 per cent in the Netherlands – Hupe and Meijs 2000: 29–30). So these voluntary sector organizations need to be taken into the argument as well. How well-focused and efficient are Dr Barnardos or MENCAP or the Transport and General Workers Union, or even the local mosque or non-conformist chapel?

In fact the third/voluntary sector itself contains a fascinating variety of organizations. At the non-profit, charitable end it embraces organizations which are very much concerned with public rather than private purposes – protecting the natural heritage, promoting research into cancer or even just providing a local centre for vulnerable teenage kids who might otherwise get involved in street crime. At the other end stand co-operative and mutual organizations which are working for the material good of their own customers/members, and which may distribute financial surpluses to these members. At the time of writing the largest banks in France and the Netherlands are 'co-operatives' (Credit Agricole and the Rabobank). Somewhere between socially-oriented charities and commercially-oriented co-ops there are non-profit organizations which may nevertheless accumulate considerable financial surpluses but are obliged to reinvest these rather than hand them out to shareholders, as would ordinary for-profit companies in the market sector.

One final point is that even commercial sector, for-profit companies are not necessarily purely 'private'. The largest European car manufacturer, Volkswagen, has the state government of Lower Saxony as its biggest shareholder (18.6 per cent at the time of writing). The Airbus Industrie company, which now rivals Boeing as a constructor of airliners, describes itself as 'a 20.5 billion euro turnover private sector enterprise' (http://www.airbus.com (accessed 28 June 2002)) but that is not how it has been viewed by its main rival, the US company, Boeing. American sources refer to it as 'a government-funded consortium', and a top Boeing executive was reported as saying that his company competed at a disadvantage against Airbus's 'impermissible government subsidies' (http://seattlepi.nwsource.com (accessed 28 June 2002)).

Argument E is that competition is the crucial difference – that it provides a sharp spur to improvement in the private sector but is fatally absent in the public sector. We can divide this argument into two parts. First, factually, is it the case that the private sector is always competitive and the public sector always sheltered? Second, is it true anyway that competition is a uniquely powerful predictor of efficiency and good performance?

To the first question we can answer that, no, it is not true that the private sector is always competitive (and neither is it true that the whole of the public sector is sheltered from competition). When public sector monopolies in, for example, telephone communication or water supply were privatized during the 1980s and 1990s there was often a period when these organizations continued to dominate their market, and where, according to classical economic theory, they were therefore able to earn excess profits and operate in a less-than-optimally efficient fashion. Of the UK experience one expert says that: 'Returns to investors were high in the early years of privatization because of the underpricing of shares when the firms were floated and because the industries were privatized at a time when there was little competition' (Parker 1999: 107). However, he adds that 'since privatization competition has developed speedily in telecommunications, gas and electricity', though indicating that this beneficial development has much to do with the determination of government regulators (Parker 1999: 100).

We may also note that many important sectors are characterized by oligopoly rather than open competition (more and more according to van Tulder, van den Berghe and Muller 2001). Competition certainly exists in oligopolistic markets, but it tends to take a very different form from that portrayed in the economic textbooks for open competitive markets.

As for the second question (the power of competition to promote efficiency), there is little doubt that this is a very widely shared belief, both among economists and the wider public. However, one review by an economist suggested that: '. . . general belief in the efficacy of competition exists despite the fact that it is not supported by a large corpus of hard empirical evidence in its favour' (Nickell 1996: 725). Nickell found that there *were* both theoretical reasons and empirical reasons to support the connection between competition and efficiency, but that this evidence was certainly not as overwhelming and conclusive as one might think. There was still room for debate and doubt.

In fact it looks as though competition can have a variety of effects, depending on the circumstances. In some circumstances it can lead to the development of new products and services, and to an expansion of consumer choice. In others it can drive *down* standards and variety, as some people believe has happened with television and films. Very stiff competition can make some organizations strive to reduce costs and risks by producing a basic, low cost service for the most obvious consumers, while abandoning more complicated services or more difficult clients. Patents, for example, can be seen as a form of temporary monopoly designed to give researchers and inventors protection from early competition, so that they will have sufficient incentive to go on trying to innovate. Nevertheless, it is very widely believed that serious competition, or the threat of serious competition, is one of the most effective stimulants to increasing productivity, all other things being equal.

Finally, economists have long recognized that there are certain types of service or product where it may be impossible to create or sustain strong competition anyway. These are usually called 'public goods', and are particularly those where it is impossible or very difficult to exclude individuals from the consumption of the good, once it is provided. Examples include clean air, national defence, street lighting, etc. Herbert Simon referred to them in the extract from his 2000 speech in Washington (see above, p. 2–3). The point here is that, even if competition *was* shown to be a magic wand, there would still remain important goods or services where competitive private sector provision would be hard to put in place. This is one of the reasons why such 'public goods' have very often and in many countries been provided by public authorities rather than the market sector. Alternatively, even if they are not actually *produced* by the public sector, such natural monopolies are likely to be strongly *regulated* by the public sector. Regulation is a branch of public sector activity which seems to have grown in importance and complexity since a number of countries launched privatization programmes during the mid-1980s (Baldwin and Cave 1999).

Box 1.1   Is the weather public or private?

For most English people of my generation the weather is obviously *public*. After all, weather 'happens' in the air – which is surely a public space – and its vagaries are reported to us by the 'Met. Office' – a government agency. Most of us, I suspect, associate the Met. Office with the TV or radio news, on which widely-recognized figures such as Michael Fish or Isobel Lang read the weather forecast, accompanied (on TV) with an ever-more sophisticated array of visual aids. All this is close to the heart of daily life (the English are famous for their eagerness to discuss the weather) and may appear to be innocently public, wholesome and uncommercial.

The truth is considerably more complicated. Meteorology is quite serious money, for several reasons. First, collecting the data is expensive. One needs satellites, aircraft and computers. Then one has to employ well-paid scientists to build models of climatic systems and interpret the data. Second, the weather is definitely a saleable product. Apart from Michael Fish talking to all of us after the TV news, many organizations will pay good money to obtain specialized forecasts, because the weather directly affects their lives and livelihoods. Airports and airlines, farmers and traffic managers, companies organizing big events such as motor races or golf tournaments – all need the best possible forecasts to arrive on time and in an easily understandable format.

A moment's thought will also indicate that the weather itself is not neatly organized into national units. It comes and goes without regard to political or adminis- trative boundaries. Today's weather in London may be tomorrow's in Cologne. If the Met. Office only collected data from or over the UK, they would not be able to make very good forecasts. So there needs to be – and is – considerable international traffic in data and forecasts. Generating and managing this traffic is a complex mixture of public non-profit, public for-profit and commercial (private) organizations. Listen to the following extract from an interview which a colleague of mine conducted recently with a Dutch meteorologist. He had worked for the Dutch meteorological office (Koninklijk Nederlands Meteorologisch Instituut, or KNMI). Later he had transferred to a Dutch commercial company which sells weather forecasts:

> Every [national] institute has their own network [of data collection instruments] and a monopoly of observations in their own country and provides the world with their observation set. For example, Great Britain has recently given their observations for free, and that is good. Well, KNMI is busy trying to get to that point . . . but they are not there at this moment. Well, when we started this [commercial] company we had to buy 800,000 guilders [363,000 euros] of data: that's almost 15 per cent of our company value! So that is very huge. Well, we have brought that back to 5 per cent, or something like that, by just getting the data out of the [United] States. And we are able to do that because we are part of a Japanese company which has companies in a lot of countries, for example also in the USA. So in the US the data is free. So that's how it works.

(Smullen 2002)

As this quotation implies, the status of national meteorological institutes, and their relationships with commercial activities, vary a good deal from country to country. For example, in the Netherlands during the 1990s it was decided that it would be wrong for the KNMI to operate profit-making commercial services, so that part of its operations was privatized. Despite this, however, they continue to sell certain data and services (for example, to the air traffic sector) although in doing so they are supposed only to cover their costs, not make a profit. In the UK, by contrast, the Met. Office was given trading fund status in 1996, and, according to its Business Director, 'The Met. is run as a business, so profitability is important for its very existence' (research interview, October 2000). In fact, about 20 per cent of the Met.'s total running costs are offset by its commercial earnings. The Swedish Meteorological Office stands somewhere between the 'purity' of the Dutch and the commercial-mindedness of the British. It does engage in some commercial activities (at least up to the time of writing) but organizes itself in such a way as to maintain a strong internal distinction between its government-oriented tasks and its commercial tasks.

All these organizations are also members of international organizations of various kinds, such as the EUMETSAT (European Meteorological Satellite) Council. And in most countries they work alongside at least a few commercial forecasting companies, some of which have international ownership structures or other links (as we saw in the Dutch case). Such companies frequently recruit (or are actually founded by) staff who have previously worked for and been trained by national meteorological institutes.

Thus it turns out that 'the weather' is a complex 'product', manufactured and delivered to us citizens by a mixture of organizations, including public non-profits, public for-profits, and commercial companies. Furthermore, these various organizations are obliged by the nature of their subject and its associated technologies to operate internationally, and to co-operate as well as compete with one another.

For a more systematic look at the issue of public/private differences we can now move on from the debate in 'The Cricketers' to see what academics have had to say about the same issue – public/private differences.

Background and key concepts

It may be useful to summarize some of the key ideas which have emerged from the past 40 years of debate about similarities and differences between the public and private sectors.

Broadly speaking there have been two approaches. One has been a *normative* approach – concerned with what *should* be so, from the perspective of the author. So, for example, a recent survey of public services changes all over the world concluded that serious problems were arising because of a 'common global trend towards diminishing publicness', and that what was happening was a replacement of 'public norms (citizenship, representation, impartiality, equality and justice) with market values (consumerism, competition, productivity and profitability)' (Hacque 2001: 74). A second approach has been more *descriptive* – concerned to try to identify what *empirical* differences and similarities there are between public and private sectors (and how these may be changing), without necessarily making judgements about the desirability of these findings. For example, Hal G. Rainey first describes 'some of the most frequent observations about the nature of public organization', and then goes on to examine 'the research and debate on the accuracy of these observations' (Rainey 1997: 55).

Of course, in practice the two approaches often overlap. The normative theorists cite a good deal of descriptive evidence to support their preferred positions and values. And the descriptive theorists cannot entirely avoid values creeping in (to begin with, simply by their selection of this topic as one worthy of discussion). Nevertheless, it is worth keeping in mind the difference in intent behind the two kinds of writing: the first to argue that there is a particular kind of problem (and often that there is a preferred solution) while the second is trying for a more clinical, non-committed description of how the world is and how and why it seems to be changing.

Let us first consider some of the key concepts and arguments deployed in the normative literature. A good specimen of this can be found in a book by two British academics from the Institute of Local Government Studies at Birmingham University. In 1994 they wrote *Managing in the Public Domain*. In it they argued that:

> Although public sector organisations are a significant feature of everyday experience, understanding of their distinctiveness has all but atrophied.
>
> (Ranson and Stewart 1994: 3)

While they acknowledged significant failings in public sector bureaucracies, they vigorously resisted the suggestion – which they believed was all around them as they wrote – that private sector management was the model that should be followed everywhere. On the contrary, they asserted:

> The distinctiveness of public management is characterised by universal tasks and purposes which distinguish it from all other forms of management.
>
> (Ranson and Stewart 1994: 5)

But what *were* these differences of task and purpose? Ranson and Stewart developed a model which identified what they saw as the defining features of *public* management and which I have laid out in Table 1.1.

In my view these elements *are* distinctive, but seldom in an utterly black-and-white, absolute way. Thus, for example, *some* business people also have to deal with politicians (chairpersons and chief executive officers of big corporations, for example), though they are not subordinate to them in the same way as is a public manager. Equally, *some* managers in commercial companies have to deal with public protest (for example, when a retail chain wants to open a large new supermarket near a sleepy home counties village, threatening it with heavy truck and car traffic). Some are obliged to operate within codes of conduct or other devices drawn up with an eye to the 'social' (public) responsibility of business. And many private sector managers will be concerned with partnerships and co-operation, as well as with competition. The point is, however, that most public managers are heavily influenced by these elements for most of their working lives, while many private sector managers can usually get on with their work without having to worry too

Table 1.1   Distinctive issues for public managers (derived and developed from Ranson and Stewart 1994: 261–2)

1   *Managing in a socio-political system.* The need to understand the political process and work with elected representatives. The status and motivations of elected politicians are not the same as those of the board members of a normal, for-profit private company.

2   *Working with public pressure and protest.* Public pressure and protest are 'necessary elements in public discourse' (p. 261). In fact one could say they are signs not of something going wrong (as might be the case for a private company) but of a healthy democratic process.

3   *A sense of accountability.* Openness has not only to be accepted, but actually promoted if the particular requirements of democratic *public* accountability are to be met.

4   *Understanding public behaviour.* The 'public' are not only customers, but also citizens, taxpayers and voters. Their relationships with the public manager therefore tend to be more complex and multi-dimensional than those of a customer with a commercial company.

5   *The management of rationing.* Many public managers are in the position of having to ration services – to say who comes first in the queue or who qualifies and who doesn't. Private sector managers are less often in this position – if there is high demand for their product the answer is to make more of it, a solution which is often not available to the public sector manager.

6   *The management of influence.* Rather than competing with other organizations, public sector managers are frequently required to manage co-operative relationships, or to construct partnerships.

7   *Assessing a multi-dimensional performance.* The performance of public sector bodies can seldom be reduced to simple, single measures such as 'profit' or 'efficiency' or even 'customer satisfaction'. Public sector managers must accustom themselves to working at tasks which are judged against multiple, and sometimes conflicting criteria. (For more on this point, see Chapter 5.)

8   *Understanding a wider responsibility to a changing society.* '[M]anaging in the public domain needs an understanding of societal change as necessary to a learning society' (p. 262).

much about them. Furthermore, some of these elements – the demand for public accountability for example – directly affect virtually all public managers, and only a minority of private sector managers.

At this point it should be acknowledged that the views of Ranson and Stewart were far from the only perspective on these issues. Indeed, one reason why their book was written at that particular time was that a climate had developed in which it was frequently assumed or asserted that there was *not* much that was distinctive about public management, except, perhaps its sluggishness and inefficiency. For proponents of this view (the Daves of the 1980s, who happened to include the Prime Minister of the day) the answer was a wholesale importation of private sector management techniques and ideas into the public sector – plus extensive privatization of hitherto publicly-owned utilities and services. The consequences of this approach will be discussed further in later chapters, especially Chapters 2 and 6.

In fact, the debates which took place during Mrs Thatcher's prime ministership can be seen as a local manifestation of a wider debate which has been going on for many decades, and which continues today. Not just right-wing politicians, but many distinguished organization theorists have taken the view that the most important features of organizational life (for example, the size of an organization, or the degree to which it is specialized) are common variables for both public and private sector organizations (Rainey 1997: 55–60). Against them many other academics and practitioners have stoutly maintained that there both should be (normatively – as with Ranson and Stewart) and are (descriptively) major, enduring differences. So there is and has been a large debate and controversy about this question. As indicated in the introduction to this book, I take the 'differences' side, but I do not think that the differences are simple. Rather, I would argue that they are multiple, and present to very varying degrees in different organizations and parts of organizations. To explore this further we can now move on to the findings of the more descriptive literature.

In many countries the last two decades of the twentieth century witnessed vast changes in the ways in which public services were provided (Pollitt and Bouckaert 2000). These reforms (which are continuing) have certainly affected the border between the public and private sectors, and in a variety of ways. For example:

- Many publicly-owned industries have been privatized – that is, their assets have been sold on the stock exchange and they have become for-profit private corporations. This process has been particularly far-reaching in New Zealand and the UK, but has also affected, for example, France, the Netherlands, Sweden and the USA. Most dramatically, huge swathes of industry were privatized in the former Communist countries of eastern and central Europe.
- Many other public services have been 'contracted out'. This means that the public authorities still retain responsibility for seeing that the service is provided, and still pay for it and set the standards and requirements for it, but the actual work of delivering the service is undertaken, on contract, by some other organization.
- In many OECD countries 'public–private partnerships' (PPPs) have become very fashionable, especially in the areas of urban regeneration, transportation and other infrastructure (see, for example, Lowndes and Skelcher 1998).

In these cases public objectives are pursued by partnerships between fully public organizations (often more than one level of government is involved), for-profit commercial companies and non-profit voluntary organizations (for official government enthusiasm about partnerships, see Prime Minister and the Minister for the Cabinet Office 1999).

- Some countries have also developed 'market-type mechanisms' (MTMs) for use *within* the public sector. These are devices which, in one way or another, oblige public sector organizations to compete with one another. For example, the Conservative administrations which governed the UK from 1979 to 1997 introduced an 'internal market' to the National Health Service, and also encouraged state schools to compete for students (Pollitt, Birchall and Putman 1998; more generally, see OECD 1993).

The impact of these, and other, changes has been to complicate the borderline between public and private, and to lead some theorists to talk about the 'end of big government' and the 'hollowing out of the state'. For the UK, Rod Rhodes argues that the reforms of the Conservative governments of 1979–97 led to a 'hollowing out' of central government in which organizational structures were fragmented, public accountability obscured and the government's capacity for strategic steering was reduced (Rhodes 1997). For the United States, Mark Peterson argues that 'continuing attempts to privatize its administration could put much of the big state, including its social programs, in the hands of big business' (Petersen 2000: 251). For Sweden, Michele Micheletti shows that, while central government may have shrunk somewhat, 'Government is becoming even larger at the lower levels'. However, the public–private border is nevertheless becoming more complex because 'Responsibility for service democracy is increasingly shared with other societal actors' (Micheletti 2000: 265 and 275).

The studies just mentioned are of particular countries at particular stages of development. They are descriptive but they do not *directly* address our question about what is enduringly *different* about the public sector. They show what changes are taking place, but they do not much interrogate the underlying concepts and dimensions of 'publicness' and 'privateness'. However, there is another section of the literature which does precisely this, and it is to these works that we will turn in order to conclude the present chapter.

We can begin with a recent article by Professor George Boyne of Cardiff University, entitled 'Public and private management: what's the difference?' (Boyne 2002). In this piece he takes a pretty sceptical line on public–private differences. He points out that most of the empirical studies of such differences are American, their data were collected 20 or 30 years ago, and tended to concentrate on the views of senior managers – people at the level of the organization where differences would probably be greatest (cleaning the floors for the government is probably not tremendously different from cleaning the floors for Rank Xerox or Royal Dutch Shell). These are all strong criticisms, and Boyne identifies other methodological weaknesses as well. He then shows that, from a statistical point of view, the strength of support for several of the key hypotheses (for example the idea that the goals of public organizations are more complex or that they are more open to public influences) is very poor.

However, Boyne does not draw the conclusion that there are no differences. His main point is, perhaps, that the evidence – either way – is much shakier than many people suppose. In his conclusions he says that the statistical evidence *does* seem to support at least three aspects of difference:

- Public management is more bureaucratic (in the sense of having more 'red tape').
- Public managers do have stronger values in favour of serving the community – there does seem to be a 'public service ethos'.
- In the public sector there tends to be a weaker commitment to the manager's employing organization, possibly because there is often only a very weak link between performance and individual rewards.

Boyne also acknowledges that more qualitative research methods seem to indicate the existence of other significant public–private differences, including:

- In human resource management policies.
- In the management of ethical issues.
- In styles of decision-making.

Near the beginning of this chapter there was a quotation from one of the most prolific writers on public–private differences, Professor Hal G. Rainey of the University of Georgia. Like Boyne, Rainey is mainly interested in empirical evidence. His conclusion, having reviewed the fruits of his own work and that of many other researchers, is that there are very significant public–private differences. However, he is also careful to acknowledge that there are other factors, such as organizational size or the nature of the task itself, which can heavily influence the nature of management whether the organization is in the public sector or the private. This having been said, Rainey provides an extremely useful summary of the main differences which it has been asserted as existing between public and private management. In Table 1.2 I have simplified and adapted Rainey's synthesis.

In Table 1.2 one can hear many echoes of the earlier discussion in this chapter. For example, the idea that public organizations have to work with greater goal ambiguity is precisely what Dave was saying to Giles. And the expectations of greater openness and accountability were important elements in the work of Ranson and Stewart discussed above and summarized in Table 1.1. We should be clear, however, that Rainey is *not* saying that all these alleged differences actually exist, or that they permit us to draw a firm, neat line between the public sector and the private sector. On the contrary (and like Boyne) he is attempting to draw a far more complex and graduated picture. He argues that many of these factors should be seen as variables on a scale, not binary variables which can be marked 'present' or 'not present'. Each particular public sector job can be characterized in terms of its position with respect to each of these variables. One can therefore think in terms

Table 1.2 Distinctive characteristics of public management (extensively adapted from Rainey 1997: 73–4)

Environmental factors
1   Not a market environment – revenue comes from budgetary appropriations, not sales of goods and services
2   Presence of elaborate formal legal constraints
3   Presence of intensive political influences

Organization/environment transactions
4   Public organizations produce 'public goods', and tend to deal with situations where there are significant 'externalities' (effects on others who are not directly producers or consumers of the service in question)
5   Public services are often monopolistic and/or coercive
6   Public activities tend to have a very broad impact, and often carry a high symbolic significance
7   Public managers are subject to more intense public scrutiny
8   Public managers are expected to have higher degrees of fairness, honesty, openness and accountability

Organizational roles, structures and processes
9   Greater vagueness, intangibility or unmeasurableness of goals. Also greater multiplicity of goals and a higher incidence of conflict of tension between goals
10   General manager roles involve more political, expository activity. More crisis management
11   Less decision-making autonomy, less authority over subordinates
12   More red tape – more complex organizational structures and procedural requirements
13   Strategic decision-making more vulnerable to interruptions and interventions by external groups
14   Fewer extrinsic incentives (for example high pay and benefits packages) and a weaker link between performance and rewards
15   Different, more community-oriented work-related values (the 'public service ethos') but also lower work satisfaction
16   Greater caution, reluctance to innovate

of multi-factorial 'degrees of publicness'. One job – let us take Giles' position as a local authority social worker – may be highly 'public', because:

- It does not have a market for its outputs, and receives a budget appropriation not closely related to its measurable performance (but perhaps rather to estimated 'need' in the community).
- It is subject to elaborate legal and other formal constraints.
- It may be subject to intense political influence (especially if anything seems to go wrong).
- It involves coercion of citizens.
- It has high symbolic significance.
- It is subject to considerable goal ambiguity.

And so on (the list could easily be extended).

On the other hand, another public management job – let's say the purchasing manager for a government department – may be much less distinctively 'public'. If this job involves buying office furniture and equipment, arranging cleaning and maintenance services, and so on, then it is quite possible that the occupant will be more concerned with the ordinary commercial law surrounding contracts and purchasing than with any special legal constraints; will seldom have any contact with politicians; will never have to coerce a citizen; and will operate with a clear set of goals to do with efficient purchasing so that suitable items and services are purchased in a timely fashion at the lowest possible price. In short, the purchasing manager's job will be very similar to that of a purchasing manager for a big private corporation – except that somewhat stronger requirements for public account-ability may apply.

Both Boyne and Rainey are therefore warning readers not to succumb to the temptation to generalize beyond the evidence. Both see 'publicness' as multi-factorial, and present to a greater or lesser extent in different organizations and jobs within those organizations. Neither would have much patience with the sweeping stereotypes used by Dave (or, for that matter, Giles) in the conversation which opened this chapter. I would go even further than Rainey's disaggregation in Table 1.2, because I think that sometimes it bundles together different variables which need to be examined separately – for example, item 5 in the table couples the coerciveness of some public services with their monopolistic character, whereas I would see the two as analytically separate. One can have a public service which is coercive without being monopolistic and another which is monopolistic without being coercive. But these are perhaps details. Overall, Rainey is convinced that the cumulative differences *are* significant. Yet he is quite ready to concede that there are many jobs and organizations which exhibit 'hybrid' symptoms (and, indeed, that, with recent reforms, the hybrid zone is probably growing).

Finally, we should note that the picture is a dynamic, not a static one. Boyne pointed out that many of the empirical studies on which he (and Rainey) based their analyses were now more than ten years old. That is a major limitation in a world where intensive reform programmes have been focused on changing some of the very factors which are said to distinguish the public sector manager (for example, changes have been made in many countries to give the manager more delegated autonomy and authority over subordinates – see the discussions in the next chapter). In other ways, however, it could be supposed that the differences have intensified – for example, the pressure on public managers to be 'open' and to expose their reports, decisions and results to public scrutiny is probably greater than ever before.

By way of a personal conclusion, it may be of interest to refer to a visionary book that was written almost two hundred years ago. Robert Owen, founder of a model industrial community at New Lanark on Clydeside, published *A New View of Society* in 1813. Near the beginning of this work he insisted on a first principle, namely that:

> Any general character, from the best to the worst, from the most ignorant to the most enlightened, may be given to any community, even to the world at

large, by the application of proper means; which means are to a great extent at the command and under the control of those who have influence on the affairs of men.

(Owen 1813/1991: 12)

Owen, pioneer socialist, feminist and ecologist, was clearly an optimist (a self-taught optimist, neither an academic nor a technocrat). His optimism was by no means always fulfilled – for example, his second model community, 'New Harmony' in southern Indiana, quickly fell apart in factionalism. In a sense, many recent management gurus are his intellectual descendants. They, too, believe that even struggling organizations can be given a good character if only leaders will apply the appropriate methods. From this perspective, Owen, therefore, could be seen as one of the great-great-grandfathers of generic managerialism. From another, however, he was certainly not; he always insisted that 'good character' could only be had through a collective and egalitarian approach – a complete moral and educational *context* which stressed interdependence and which rose above the competition of individual interests.

Perhaps the need for a similarly *contextual* approach is, after all, one of the differences between public management and management in the for-profit sector? The public sector context is – often, though not always – different. The public sector, if it is to retain legitimacy in the eyes of citizens, has both to practise and visibly to display values of equity, impartiality and a certain moral enlightenment which are not *central* to the commercial marketplace, even if they are sometimes found there. Managers in the public sector (or, at least, in those roles which have a high degree of 'publicness') therefore face a more complex task than their commercial counterparts. Like their market sector cousins, they must strive for improvements in efficiency, effectiveness, reliability and quality. But they do so in a different context – one in which the exercise of democratic and communal values takes a much more salient place. Increased efficiency cannot substitute for these values. Increased efficiency may be both admired and desired, but it cannot be traded-off against public trust – or, at least, not very far. Increased efficiency will not even bring political legitimacy – the public are too smart to believe that making the trains run on time is a sufficient manifesto for government. Once the public official loses his or her *ethical* distinctiveness, there is no longer any reason for the public to regard the sector named after it as deserving of any particular respect, effort or loyalty. But without some such recognition by the public themselves of the *special* authority of government, and the link between public authority and the solution of certain types of collective problems, the business of government becomes immeasurably harder – some would say impossible.

Guide to sources

Generally speaking, there has been a lot of abstract speculation about differences between the public and private sectors, but rather less in the way of actual empirical confirmation or refutation of those abstract propositions. (To put this another way, the temptation to write normative analyses has often taken precedence over the more strenuous business of actually collecting detailed facts about how the world actually is.) For example, it has frequently been said that public sector organizations have more complex and ambiguous goals than private sector organizations, but that assertion has seldom been tested (Rainey and Bozeman 2000).

An attempt to test the evidence rigorously was made by Boyne (2002). He found 34 empirical studies, of which 28 were American. These included a classic series by Hal Rainey (for example: Rainey *et al.* 1976; Rainey 1997; Rainey and Bozeman 2000), which should probably be consulted by anyone who really wants to get into this subject in depth.

More normatively-inclined discussions include Ranson and Stewart's *Management in the Public Domain* (1994) and Shamsul Hacque's (2001) bold attempt to survey both the developed world and the developing world in his major article 'The diminishing publicness of public service under the current mode of governance'.

There have been many studies of privatization. As mentioned above, some of these are briefly reviewed in P. Jackson 2001. A useful full length study of the effects of privatization on economic performance can be found in Martin and Parker's (1997) *The Impact of Privatization: Ownership and Corporate Performance in the UK*. A more recent, international study is Hodge (2000) *Privatization: An International Review of Performance*.

On the specific issue of social services, a useful recent article on the attempts to introduce market-type mechanisms to UK social services departments is to be found in Kirkpatrick, Kitchener and Whipp (2001). This analysis helps illuminate some of the key differences between a complex service such as residential care for children and a relatively standardized product such as a car or a refrigerator.

2

The 'New Public Management' – revolution or fad?

Introduction

Over the past ten years or so there has been a huge fuss over the 'New Public Management' (or NPM, as it is often abbreviated). Different commentators have argued about what the NPM *is*, about what caused it; about whether it is a global phenomenon towards which most countries are converging or something localized to just a few states; about whether the NPM delivers its promised benefits; about whether it also brings hidden disbenefits, and about whether it is now 'over' and, if so, whether something else (what?) is replacing it.

In this chapter I will try to answer at least some of these questions. The NPM that emerges from my investigations is a rather chameleon-like and paradoxical creature – something that springs up for different reasons in different places; that is 'edited', 'translated' or 'customized' for each different context in which it is introduced; that preaches a strict doctrine of performance measurement but seldom applies this rule to itself; that simultaneously promises public managers more freedom, politicians more control and public service users more choice; and that has achieved a degree of rhetorical dominance (at least in the Anglophone world) that far outruns its impacts on practice (substantial though the latter have nevertheless been). One question can be answered right away: the NPM is not just a fad. It *may* be a fad (or may have been a fad) but it is not 'just' a fad. It has already lasted too long and led to too many real institutional changes (at least in some countries) to be dismissed as merely a passing fashion. However, as I will explain later, to call it a revolution seems a bit 'over-the-top'.

The main text will be accompanied by a series of quotations from public managers. The intention is that they should provide 'the voices of the practitioners', occasionally contrasted with official pronouncements, or other voices. Most of these quotations are taken from research interviews on projects which I have worked on over the past decade. Where they come from somewhere else, the source is indicated. There is also a further brief encounter with Dave, Giles and Jeremy, who this time are talking about performance indicators in schools.

What is the NPM?

There have been many different definitions, but there is a fair amount of overlap between most of them (see, for example: Christensen and Lægreid 2001; Hood and Jackson 1991; Lane 2000; or, for a practitioner account OECD 1997). Many commentators allow that the NPM has a number of facets or ingredients, and that from one country and time to another the emphasis may vary between these. My own synthesis would be as indicated in Table 2.1 (references are indicated for each element, for those who wish to follow up in more detail). It is hard to summarize this 'package' in a single phrase, but one of the better attempts which I have seen is 'disaggregation + competition + incentivization' (Dunleavy and Margetts 2000: 13).

Table 2.1 Key elements of the New Public Management (NPM)

- **2.1.1** A shift in the focus of management systems and efforts from inputs (for example staff, buildings) and processes (for example teaching, inspecting) towards outputs (test results, inspection reports) and outcomes (standards of literacy in the community; institutions which repeatedly fail inspections being closed down) (see Pollitt and Bouckaert 2000: Chapter 4). The British Prime Minister put it like this: 'A clear focus on outcomes allows us to give freedoms back to public service workers – if a service can be accountable for *what* it achieves, we need worry far less about *how* it achieves it' (Blair 2002: 15 (original italics)).
- **2.1.2** A shift towards more measurement and quantification, especially in the form of systems of 'performance indicators' and/or explicit 'standards'. Instead of just 'trusting the doctor' one develops measures which show how often the doctor prescribes certain drugs compared with her peers, how often her patients develop post-operative complications, how long are her waiting lists, how far she complies with the best practice protocols established by the royal colleges of medicine, and so on. Similarly, for civil servants paying out social security benefits, one measures the average time taken to process a particular type of claim, and uses that measure to see which local offices are fastest or slowest (see, for example: National Audit Office 1998).
- **2.1.3** A preference for more specialized, 'lean', 'flat' and autonomous organizational forms rather than large, multi-purpose, hierarchical ministries or departments. Thus, for example, the UK, the Netherlands, Canada, Jamaica, Thailand, Tanzania and Japan all had programmes for separating out certain functions or activities and placing them in 'arms length' specialist agencies rather than carrying them on within the main body of a ministry (Pollitt and Talbot 2003).
- **2.1.4** A widespread substitution of contracts (or contract-like relationships) for what were previously formal, hierarchical relationships. Throughout Western Europe, for example, local authorities which had previously collected refuse or cleaned the streets using staff from their own works departments, turned to systems of contracting out for these functions (even if the existing unit continued to carry out the work, it now had to do so under a set of carefully-specified contractual conditions) (see Lane 2000).

Table 2.1—*continued*

- **2.1.5** A much wider-than-hitherto deployment of markets (or market-type) mechanisms (MTMs) for the delivery of public services. Famously, Mrs Thatcher introduced an 'internal market' to the UK National Health Service, and similar developments took place in New Zealand (Ashton 1999; Ranade 1997). (In both countries the market mechanisms were later toned down or removed.) During the 1980s UK local authorities were obliged by central government not only to use contracts but to do so through a process of mandatory *competitive* tendering (Ascher 1987).
- **2.1.6** Alongside the favouring of MTMs, an emphasis on service quality and a consumer orientation (thus extending the market analogy by re-defining citizen-users of public services as 'consumers'). Across Western Europe and North America literally thousands of service quality improvements projects were launched, frequently using private sector-derived techniques such as Total Quality Management (TQM) (see Gaster 1995; Pollitt and Bouckaert 1995).
- **2.1.7** A broadening and blurring of the frontiers between the public sector, the market sector and the voluntary sector (for example, through the use of public–private partnerships and/or contracting out) (see Hacque 2001; Micheletti 2000; Peterson 2000). This issue was referred to in Chapter 1, and will be dealt with more extensively in Chapter 3.
- **2.1.8** A shift in value priorities away from universalism, equity, security and resilience, and towards efficiency and individualism (see Hood 1991, and also Chapter 6 of this book).

The following quotations from practitioners echo some of the key elements referred to above, although they also indicate that in practice NPM reforms are frequently not as cut-and-dried as they may appear to be from a brief summary such as Table 2.1.

> The top priority was a change in attitude towards performance. I wanted to see more action and fewer words. Too much attention was paid to whether or not the right procedures had been followed rather than to what had been achieved. It was an attitude born of years of painful experience. When things went wrong and inquiries were conducted, the survivors were those who had followed the rule book and created their own alibis.
>
> (Lewis 1997)

In 1992 Derek Lewis was brought in from the business world to be Director General of the Prison Service. Less than three years later 'things' did indeed go wrong and he was controversially dismissed by the then Home Secretary, Michael Howard (despite the fact that he had achieved almost all the performance targets in his contract). However, Lewis did not 'go quietly'. He sued the Home Office for wrongful dismissal, and was eventually awarded an out-of-court settlement of £280,000.

> A civil servant may tell you that he is responsible for policies about the permissible levels of pollution in the waterways of Britain. That is a worthy

activity, but it does not tell you much about what he is doing. I wanted to know what standards had been set; whether higher standards were to be brought in, and when; what this would cost, and how the benefits were to be measured.

When the literacies of the Civil Service and the generalities of their intentions are turned into targets which can be monitored and costed, when information is conveyed in columns instead of screeds, then objectives become clear and progress towards them becomes measurable and far more likely.

(Heseltine 1987: 21)

Michael Heseltine held several cabinet positions in the Conservative administrations of the 1980s and 1990s, eventually becoming Deputy Prime Minister.

The following quotations come from a research interview that a member of a research team I was part of conducted in May 2002. The interviewee was a senior public servant in an UK public sector organization which supervised a number of executive agencies.

Good practice means you don't have too many key performance indicators. The public are not all that interested in knowing about the commercial aspects of [Agency X] which is why its financial director doesn't reveal it so much.

The interviewer then asks whether the ministry takes action if the agency misses a performance target. The interviewee replies by citing a case where a financial target was missed because of a change in world market prices for a particular product.

What tends to happen is that if [the agency chief executive] feels he has to do this he brings it to me and we put a proposal to the board which allows him to change his target in the light of changing circumstances throughout the year.

The above three quotations illustrate both the advantages and the limitations to the 'performance-driven' approach. In the first instance, Derek Lewis stresses how important it is, NPM style, to have some action targets rather than continuing to follow rules and procedures. But subsequently he is dismissed, despite having achieved most of his targets, because politically embarrassing events have occurred which were not written into the performance contract.

The second quotation comes from a book by a leading Conservative politician who took an unusually developed interest in management issues. One can sense – and perhaps sympathize with – the impatience of a powerful politician confronted with an endless succession of long, well-honed civil service briefs setting out 'on the one hand' and 'on the other hand' but containing little precision, and no 'bottom line'.

The third extract shows an experienced public manager, who fully supports the push towards a performance orientation, acknowledging some of the limitations of a performance indicator regime. First, one can have too many indicators, which leads to dilution of management attention. (At one time, during the 1980s, UK District Health Authorities had more than 1000 performance indicators.) Second, the public may not be at all interested in many of the indicators which, for technical purposes, the organizations wants to monitor. Third, indicator targets cannot be written in stone. There are many unpredictable developments which are beyond the control of management, and which may affect the organizations performance. If this happens it seems only fair to allow some adjustment of the target(s) in question.

In a given context, the different NPM ingredients indicated in Table 2.1 can exist anywhere along the long and winding road that runs from ideas ('wouldn't it be a good idea if we . . .') through definite plans or decisions, to accomplished and implemented practices. One can envisage a trajectory that runs as follows (Pollitt 2001a):

- Talk (about a particular reform).
- Decisions (to adopt the reform, for example, in a government white paper or Parliamentary statement).
- Implementation (actual changes in practice).
- Results (the changes in practice lead to improved results).

However, the whole process can get stuck and peter out at any point. Rhetoric may not translate into decisions. Decisions may not be fully implemented. Even where implementation has been accomplished, that does not necessarily mean that the results which NPM enthusiasts predict will actually come about. I will be using this four-stage classification at various points throughout the rest of the book.

Box 2.1   Talk and text

The 'talk' stage of management reform deserves some further comment. It is important to recognize that words have a value in themselves. 'Empty rhetoric' usually isn't empty at all – it serves some purpose and brings someone some advantage. Talk and text are our main means of *persuading* others that we have the best answers.

First, consider the position of a minister announcing a set of management reforms. She or he picks up media attention – hopefully favourable – for *announcing* the reform – in other words for talk. The announcement gives her or him the opportunity to rehearse the government's favourite values – efficiency, transparency, accountability or whatever. The white paper or speech or government decision promises modernization, improvement, progress. It refers to a better state of affairs which will be attained in the future (and which cannot be disproved today). The fact that the actual changes which have been announced will take months – or more probably years – to come to fruition is not a secret, but, on the day of the announcement it is not the most important thing either.

But if the minister's promises (of efficiency, etc.) are not fulfilled, won't she or he later have to pay the political price? Not necessarily, she or he may have moved on to another post. There may even be another government. And even if the same person is in the same job there may be little interest in what eventually, 'really', happened. Ask yourself how many times you have seen the results of an *administrative* reform occupying the media headlines? Probably there will have been other changes or new influences in the meantime. Possibly (as we will see a little later in this chapter) there has been no systematic evaluation of the changes, so that no-one can be entirely sure what has led to what, or on what scale. In short, there will be ample opportunities to smother any questioner in a blanket of complexities, uncertainties and new developments.

Now consider the work of public managers. What do they produce? In many, many cases their chief tangible output is talk and text – words. They don't lift boxes, dig for minerals or make engines; they write documents and attend meetings. Not infrequently, their careers are heavily influenced by their ability to produce the 'right' words – the sweetly written memo, the diplomatic communique, the persuasive speech to the minister or to staff, the shrewdly drafted white paper, the subtle chairing of a difficult meeting.

And what about management reforms themselves? Where do reformers get their ideas? Well, occasionally they may be brand new, original thoughts. But more often they will have been heard about from somewhere else. 'Reformers may learn about reforms to imitate through written reports, on short visits during which they are given talks about a country's experience with reforms, or more indirectly when consultants or researchers tell them about exchanges initiated elsewhere. Thus, what is spreading is not practice as such, but accounts of this practice' (Sahlin-Andersson 2001: 54).

Furthermore, the nature of these accounts can be rather varied. A common mistake for beginning researchers is that they treat all documents about topic X in the same way. But that is to compare apples with pears and pears with cucumbers. A civil service brief about, say, regulatory impact assessment, is written to give the minister something good to say, and to defend him or her from today's possible criticisms. If it is more than two pages long it will be sent back. A think-tank booklet about regulatory impact analysis needs to be more than two pages long, and it needs to show that the think tank is thinking – having bright new, policy relevant ideas. Probably it needs to suggest that there are deficiencies in the present arrangements, which require the bright new idea in order to make progress. An academic article and book about regulatory impact analysis will be longer still, and will usually include a review of the existing literature (text about other text). Unlike the civil service brief or the think-tank booklet, it does not need to come to a specific recommendation (indeed, it may avoid practicalities altogether and stay on a high plain of abstraction). And so on; to judge all three documents by the same criteria is to miss the point that they are produced for different audiences, with different needs, on different timescales. You wouldn't criticize a cucumber for being longer than an apple.

Behind the specific practices and forms of NPM (for example, executive agencies, performance management, public–private partnerships), lie some *theories* of how individuals and organizations behave. Therefore the strength of the NPM depends partly on the robustness of these underlying assumptions and hypotheses. However, it is by no means clear that such 'robustness' is present. Some of the theories look as though they may be partly or wholly incorrect (for example, some of the predictions about how performance-related pay would work in the public sector seem to have been quite mistaken). Furthermore, the theories concerned are quite a mixture (Gruening 2001) and do not necessarily fit together very comfortably with each other. One of the main lines of tension exists because of the different assumptions which underpin two major tributary sets of ideas which flow into the NPM. One tributary comes from economics (see Lane 2000) and includes a model of individuals as basically selfish utility maximizers. This is a 'low trust' vision of organizations, where contracts have to be as tight as possible and much thought needs to be put into monitoring agents in case they depart from purposes set for them in order to feather their own nests. The other tributary comes from modern management theory and embodies a rather more optimistic model of individuals, which presumes that they can be bound in to organizational purposes by vision statements, good leadership and a supportive and creative organizational culture. In this perspective, when the culture is right, staff can be trusted – indeed, they will be more innovative and productive if they are given 'freedom to manage' – especially freedom to manage themselves. They *want* to deliver a high quality service.

Furthermore, even if some aspect of NPM *is* implemented and *does* produce its theoretically-predicted improvements, it may also generate some less palatable consequences (for example, contracting out may result in economies and efficiency gains, but may also lead to less equal opportunities for employees and/or to very low wages and poor conditions). I will say more about these disbenefits a little later.

In short, the overall picture is likely to be complicated – NPM has eight or nine different elements, and each of these may work well or badly and may or may not generate additional, unforeseen or unwanted effects. This complexity is one reason (but not the only reason) why, in practice, few NPM reform programmes have been convincingly evaluated (Pollitt 1995; Pollitt and Bouckaert 2000: Chapter 5).

> At the Ministry hardly any attention is paid to these indicators. Even if performance was bad I suspect they would not react unless we pointed their attention to this.
>
> (A head of department at a Dutch agency, discussing the agency's performance indicators system, research interview, January 2001)

One final point may seem so obvious as hardly to be worth stating. The NPM is a programme of *reform*. That is, it arises from a dissatisfaction with the *status quo*, and is fuelled by an image of the faults and weaknesses of that *status quo*. So, to better understand the nature of the NPM, we need to know what it is opposed *to* – what the 'other' is that the NPM is designed to replace. Which takes us to the next section.

NPM as a triumph over bureaucracy

Most books and articles on the NPM identify the 'other' (if they identify it at all) as 'bureaucracy'. Bureaucracy is pictured as ruling the pre-NPM earth like a dinosaur. Like a dinosaur, it was too big, too slow-moving, too insensitive, insufficiently adaptable, and seriously underpowered as far as brains were concerned. Messages took too long to get all the way down the hierarchy from the tiny little head to the cumbersome feet and claws, and, by the same token, information travelled up from the ground level to the brain at an agonizingly slow pace. The large size demanded a huge and continuous supply of resources. This image fits neatly with the concerns of many western governments during the 1980s (when NPM ideas took hold). In the early 1980s they were faced with economic slowdowns, large public sectors that generated high levels of public expenditure, and increasingly well-educated and demanding citizens who were less and less prepared to accept poor service from public officials. They were also worried by reports of the speed and efficiency of the Japanese, and other emerging Asian 'tigers'. So bureaucracy was cast as the enemy of freedom, creativity and efficiency.

> Most of the medical staff . . . saw the transfer [to the status of an independent trust] as an opportunity to escape from the bureaucratic style of the former District Health Authority.

This was the view of a manager at a UK National Health Service hospital explaining why his hospital had taken the chance to 'opt out' from the management control of the local health authority, under the quasi-market reforms instituted by the Conservative Government in the early 1990s.

Osborne and Gaebler, the American consultants who wrote the bestseller *Reinventing Government*, and who helped to inspire President Clinton's National Performance Review, offered a ray of light to those still labouring in the shadow of the dinosaur:

> Yet there is hope. Slowly, quietly, far from the public spotlight, new kinds of public institution are emerging. They are decentralized, lean and innovative. They are flexible, adaptable, quick to learn when conditions change . . . And they are our future.

(Osborne and Gaebler 1992: 2)

Without getting too bogged down in administrative history, we must question the accuracy of this monochrome picture of the past. It doesn't take much research and thought to realize that the image is misleading in two important respects. First, to portray bureaucracy as the bad old dinosaur, fit only for imminent extinction, is to ignore its more positive features (including those that made bureaucracy such a popular organizational form in the first place – both in the public *and* the private sector). Second, to speak only of 'bureaucracy', in an undifferentiated way (as more than one otherwise respectable textbook does) is to overlook the fact that the public sectors of Western European and North American states for a long time contained a rich variety of organizational forms and types. We will take each these points in turn.

Bureaucracy had not grown up by accident, but because it appeared to offer considerable advantages over what went before. Bureaucracy was designed to be reliable, equitable and free from corruption. Civil servants in bureaucracies owed their jobs to merit, not patronage. They worked to predictable rules, based directly or indirectly on public laws. They treated individual cases impartially, according to these rules. In many instances they enjoyed lifelong career prospects, which, it was held, would encourage institutional loyalty and discourage opportunistic attitudes to external attractions. Big bureaucratic ministries offered the prospect of the functional integration of many diverse public activities and:

> In its heyday, the result was an elongated, hierarchical chain of command, widely regarded as an efficient means of coordinating activities by giving government a manageable span of control. Functional integration was thought to reduce administrative costs and friction, facilitate oversight by headquarters staff, reduce the number of officials reporting to political leaders, and promote uniformity in the provision of public services.
>
> (Molander, Nilsson and Schick 2002: 27)

Nor should all this be in the past tense. If you want to read a spirited recent defence of bureaucracy against its many detractors, try Paul du Gay's book *In Praise of Bureaucracy* (2000). Du Gay concludes his book thus:

> . . . it is both misguided and remarkably premature to announce the death of the ethos of bureaucratic office. Many of its key features as they came into existence a century or so ago remain as or more essential to the provision of good government today as they did then – as a number of recent well-publicized cases of improper conduct in government, at both national and supranational level, indicate only too clearly. These features include the possession of enough skill, status and independence to offer frank and fearless advice about the formulation and implementation of distinctive public purposes and to try to achieve those purposes impartially, responsibly and with energy if not enthusiasm.
>
> (Du Gay 2000: 146)

Therefore one key question is whether the implementation of NPM doctrines will undermine/has undermined some of the traditional bureaucratic virtues? You will find many echoes of this question later in this chapter but also in the discussion of ethics and values in Chapter 6. You will also find an analysis of 'joined-up government' in the next chapter. Joined-up government can be seen in part as an attempt to restore functional integration after NPM-style reforms had fragmented the former bureaucracies.

As far as the domain of bureaucracy was concerned, the hierarchical, legalistic, multi-purpose ministry was never the only creature in the public park. Large sections of post-Second World War welfare states, for example, were actually dominated by professional groups such as doctors or teachers, with administrators working only in supporting roles (Clarke and Newman 1997). And many governments included a variety of specialist, single-purpose agencies and boards that were not part of the central ministries (quite apart from the variety in local governments). Indeed, specialization was far from being the only NPM doctrine to have enjoyed one or more previous incarnations. In the nineteenth century performance related pay had been widely used for school teachers, both in the UK and the USA.

This is not to say that there was no hierarchical bureaucracy, simply that that is not *all* that there was, and that the transition to the doctrines of the 'New' Public

Management was not such a totally clean-cut break with the past. Much of it involved the creative repackaging of some very *old* administrative arguments in new wrapping paper. Hood and Jackson (1991: Chapter 8) give a systematic account of this. In fact, many of the elements that make up the NPM have echoed round administrative debates for decades, or even centuries. Consider, as one last example, the idea that bureaucracies are too much focused on rules and official positions, and not enough focused on satisfying the citizens who try to use their services. Much was written and said about this during the 1980s and 1990s, and the frequent assumption behind this outpouring was that quality-for-the-customer was a new preoccupation, learned from private sector advances, especially Total Quality Management (TQM) and its multiple forms and derivatives (see, for example: Pollitt and Bouckaert 1995). Here is a typical statement:

> The customer-satisfaction criterion applies with as much force to govern-ment as to business. In the past the failure of public enterprises generally to pay sufficient attention to customer attitudes and citizen relations has been the aspect of public administration which is most inefficient and open to criticism . . . .

It sounds good. The kind of thing we are all now supposed to believe. Thanks to NPM many public organizations have developed systems and procedures to ensure precisely such a customer focus (citizens' charters, standards of customer service, better complaints procedures, and so on). The only small surprise is that the above text was penned in 1936, by an American, Marshall Dimock (Dimock 1936: 126).

What caused the NPM?

There has been a lot of loose talk about the *inevitability* of NPM. Various candidates have been advanced to explain why it had to be. 'Globalization' has been a favourite. 'Rising expectations' has also often been cited, and rapid developments in 'infor-mation and communications technologies' (ICTs) are frequently mentioned. A number of accounts draw a picture in which, under economic pressures from 'globalization', political pressure from disgruntled citizens and technological pressure from new ICTs, bureaucracy was bound to collapse and be replaced by something similar to NPM.

Explanations of this type, although occasionally popular with political speech writers and some academics, are (to my mind) deeply inadequate. To begin with, even if the picture of unstoppable forces for change was an accurate one, it still does not explain why the NPM model gets chosen rather than some other post-bureaucratic model of reform. The 'unstoppable forces' argument may just explain why bureaucracy has to change, but it does not explain why one particular type of change should be the one that is usually chosen.

But there are also other objections to the 'unstoppable forces' argument, of both a philosophical and an empirical character. Philosophically, it is an explanation that leaves no room for human agency or choice. Governments just have to do what they have to do. Most social scientists (including me) don't like this kind of 'deterministic' explanation. It isn't (we think) how the world works (or, at least, not in the case of something as subjective and plastic as management reform). Furthermore, empirical evidence shows that not every country faces the same economic conditions, that not all countries have adopted the NPM (see more details in the next section) and that the specific connections between economic conditions and NPM are hard to show. (To take just a few examples, while it is true that New Zealand launched its 1984 reform programme on the back of an acute economic crisis, the Finnish government launched its 1989 public management reforms during a period when the Finnish economy was doing rather well, and President Clinton implemented his National Performance Review during one of the longest sustained booms the American economy has ever enjoyed, see Pollitt and Bouckaert 2000). 'Globalization' is not one thing, but several (economic, cultural, technological, etc.). Even when the economic component is separated out, it does not appear to affect all countries to the same degree or in the same way. In short, the detailed evidence for economic pressure and changes in ICTs do not seem to match well with actual management reforms. As for 'rising public expectations', while these have no doubt played their part as a background influence, I have yet to see a single sustained analysis connecting measured changes in public expectations with specific political initiatives to reform public management. Again, once one gets down to the specifics, there is no clear 'fit'.

There is at least one other explanation of the coming of the NPM, and that is that it was a kind of 'New Right' political plot. Neo-conservative politicians gain power and dismantle the state apparatus so as to favour their business allies with tax cuts and privatizations. What is left of the state machine is subjected to business-type disciplines such as competitive tendering, performance measurement and performance related pay. Thus NPM is seen not as economically inevitable, but rather as a chosen ideological strategy. In favour of this view, the finger is often pointed at the early enthusiasm for NPM-type reforms exhibited by Margaret Thatcher (UK), Ronald Reagan (USA) and Brian Mulroney (Canada) – all 'new right' politicians.

Unfortunately for its proponents, this explanation doesn't work very well either. Some of the most radical NPM initiatives have been launched by social democratic or labour governments – especially in Australia and New Zealand. Christensen and Lægreid (2001) analyse change in four countries where reforms were mainly the work of centre-left governments, not the new right). Neither have social democratic/labour governments in countries such as Sweden or the UK been at all keen to reverse most of the reforms carried out by their more conservative predecessors.

If these simple explanations are too simple, then what more convincing account can we put in their place? There is considerable academic debate about this. My own preferred version (see Pollitt and Bouckaert 2000 and Pollitt 2001b for extended justifications) goes like this:

- NPM has not been 'caused' so much as chosen. However, the choosing has not been determined solely or even primarily on the basis of new right ideological prejudices.

- It has been chosen by practitioners – mainly politicians and public servants, though also with some influence from management consultants and academics – who have been less concerned with purity of theory than with solving (perceived) practical problems.
- . Practitioners' choices have varied from time to time and place to place, but elements of the NPM have been a popular choice in many countries. This popularity probably stems from a variety of features. One important one is that NPM reforms promises to save money – by downsizing and efficiency gains. Another is that it promises better control for politicians: public sector organizations will have clearer targets and better performance measures so it will be easier to see if they are achieving what they have been told to do.
- There has also been an element of fashion – of copying – in the spread of NPM ideas. It has sometimes seemed like 'the only show in town', internationally. It has been promoted by some national governments (notably the UK and the USA), by management consultancy firms and by influential international organizations such as the OECD and the World Bank. The basic ideas are fairly simple – understandable to politicians and senior civil servants, neither of which groups tend to contain many individuals who are very deeply trained or experienced in organizational theory or design (Pollitt 2001b: 940–43; Powell and DiMaggio 1991).

Is the NPM a global wave?

Perhaps the most famous book on public management of the past two decades – Osborne and Gaebler's *Reinventing Government* – saw the NPM as both global and inevitable (Osborne and Gaebler 1992: 325–8). A number of scholars agree that it is a global movement, even if they may shy away from the idea that it is 'inevitable' (see Kettl 2000 for a well-argued and well-informed statement of this position). I disagree, partly for reasons which have already been mentioned in the previous section and partly for other reasons. My scepticism is founded on the following observations:

- Some governments (including those of some big, important countries such as Germany and Japan) have been very reluctant to embrace NPM ideas.
- Many other countries (for example Canada, Norway, Finland, the Netherlands, Denmark) have moved cautiously and selectively, taking the bits they find useful, but not buying the whole NPM package. (Since the late 1990s Japan has perhaps also moved into this category of 'cautious selectives'.)
- Alongside NPM reforms, other reforms of a more classical kind have continued, although they have tended to receive less attention from scholars and politicians than the NPM.
- Where countries have adopted forms of the NPM this has by no means always led to significant and lasting changes of practice. NPM talk and NPM-type decisions have often outrun the actual adoption of NPM working practices. Often, also, the results of NPM reforms have remained obscure –

the promised gains in efficiency or service quality have proved elusive or at least debatable (Pollitt 2001b).

•   There are also a significant number of cases where governments have stepped back from NPM reforms because of dissatisfaction with the apparent results. In both New Zealand and the UK governments have tried to make their health care systems more efficient through the use of market-type mechanisms but, after a few years, have reversed some elements of this trend. There are also signs that what was probably the most famous agencification programme in the world – the UK Next Steps programme of the late 1980s and 1990s – produced effects which were unpalatable to New Labour ministers in the late 1990s and early twenty-first century. Attempts were made to pull a number of agencies back closer to ministerial control, and a programme for 'joined-up government' was launched to counteract tendencies of fragmentation and to bridge the growing gap between policymakers and operational managers (see Chapter 3 on joined-up government, and Office of Public Services Reform 2002).

However, I would concede that my differences with scholars such as Kettl are, in some part, semantic. How wide does the spread have to be before NPM is seen as 'global'? How deeply do the reforms have to penetrate actual practice? How long do we have to wait before we decide whether 'cultural change' has actually taken place? These are all subjective judgements, so let me conclude this section by conceding that NPM ideas *have* had a wide influence, and that many reform decisions in many countries have been clearly connected with one or more of the NPM elements identified near the beginning of this chapter. There are certainly broad trends in ideas, but the interpretation and implementation (and the results from that implementation) have been far patchier, messier, diverse and reversible than a reading of enthusiasts such as Osborne and Gaebler (1992), or even Lane (2000) would lead one to believe.

The impacts of the NPM – benefits

NPM doctrine lays considerable stress on the need for managers to have clear targets and a good system of performance indicators that will show how closely targets are being met. It also emphasizes cost consciousness – the need to use resources efficiently so as to obtain the maximum output for any given level of input. It is curious, therefore, that many if not most NPM reformers have seemingly failed to apply these doctrines to themselves. That is to say that many NPM reform initiatives have been launched and carried through with only a very general idea as to what was to be achieved, with little attempt to estimate the transitional costs of the reforms themselves, and with only limited attempts to confirm, track and measure the purported gains. It seems that at least some of the architects of the NPM were so confident of the benefits of the reforms that they were content to leave the results as matters of faith rather than issues to be checked and evaluated (Pollitt 1995).

This seeming over-confidence (or perhaps just lack of interest) is, however, only one part of the story. Evaluation – particularly of management changes – is by no means a straightforward or simple task (see Chapter 6 for a deeper analysis of the challenges of evaluation; also see Boyne *et al.* 2003). Governments can be partially forgiven for not having produced clear 'balance sheets' for NPM-style reforms. To illustrate this point, consider what might be involved in a full assessment of a programme of NPM reforms. First, the aims of the reform would need to be very clearly specified. Then the state of play *before* the reform would need to be closely measured – the inputs, unit costs, outputs, outcomes, service quality and so on. Subsequently, after the reform was in place (and – importantly – had had a reasonable time period to settle down) the same parameters would be measured again, to provide a classic *before and after comparison*. Such a comparison should include an analysis to demonstrate, as far as possible, that changes in the inputs, unit costs, outputs (etc.) were due to the reforms themselves and not to some other change in the environment. (For example, the improved performance of a public agency concerned with finding jobs for the unemployed might be due not so much to its reform as to a general improvement in the economy.)

This is not all. One would also want to know about the costs of the reform – both the direct costs (consultants, training courses, new ICTs, etc.) but also about possible indirect effects such as a lower standard of service during the transitional period when the organization(s) concerned were in a state of upheaval and change. (It is quite common for reforms to lead, temporarily, to longer waits for citizens to receive replies to enquiries or decisions on applications.)

In practice the conditions for evaluations of this kind are seldom satisfied. More commonly, one or more of the following eventualities make it difficult to carry out a proper comparison:

- The original objectives of the reform were specified only vaguely (if at all) so that it is hard to know exactly what should be studied and measured.
- No-one carried out a proper analysis of the relevant parameters before the reform, so that there is no 'baseline' against which later performance can be compared. This failure can be because no-one thought of it, or because reformers are anxious to get on with their reform, and so are unwilling to wait while a study is done of the *status quo ante*.
- The reform consisted of several simultaneous changes (for example, new ICTs, new quality techniques, new budgeting and/or accounting procedures) thus making it more difficult to say which elements have been most influential/successful, and which less so.
- The costs of the reform itself were not measured, or were only measured in a very crude and narrow way. 'Transitional problems' were not properly taken into the equation.
- The size and shape of the organizations concerned were themselves altered, so that a before and after comparison is no longer comparing like with like.
- The outcomes of the changes were likely to occur only over a period of many

years, but the evaluation was carried out soon after the reform, and probably thus understated what might eventually be achieved.

And so on. When, in the mid-1990s, I was part of a team investigating twelve UK local service delivery organizations that had undergone NPM-style reforms (hospitals, schools and housing organizations) I discovered that even simple before and after comparisons were virtually unknown (Pollitt, Birchall and Putman 1998: 164–6). On the rare occasions when governments have attempted broad-scope evaluations of NPM reform programmes – as did happen in Australia and New Zealand – even well-resourced evaluation teams were unable to come to any firm conclusions about the precise savings or efficiency gains that could be attributed to the changes under scrutiny (Pollitt 1995). Indeed, even the concept of a 'saving' is quite wobbly – it can mean a variety of different things to different people (Pollitt and Bouckaert 2000: Chapter 5). One leading American scholar who is generally favourable to NPM reforms wrote that 'no good reliable data are available in any country regarding the savings that the reforms produced' (Kettl 2000: 51)

The result of this state of affairs is that our impressions of the impacts of some of the biggest programmes of NPM-type reform, for example, in New Zealand and the UK, are just that – impressions – not conclusive or carefully assessed 'results'. Of course, that is not to say that they had no results, simply that some of the big questions about overall efficiency gains, or, indeed, about the costs of reform, cannot be answered with any certainty. There are many useful data about particular organizations, such as changes to unit costs or response times or user complaints or productivity measures or quality scores, and these help us form part of the picture (Pollitt and Bouckaert 2000: Chapter 5 discusses these and offers some examples). A brutally brief summary of these scattered pieces of information might look something like this:

- In certain specific cases there is reasonably convincing evidence that substantial 'savings' (economies) were achieved. But in others expected savings were not realized, or not on anything like the scale originally predicted.
- Similarly, there are certainly cases where process improvements took place – that is applications were processed more quickly or waiting times were shortened or fewer mistakes were made.
- There are also examples of considerable gains in efficiency (although there other examples where 'efficiency gains' are claimed, but without the support of any real input/output ratios – during the 1980s 'efficiency' became one of the most promiscuously used words in the administrative lexicon).
- Effectiveness is particularly difficult to measure, and sometimes requires long time periods before it can be fully assessed. Cases of demonstrated improvements in the effectiveness of programmes, linked directly to management reforms, are fairly rare.
- Evidence of cultural change (shifts in attitudes and values) is mixed, but in some cases it does seem to have occurred. Whether such shifts are desirable or not is a more complicated and subjective question (see Chapter 6 for a discussion of the effects of NPM on values and ethics).

- Claims of improved management capacity and/or flexibility are made quite frequently, but these are rather abstract concepts, which are difficult to pin down and measure. No doubt some of these claims are true, although in other ways NPM reforms can sometimes *increase* bureaucratic regulation, particularly in terms of audit, inspection and monitoring (see next section, and Hood *et al.* 1998).

This may seem a fairly down-beat assessment of the benefits. It is. There is no shortage of more optimistic opinions. If you want to try a couple, to balance against my more sceptical account, you could look up one of the UK government's annual reports on the Next Steps agencies programme (Chancellor of the Duchy of Lancaster 1997 is a good example) or an academic analysis of prize-winning improvements (Borrins 1998). But don't forget the cautionary words (above) concerning the difficulty of making sound before and after comparisons – and sound attributions of cause.

Walking home from 'The Cricketers'

[*Dave, Giles and Jeremy leave 'The Cricketers' and begin their walk home. It is a fine, moonlit night, with the distant slopes of the North Yorkshire Moors bathed silver and grey. At the first corner, bidding farewell, Giles takes the left turn and the other two go right. They stroll down a street of decent modern houses, each with its Vectra or Focus or (occasionally) sports utility vehicle parked on its drive. Most lights are out, and the street is silent. The scent of summer gardens hangs in the air.*]

Jeremy: You were a bit tough on poor old Giles, weren't you?

Dave: Did you think so? No harm intended. Anyway, we go back a while, him and me. I don't think he will have taken it wrong. But sometimes his 'holier than thou' attitude gets up my nose. I was interested in what you were saying about teaching, though. Has it really become that heavy? Tricia's school – Green Lane – *seems* alright, but how would we really know?

Jeremy: Tricia's school probably *is* alright – they've got pretty good SATS and Jenny, the head, is a smart operator. But she's young and energetic whereas I suppose I just got tired of it – of the endless change and pressure, of having to spend so much of my time fielding the latest initiative from the ministry or the local authority – things that sometimes would come and go like pop groups.

Dave: What are SATS?

Jeremy: Oh, sorry – teacher talk. SATS are the standardized national tests which all schools have to carry out on their pupils. They are part of the National Curriculum, which was introduced in the late 1980s by the Conservatives. So there are SATS at four stages in every child's school career. I was talking about the second stage – 'Key Stage 2' – which is the level of attainment expected for most 7 year olds. I suppose this is the one your Tricia will have taken recently. She would have been tested in English, maths and science. These are tests for individual children, and are supposed to show which are ahead and which are behind the standard set. But, SATS are also used to judge schools. The SAT scores for each school are displayed on the Department of Education's website, and once a year the papers have a field day publishing tables and praising or damning the 'best' and the 'worst' schools in the country. This puts terrific pressure on some heads.

Dave: So what SATS did Green Lane get?

Jeremy: Can't remember the exact numbers, but high. Well above the local authority average and also, I think, above the national average. You can check it out on the website.

Dave: So what's wrong with SATS, then – I get the impression you don't like them?

Jeremy: No – they're OK. I'd much rather have them than not have them. What I don't like is the way they are sometimes misused – and the negative effect they can have on a school that is trying really hard.

Dave: Like what?

Jeremy: Well, once you get below average scores, some of the parents – often the most active ones – begin to transfer their children elsewhere. And it becomes harder to recruit good staff. It can even affect local house prices. Mind you, many, probably most of the parents don't know what a SAT is or, if they have heard about it, don't really understand the meaning of the measures. And the local authority starts to ask questions and put pressure on the head.

Dave: But, I mean, couldn't that be a good thing? If the results aren't up to much, then shouldn't there be questions and a bit of pressure?

Jeremy: Maybe, but the trouble is that the cold statistics don't tell you anything about *why* the school is below average. For example, if the national average in a subject is 70 per cent and a school in a really rough, run-down area is getting 60 per cent it is probably doing brilliantly. Whereas a posh school in a leafy professional suburb – like where we are now – could get 75 per cent but actually be slacking. Most educationalists understand this, but some politicians and a lot of media people don't. And they can stir up the parents. Which makes *doing* something about a low score even more awkward. In my experience it is extremely difficult to shift SAT scores up much anyway, but the only places where I've seen it done have been where the head, the staff, the governors, the parents and the kids themselves have got together and made a sustained effort. But bad publicity and parent anxiety makes it more rather than less difficult to get that kind of co-operation off the ground.

Dave: So I should really be keeping track of these SATS – quizzing Tricia's teacher about their scores?

Jeremy: I wouldn't make a fetish of it. As long as Tricia herself is happy and is getting decent marks. And anyway, on the level of the individual child, rather than the whole school, change can happen so quickly – especially when they are just 6 or 7. They team up with some special friend, their confidence grows and their scores zoom up. Or they become a victim of bullying and their scores crash. Or they just like their new teacher, and blossom in the classroom. The tests don't help you sort any of this out – what you need is a good teacher who knows each child and keeps in contact with the parents so that they all have a better picture of what is going on in the child's life. So if Tricia is your concern, there's not much point giving the whole school the third degree – unless you want to become a parent governor, that is.

Dave: Stranger things have happened.

Jeremy: Well, I think you'd make a good one. You're just bolshy enough. But then you'd soon see my point about the context being important. And it wouldn't just be test results you would be looking at. There's a whole range of school indicators – truancy rates, exclusions, pupil mobility, number of pupils on Special Educational Needs, numbers of complaints – it's endless. But even when you've studied the lot there's still the question of who is going to do what about it. From a head's point of view – or a governor's – the indicators come somewhere near the *beginning* of managing the school, not the end.

[*They reach Jeremy's house. An impeccable front lawn is bordered with carefully tended rose beds.*]

Dave: So, all in all, you're glad to be out of it?

Jeremy: Well, I know I said that in the pub, but actually it's a bit more complicated than that. For the first six months after I retired, it was great! I just did whatever I felt like – I could hardly believe it, after 35 years' grind. But, to be honest, now I'm getting bored. Sure, the garden is in great shape, but is that supposed to be the limit of my ambition? I miss it – all of it, including the hassle. I mean, basically, I never lost my interest in teaching kids. And then, later, becoming a head with a management task made it even more interesting – can you believe? I think my dream would be to go back to being a head, but just for three days a week, and with the right to tell the inspectors to piss off and come back next year, when I'm ready for them. Some tests, yes, but not as prominent as they are today. And with great staff, of course, and keen, inquisitive kids – plus maybe a smattering of difficult ones – just enough so that the staff could give them real individual attention.

Dave: Sounds good. Better than flogging the latest Nissan.

Jeremy: Yeh, but it also sounds like a dream. Time for bed. Goodnight.

Dave: Night.

If you would like to look up the school league tables for SATS, visit the Ministry's website, http://www.dfee.gov.uk/performance. A small extract from the tables showing the actual Key Stage 2 tests of May 2000 is shown in Table 2.2. It refers to a handful of schools in the same part of the country that Dave, Jeremy and Giles come from.

From Table 2.2 one may notice a number of features:

- The LEA average performance is for all three subjects below the English national average (this is a north-eastern local authority in an area of long-standing industrial decline and population loss).
- The average marks in science are in every case higher than those for English and maths (nationally and locally).
- Within the LEA there is a very wide range of scores from individual schools. Abingdon and Brambles are well below both the LEA and the national averages. Green Lane and Marton Manor are well above both the LEA and the national averages. (Those who know the area will also know that Abingdon and Brambles are both in rather run-down, low average income areas, surrounded by poor housing, whereas Green Lane and Marton Manor enjoy more well-to-do, middle-class catchment areas.)

The full tables (on the website) also provide a useful historical perspective, so that one can see how the achievements of pupils at each school have changed over the previous four years.

In tables such as this one can see both the advantages and the limitations of the 'targets and measurement' approach which is so characteristic of the NPM. To be able to compare similar institutions against some standardized tests raises the level of debate as compared with the previous situation, in which people often had only qualitative impressions of how well or badly a school was doing. Quantitative

Table 2.2   Performance tables: Key Stage 2 test results for selected schools in northeast England (selected and edited extracts from the Department for Education and Employment website, http://www.dfee.gov.uk, June 2002)

	Total pupils	English L4+	English A/D	Maths L4+	Maths A/D	Science L4+	Science A/D
Abingdon Primary	47	45%	0%	49%	0%	64%	0%
Brambles Primary	40	55%	0%	48%	5%	65%	3%
Green Lane Primary	93	87%	2%	89%	3%	90%	2%
Marton Manor Primary	27	96%	0%	93%	0%	96%	0%
LEA average	–	69%		66.9%		79.9%	
England average	–	75%		72%		85%	

Explanation of abbreviations:
LEA = Local Education Authority
L4+ = Pupils reaching level 4 or above. Level 4 is the level of attainment expected of pupils at the end of Key Stage 2 (that is it is *not* an average)
A/D = pupils absent or disapplied

measurements open up many kinds of question and, potentially at least, put parents in a stronger position to ask teachers and heads about disparities between local schools.

At the same time, the apparent 'hardness' of the figures can easily lead the uninitiated (or those with an axe to grind) to draw dramatic but unwarranted conclusions. It could, for example, lead a parent to conclude that Brambles was just a bad school, compared with Green Lane, although a better informed inter-pretation would be that the different types of intake would have a lot to do with the different results. At a school like Brambles the children may suffer a number of disadvantages as compared with the children at Marton Manor. The lower average incomes of their parents may mean fewer books and computers at home. There may also be more large or single parent families where the parent(s) are under such pressure that they find it very difficult to spend much time in edu-cational activities with each child. There may also be localities with a high proportion of ethnic minorities whose first language is not English. Furthermore, the higher income parents who predominate at the 'middle-class' schools are more often in a position to pay for private tuition to supplement the efforts of the school (there is evidence that the amount of private tuition in England may have risen in line with increasing affluence and the increasing prominence of the SATS).

SATS could also lead to complacency – the staff at Brambles could say, in effect, 'oh well, it isn't surprising that we get low scores, and there is really nothing we can do about it'. The difficulty is striking a balance between using socio-economic factors as an explanation for *some* differences and using them as an explanation for *all* differences. To try to encourage a more sophisticated debate among schools the Ministry circulates a Performance and Assessment Data (PANDA) report once a year, in which schools are compared with other schools which are similar, socio-economically. This kind of analysis usually shows that there are some schools which achieve high results despite adverse socio-economic con-ditions in their immediate localities. So this raises the crucial question 'what are they doing that other schools are not?' Such PANDA reports are thus used as a starting point when schools are inspected.

The impacts of the NPM – disbenefits

First, it should be pointed out that the discussion above concerning the difficulties of adequately evaluating management reforms applies to the disbenefits just as much as it does to the benefits.

Second, it is clear that in each category of benefit achieved, there were dis-appointments and failures as well as successes. For example, if we take process improvements we can find the huge re-engineering project at the US Social Secur-ity Administration failed to meet most of its targets (Thompson 2000), while the UK Department of Social Security's 'Operational Strategy' of the late 1980s and early 1990s fell well short of both its savings and its quality of service targets (National Audit Office 1999: 25). So the question seems to be not 'does NPM work?' but rather 'under what *conditions* does this or that element *within* NPM work, and under what conditions is the same element likely to fail?'

Let us begin by re-visiting the core idea of setting output and outcome targets, and holding people responsible for their achievement. Surely this is a good thing? Well, yes, but . . .

> some ministers argue that the targets [that is the targets of their own government!] are too ambitious and fear that the government has made a rod for its own back. They want to scrap some pledges not under the Government's direct control, such as those requiring a change in people's behaviour.
>
> Some Cabinet ministers have told Downing Street it would be unfair to judge them against targets they inherited when they took over new briefs after last June's general election and which they played no part in setting.
>
> (Grice and Russell 2002: 1)

This report of ministerial unrest may simply confirm your scepticism about politicians – they promise things and then, when the time to deliver approaches, they want to slide out from under their original commitments. On the other hand, there could be some serious concerns behind the unrest. Here are just a few:

- As the first part of the quotation indicates, it does not seem logical for government to take the whole of the responsibility for achieving outcome targets which are not by any means entirely within their control (usually because the 'result' depends at least partly – if not mainly – on other factors which are beyond the direct control of any government). Targets involving behavioural change often fall within this category. For example, a government concerned with AIDS (and other sexually transmitted diseases) may launch (and have launched) campaigns in favour of 'safe sex' (the use of condoms and the avoidance of sexual practices which pose a high risk of mutual infection). But we can hardly expect governments to take the whole responsibility for this. Individuals ultimately make their own decisions about their sexual behaviours, and, short of a government camera in every bedroom (and car, etc.) the public authorities cannot either monitor or directly intervene in what goes on.
- Even where the government *has* a greater degree of control, working to targets can cause perverse effects as well as beneficial ones (Smith, 1996). It can lead to an over-concentration on what is precisely quantifiable (for example, costs, numbers of licences issued) and an under-concentration on other aspects which are not so easily measured and rendered into the form of a target (for example, the friendliness of officials dealing with members of the public, the quality of decisions, equity of treatment between many diverse applicants, and so on). It may also encourage a kind of 'tunnel vision' in which departments and agencies intensively pursue their own targets, and become less willing to co-operate with other organizations which work on the same issues. One recent example was the way in which schools, pursuing

their educational attainment targets increased the number of disruptive students who they excluded, leading to a rise in criminality among young people, thus adversely affecting the target attainment of law enforcement agencies (DETR 2000: para 1.7). Finally, linking the achievement of targets to rewards, punishments and status may even encourage outright cheating. As this chapter was being written, the British newspapers were full of pieces about how teachers were deliberately breaking the rules in order to achieve better exam results for their particular students. 'Hundreds of teachers cheated in last month's Sats (standard assessment tests) by helping their pupils or even altering the final answers . . .' began one headline article (Smithers 2002: 1).

'Targetitis' is not the only pathology linked to the NPM. Academic studies, audit bodies and parliamentary investigations have revealed a number of other worrying aspects as follows.

- The more 'arms-length' or 'autonomous' relationships involved in agencification and contracting need careful handling. It is very easy for them to get out of balance so that there is *too little accountability* – managers are given so much freedom that there is some erosion of democratic control. 'In the public sector the rise of "quangos" and other forms of semi-independent agencies has created major gaps in the system of parliamentary accountability' (Bovens 1998: 229). (Accountability is discussed further in Chapter 3, and extensively in Chapter 4.)

- Balance can also be lost in the other direction, that is, *too much* regulation and monitoring can be imposed. A number of commentators have remarked on the way in which increasing nominal autonomy for public sector managers has in practice been accompanied by a significant intensification of different forms of monitoring. Professor Mike Power wrote an influential booklet entitled *The Audit Explosion*, and followed it up with a more extensive work, *The Audit Society* (1997). He argued, not only that auditors were greatly expanding their field of operations, but also that their claims to be able to produce well-founded, 'objective' knowledge were very shaky. A little later a group of London School of Economics academics showed that the regulation of the public sector appeared to have grown rapidly, and in a fairly unco-ordinated way. They described how NPM-style reforms in the UK had been accompanied by an ever-larger army of 'waste-watchers, quality police and sleaze-busters' (Hood *et al.* 1999). The UK may be the most pronounced case of this particular pathology, but some symptoms are also visible in other countries, especially in the field of quality accreditation and inspection. This is one of the things Jeremy, the headteacher, was complaining about in the pub and on the walk home (see earlier this chapter, and Chapter 1).

- There are considerable worries about the way in which NPM reforms *fragment* institutions into many specialized parts. Instead of one, big, multi-purpose ministry one now has a smaller, 'core' ministry, several semi-autonomous specialized agencies, a public–private partnership or two and maybe dozens of contracted out support services – cleaning, catering, building maintenance, computer operations, accountancy and so on. It can be more difficult to 'steer' this flotilla of separate organizations, and therefore more difficult to achieve an integrated service or a 'joined-up' policy (see the discussion of 'joined-up government' in the next chapter).

• It is said that the NPM has encouraged a weakening of the 'public service ethic'. As the security of their employment has diminished, and the pressure on them to produce results has increased, public officials are said to have become more instrumental and calculating in their attitudes. They won't 'go the extra mile' unless their contract specifies it, or some extra bonus or privilege is provided as reward. They are no longer as careful – indeed they *cannot* be as careful – as formerly in their dealings with the commercial world, or so it is claimed. They are no longer as unquestioningly loyal to the minister, being prepared to speak out if they believe they are being asked to 'carry the can' for the negligence or incompetence of politicians (remember the case of the Director General of the Prison Service who sued the minister for wrongful dismissal, mentioned earlier in this chapter?). It is very hard to assess how widespread these developments have been, but I have attempted a more detailed discussion of them in Chapter 6, 'Values, ethics and motives'.

In conclusion, then, what can we say about the relationship between the benefits and disbenefits of the NPM? First, it is important to admit that both are real – this isn't a simple situation where one side is right and the other is wrong. Second, we saw that the connections between specific NPM-type reforms and specific types of result (whether good or bad) are often uncertain, and appear to depend on a variety of factors, including the type of activity in question and certain key features of the context. Third, it looks as though some (but not all) the benefits are directly linked to some (not all) the disbenefits. That is to say, in order to gain the benefit, one is obliged to incur at least some of the disbenefit – there is a trade-off between the two results. Thus, for example, radical downsizing in order to yield savings and promote efficiency is also very likely to damage staff motivation and morale. Or closely linking the status of an organization, or its budget, or the careers of its staff to measured aspects of performance is similarly very likely to focus attention and energy on those measured aspects (good) but is also likely to distract staff from other, unmeasured aspects of performance and may well tempt some to manipulate the data that go into the measures (bad). Thus to remedy one type of error (failing to measure results) may increase another kind of error (a narrow, manipulative approach to a few particular statistics). These situations where there is a 'duality of error' are tremendously difficult to discuss openly, and especially so in an adversarial political environment (Hammond 1996: Chapter 2). Not all such tensions are genuine trade-offs, however. In some cases it is possible to manage in such a way as to gain the benefits while guarding against the disbenefits (Pollitt and Bouckaert 2000: Chapter 7). For example, promoting greater flexibility of treatment of clients by public services *can* generate mistrust if it is poorly explained and badly managed. But this does not appear to be a *necessary* connection: with better management the advantages of flexibility can be reaped without damaging the public's trust in the service.

What emerges from this discussion, therefore, is a pressing need for careful analysis of the specific activities, the goals which are set for the particular reform, and the context in which it is to take place. The NPM may well yield considerable benefits, but not if it is applied in a mechanical or formulaic way, without regard to circumstances. It is a tool that can work well for certain tasks but may prove clumsy or even destructive when used for others.

Is the NPM finished?

Recently, some academics have claimed that the NPM is dying or dead – that is was a late-twentieth-century phenomenon which is now over and done with. For example, the editor of the International Public Management Network's electronic *Newsletter* wrote that 'the tide has changed and the era of comprehensive experimentation with NPM-type reform is coming to a close' (Jones 2001). Such commentators tend to portray the NPM as a rather mechanical approach, focused mainly on targets, savings, efficiency and other concerns of 'internal management'. It is being superseded, they say, by more externally-oriented approaches. These include 'governance', 'joining-up', networks and partnerships – all of which are examined in the next chapter. Here I will briefly assess the proposition that the NPM is, or is almost, a thing of the past.

My own experience suggests that the NPM is by no means 'over'. It may be beginning to seem like 'old hat' in some of the pioneer countries such as New Zealand and the UK, but elsewhere it is still regarded as a central plank in modernization. When I visited Japan in the early part of 2002 most of the Japanese civil servants and academics I met wanted to talk about the NPM. They saw their current wave of reforms, both in central and local government as being informed by NPM ideas and used the term itself – 'NPM' – constantly. As I write this section, in Finland, I am also conducting interviews with senior Finnish civil servants on the subject of central government agencies. They – and their Swedish and Dutch counterparts – are actively concerned with improving the 'steering' of agencies by ministries, mainly by moving towards a tighter set of contract-like agreements, incorporating sharper, more closely measured performance targets. In other words, a fairly NPM-ish agenda. In Finland this process has now been going on for more than five years, but there is still a need to refine and improve the steering instruments. Similarly, NPM-style budgeting, accounting and auditing reforms are proceeding in a number of EU member states, and the European Commission itself is in the midst of a reform programme which includes some NPM-like elements (though not as many as some of its critics would like). In many parts of the developing world, also, NPM ideas are still being very actively implemented. Consider the programmes to create executive agencies in Jamaica and Tanzania or the setting up of independent tax collection agencies in a number of Latin American states (Pollitt and Talbot 2003).

Even in the pioneer Anglo-Saxon 'heartlands' the NPM is not 'over'. While other slogans (partnership, e-government, joining-up) may have taken over the reform headlines, the NPM-ish inheritance of the past decade and a half is not being seriously challenged. Here and there there may have been a little pulling back (some agencies have been drawn back closer to ministers, some experiments with market-type mechanisms in human services have been discontinued or toned down) but the main shift towards a more decentralized, contractualized, output-oriented system remains undisturbed. New types of reform are usually being added on to the NPM inheritance: they are not replacing it.

Summary: does NPM work?

It is very hard to draw general lessons from the mass of material which has poured forth over the past decade or more. On the one hand it is pretty clear that NPM approaches have worked quite well for some services in some jurisdictions at some times. On the other, it seems equally clear that NPM *isn't* an irresistible wave (see above) and that often its claimed benefits are hard to discern in practice. Indeed, when inappropriately applied or incompetently implemented it can generate significant disbenefits, not to say disasters.

So it seems we need to be more precise with the question. Perhaps 'which bits of the NPM work under what circumstances?' would be a more fruitful way of approaching the subject. But even that is a very hard question to answer. There are so many possibly influencing variables – the previously prevailing political and administrative cultures, the available resources, the type of function undergoing reform, the quality and stability of the managers who implement the changes, the influence of accidents and disasters – and so on (Lynn, Heinrich and Hill 2001; Pollitt and Bouckaert 2000: Chapter 2). Many studies take into account only one or two of these factors, so it is hard to know how widely their findings can safely be generalized. This situational complexity is a theme which will recur fairly frequently throughout the rest of the book, and will be the subject of some particular discussion in the final chapter.

My own (necessarily partial) reading of the evidence suggests that there may be some connection between the situations in which NPM seems to work well, and the ideas about publicness and privateness which were explored in Chapter 1. There, you may recall, a multi-factorial, graded view of publicness was put forward (see Table 1.1 and the discussion of the work of Rainey, Boyne and Ranson and Stewart). My suggestion would now be that NPM stands a better chance of realizing its claims when it is applied to activities of 'low' or 'medium' publicness than if it is used to reform a task of high publicness. Thus one might expect the NPM to encounter greater difficulties when applied to local authority social work than when applied to the purchasing function in the Ministry of Transport (to echo the example which was spelled out in Chapter 1). For the same reason it would be easier 'to NPM' an agency which issued driving licences or collected taxes than to do the same to the courts system or an overseas embassy. In one way this should not be surprising, since many of the elements of NPM (Table 2.1) are drawn from the private sector, so they should more easily fit functions which are closer to the private sector in terms of their basic characteristics. However, I should quickly add that my interpretation is both tentative and approximate. All I am suggesting is a loose connection, not a mechanical formula which can be 'read off' from a chart. And, of course, even if true, this would only be a start. The next steps would be to map out in detail which elements of 'publicness' seemed the most toxic towards NPM, and why, and then to test these suggested relationships empirically.

Guide to key sources

As indicated at the beginning of the chapter, the list of publications on NPM is very long indeed (and quite a few have already been cited in the main body of the chapter) so my selection here is fairly brutal.

If you want to see some of the earliest accounts – ones that were subsequently repeatedly referred to – then you should first look at two pieces by Christopher Hood, the 1991 article 'A public management for all seasons?' and the final chapter of his book (also 1991) with Michael Jackson, *Administrative Argument*. These two were sharp analyses of the logic and/or values which characterized the early NPM. My own early contribution *Managerialism and the Public Services* (2nd edn, 1993) also looked in some detail at the actual development of specific reforms, comparing the UK with the USA.

But the literature has come a long way since then. An intense conceptual analysis is offered by the Swede, Jan-Erik Lane (2000), who, in his *New Public Management* sees contracts as the heart of NPM, and is generally sympathetic to its achievements and potential. Lane builds quite an elaborate model of what (he thinks) NPM is. Two more sceptical – and more empirically grounded – accounts are Tom Christensen and Per Lægreid's (2001) *New Public Management* (yes, the academics are running out of titles – indeed, there are actually several books with the same main title) and my work with Geert Bouckaert (2000) *Public Management Reform: A Comparative Analysis*. The first compares Norway and Sweden with Australia and New Zealand, while the second compares ten countries: Australia, Canada, Finland, France, Germany, the Netherlands, New Zealand, Sweden, the UK and the USA. Boyne et al (2003) is one of the few detailed evaluations of the NPM. On a more conceptual/less empirical level Gruening's 2001 paper 'Origin and theoretical basis of New Public Management' offers a more complex account than Lane's somewhat single track interpretation.

NPM has also had a considerable impact – not always beneficial – on the developing world, and on the transitional democracies of central and eastern Europe. Useful sources on the developing world include Willy McCourt and Martin Minogue (2001) *The Internationalization of Public Management: Re-inventing the Third World State* and Nick Manning's (2001) article 'The legacy of the New Public Management in developing countries'.

3

Partnerships, networks, joined-up governance, the information age (and all that)

Introduction

Since roughly the mid-1990s a new, soft-focus image of government has emerged and become very popular (at least on the lips of politicians in several countries, and in certain academic circles). If early NPM was a tough, performance-oriented affair, with economy and efficiency as the watchwords and reform of bureaucracy as the target, the mood of this new approach to governing has been more externally-oriented, with ministers and civil servants apparently taking on the roles of good neighbours to all sorts of other groups and organizations in society. Government is now a good neighbour – someone who informs you about new developments that might affect you, co-operates with you, enables you to realize your own projects, supports you when you are in difficulty, learns from your experience – but hardly ever, it seems, orders you about or invokes the law to force you to do something you don't want to do. Furthermore, this good neighbour has a computer. Networking, partnering, 'joining-up', involving the public and other 'relational' approaches can all be lubricated by the wonders of modern information and communication technologies (ICTs). This is 'governance' – a set of (allegedly) new ideas of 'the involvement of society in the process of governing' (Pierre and Peters 2000: 7).

In this chapter the (related) terms 'governance', 'networks' and 'partnerships' will each be explored and interrogated. There will also be some consideration of the contribution which modern information and communication technologies (ICTs) can and do (and can't and don't) make to these new forms and styles of government.

A few snippets from Mr Blair's 1999 white paper *Modernising Government* will help illustrate how these sorts of terms have begun to colonize political and administrative discourse:

> The information age offers huge scope for organizing government activities in new, innovative and better ways and for making life easier for the public by providing public services in integrated, imaginative and more convenient ways . . . .
>
> (Prime Minister and Minister for the Cabinet Office 1999: 9)

Distinctions between services delivered by the public and the private sector are breaking down in many areas, opening the way to new ideas, partnerships and opportunities for devising and delivering what the public wants.

(Prime Minister and Minister for the Cabinet Office 1999: 9)

The Government will take its drive for more joined up and responsive services further by:
actively encouraging **initiatives to establish partnership delivery** by all parts of government . . . .

(Prime Minister and Minister for the Cabinet Office 1999: 32, original emphasis)

The Government must bring about a fundamental change in the way we use IT. We must modernise the business of government itself – achieving joined up working between different parts of government and providing new, efficient and convenient ways for citizens and businesses to communicate with government and receive services.

(Prime Minister and Minister for the Cabinet Office 1999: 45)

And so on – there are metres and metres of this kind of stuff in the official pronouncements of the 1997–2001 Labour Government. But what are we to make of it? It *sounds* good (indeed, like virtue, it sounds quite unopposable), but what, in concrete terms, does it mean? Will it work? If it is so logical and sensible, why wasn't it done before? Are there hidden costs? This chapter will attempt to pry behind the somewhat bland frontage of the 'new governance' in order to investigate these and other questions.

Partnerships in Middleton

[*The scene: a meeting of the Borough of Middleton's Strategic Partnership Board in the spring of 2002. Middleton is a medium-sized town in northern England. The Strategic Partnership Board was created a year ago, and consists of elected councillors plus representatives from some of the organizations which are involved in partnerships with the council – such as the residents association of a town centre district that is being redeveloped, a senior police officer for the Crime and Disorder Group and the director of a string of playgroups, who is on the Early Years Development and Childcare Project.*

The idea of the Strategic Partnership Board (SPB) is that it will take an overview of the (many) partnership arrangements with which the council is involved. It will try to develop an overall policy towards partnerships, and to identify and spread 'best practice'. The SPB is chaired by Elizabeth Padgett, a Labour councillor and Deputy Leader of Middleton Council. It is serviced by the Middleton Corporate Management Team, who is represented at this meeting by Tariq Ramzan, a Senior Policy Adviser.]

Tariq Ramzan: Our first agenda item today is the report from the District Audit on partnership working in Middleton. I would like to ask David Whitehouse, who led in the production of the report, to introduce it – David?

David Whitehouse: My name is David Whitehouse, and I work for the District Audit service. [*The lights go down and he flashes up his first PowerPoint screen.*] Three months ago you asked us to produce an overview report on partnership working in the town, with a view to developing the council's policy towards partnerships, and sharing best practice. You have all received copies of my report, so I would like to take this opportunity simply to pick out the highlights.

First, it should be acknowledged that Middleton has considerable experience in running partnerships. As many as 25 different partnerships were identified in our study, and some of those have been in existence for five years or more – in other words long before the present government began to lay such great emphasis on the desirability of partnership working.

[*His next PowerPoint screen shows a long list of partnerships, including the Arkwright Street Redevelopment Partnership, the Crime and Disorder Group, the Early Years Development and Childcare Partnership and the Gay and Lesbian Rights Partnership.*]

However, despite some pioneering work, of which the participants can be proud, we also found a lack of communication *between* partnerships, and a lack of uniformity in the approach to the ways in which partnerships should be managed. We believe therefore – and this is our prime recommendation – that there is a need to develop a corporate approach – a corporate model of effective partnership working.

Second, we found some confusion as to what was and what was not a partnership, and we therefore suggest that the council should develop and agree a clear definition of what constitutes a 'partnership'.

Third, we found that a number of members and officers were unsure of their roles in relation to partnerships. For example, a councillor might act as a member of a partnership, or as a member of a scrutiny committee that reviewed a partnership, or as a local ward representative asking questions about a partnership. There is, therefore, a clear training need. Both members and officers need to be supported with a proper training programme that will clarify the different roles that can be played in and around partnerships, both for members and for officers.

Fourth, we came to the conclusion that the lack of communication between partnerships might mean that useful lessons were being lost – oh! [*At this moment the PowerPoint develops a hitch and David Whitehouse cannot coax his next screen to appear. After wrestling with it for a minute or so he gives up, and switches the computer off.*] Well, I'm sorry about that, but I will continue without the visual aids. Uuum . . . . Yes, as I was saying, there really needs to be a central point that ensures that good practice ideas are spread from one partnership to the others, and that information about problems is also shared, so that different partnerships don't go on repeating similar mistakes.

As you will see from the report, these were our main conclusions.

Elizabeth Padgett (in the chair): Thank you Mr Whitehouse. We are grateful for your useful study. May I now invite SPB members to comment? Yes, Harriet?

Harriet Roberts (A Labour councillor, and member of the Early Years Development and Childcare Project): I'm sure this is right. Partnerships are the way forward for modern governance, and we must learn more from each other about how they work best. It's common sense – I support the recommendations in the report.

Bill Paisley (Managing director of a local construction company, and involved in the Arkwright Street redevelopment): Well, I don't want to pour cold water, but I have to confess I still don't really understand what it's all about. Reading the report I gather that we don't really know what partnerships are, but we are nevertheless sure that they are 'A Good Thing' and that we must have more of them. Then – and this sounds a bit bureaucratic to me – we get into training courses and secretariats to spread good practice. I may be naïve, but I want to ask why? What do we expect to gain from comparing a town centre redevelopment project with childcare arrangements or the protection of gay and lesbian rights? They are all so different. We are all busy people, so it seems to me we need some more concrete aims in view than just sharing experiences and setting up more training courses.

Sharon Shaw (A Lib-Dem councillor, known for her opposition to the commercial expansion and new car park envisaged in the Arkwright Street redevelopment): I wonder if Mr Paisley isn't missing the point? Isn't it precisely *because* we don't really know what partnerships are that we need to get together and share ideas? Plunging ahead down our own tracks is exactly what we are trying to get away from. [*Murmurs of assent from Harriet Roberts.*]

Bill Paisley: But it's all so vague! Of course we could sit round sharing ideas about all manner of things that we don't yet understand, and I grant you that occasionally something good would come out of it. But that isn't the point. I'm interested in results – and I think that's what the council says it's interested in as well. And time is the scarcest resource – for some of us anyway. [*Here he glances meaningfully at Sharon Shaw, who is the wife of the senior partner in a local law firm, and has no paid employment other than her role as a councillor.*] So I want us to use it in ways that are focused on getting some concrete outcomes. In that context learning how better to define partnerships doesn't figure very high up my list of priorities.

Inspector Ronald Genue (police representative on the Crime and Disorder Group): With respect, Madam Chairman, the point about time and effort is a real one. In the police force we already have six local Partnerships Against Crime and a School Liaison Committee. When our officers are attending these meetings that means they are not on the beat. If now we are going to add training courses and further cross-partnership meetings of various kinds I am not sure where we will get the manpower from.

Harriet Roberts: Or womanpower.

Ronald Genue: Quite.

Elizabeth Padgett (from the chair): Mr Whitehouse, it might be useful if you could put a little more flesh on some aspects of your report. What do you really mean by a corporate approach, and could you give us some examples of the kinds of lessons that could be learned from one partnership by another?

David Whitehouse: Certainly. By a corporate approach I mean that different partnerships should be run on the same basic principles, within a single local philosophy. I also mean that care should be taken to ensure that the decisions of one partnership should take account of the decisions of the others, so that both duplications and contradictions are minimized. As for lessons to be learned, I think that the Crime and Disorder Group, for example, did some excellent work on developing common priorities for fighting crime. And the Early Years Partnership has evolved an interesting way of running its meetings, with equal speaking times for all members of the group.

Bill Paisley: Mr Whitehouse's answer illustrates my point rather well. It *assumes* that everything should be connected to everything else – that the decisions of one partnership should always be made in the light of the decisions of all the other partnerships. But this is crazy! Does it mean that when I'm negotiating over what kind of shops to have and what type of car parking provision to make in the Arkwright Street development I should be checking back all the time with the Gay and Lesbian Rights Partnership? I mean – we'd never get anywhere at all. Now if you suggested that I talk a bit with other town centre redevelopment projects, then that would make more sense. But I've already done that – and not through this Partnership Board, because the most interesting schemes aren't in Middleton. No, I've done it off my own bat, through my own networks, just as I imagine some of the other partnership representatives here will have done on their own accounts.

David Whitehouse: I don't think anyone is suggesting that every partnership needs to talk to every other all the time.

Bill Paisley: Then what *are* you suggesting? Your report doesn't offer any criteria for selecting when to talk and what to talk about. What is a strategic issue and what is not? Can you help us a bit more with that?

David Whitehouse (glancing rather pleadingly towards chairperson Padgett): Well, for example, relations with councillors – how they are going to relate to the partnership – that's a general issue.

Harriet Roberts: Absolutely – that's the key to a democratic approach.

Bill Paisley: It may surprise you to know that this was one part of Mr Whitehouse's report that I rather agreed with. I mean the bit where he said that some councillors seemed rather confused about what their roles were – members of partnerships, lobbyists, critics who stand outside the process, or what. I won't name any names, but there are one or two who have tried to jump from one role to another and then another, as it pleases them, with respect to the Arkwright Street project. But I doubt whether going to a seminar with them will change that – that's just politics. I've already told at least one councillor what I think of all this dancing around, but I doubt if it will make any difference. There's some what want to get things done and some who'd rather just talk about it.

Elizabeth Padgett (just getting in ahead of a now quite agitated Sharon Shaw): Well, this is a useful debate, but we have 12 further items on the agenda this evening, and we must get on. I propose that we note the District Audit report with thanks and remit the Corporate Management Team to come forward to our next meeting with some concrete, costed proposals for selected information sharing and training events. I would ask the Corporate Management Team to bear in mind Mr Paisley's remarks, and select only those issues or themes where they believe there is a real chance of positive synergies. Is that acceptable to the board?

[Most heads nod. No-one objects. Tariq Ramzan turns to his assistant and mutters behind his hand: 'Fudge, fudge, fudge. They can't agree so they ask us to come up with a solution. Round we go again.']

Partnerships: the academic literature

There is a large and rapidly-growing academic literature about public–private partnerships. It is an international literature, including notable contributions from individuals and groups in the UK (for example: Huxham and Vangen 2000b; Lowndes and Skelcher 1998; Osborne 2000), the USA (Bardach 1998; Rosenau 2000) and the Netherlands (Teisman and Klijn 2002). It covers, inter alia, basic motives for partnership, the processes by which partnerships are formed, how they evolve, what kind of results they achieve, and how they may be evaluated. Since the late 1990s there is even an *International Journal of Public–Private Partnerships*. As one reads this literature a number of basic points rapidly become clear, and these stand in some contrast to the rosy-hued views purveyed in some official statements. Some partnerships work well, other do not. Difficulties are commonplace, even if they are often surmounted. When Mr Blair's white paper says that his government will encourage 'initiatives to establish partnership delivery by all parts of government' (see the first section of this chapter) it sounds as though partnerships are a well-understood, all-purpose piece of managerial technology. The main message I draw from the academic literature is very different – that 'partnership' is a very variable concept, that it is often not well-understood, and that, while it seems to work reasonably well under certain conditions, there are many situations in which it should probably not be the government's first choice of organizational form.

The motives for partnership

Linder (2000) provides us with a useful list of six different meanings which can be conveyed by the term 'partnership'. In Table 3.1 I have converted these meanings into motives, changing Linder's terminology slightly, to try to show the wide range of rationales that can lie behind partnership formation.

It should immediately be apparent from Table 3.1 that there are some tensions between the different motives, and that a single partnership is unlikely to be able to satisfy all these motives simultaneously. Motive 5 (downsizing), for example, is one usually held by neo-liberals and others who wish to 'minimize' the state because they don't trust it to act efficiently or fairly (Pollitt and Bouckaert 2000: Chapter 8). However, motives 1 (modernization) and 3 (legitimacy) are both concerned with *strengthening* the state, and making it more efficient and trusted.

Table 3.1   Motives for partnership formation (loosely based on Linder 2000)

Motive	Comment
1 Management reform and modernization	By working in partnership with the private sector, public managers will learn how to run programmes more flexibly and efficiently
2 Attracting private finance	By partnering, public agencies will be able to tap into private finance, enabling them to pursue projects which could not (yet) be afforded from public budgets alone
3 Public legitimacy	Participation in a partnership is seen as a good in itself – symbolic of a pooling of talents from government, the market sector and the voluntary sector in the pursuit of worthy public purposes
4 Risk shifting	Private partners assume part or the whole of the financial risk associated with projects. Similar motive to 2, above
5 Downsizing the public sector	Like contracting out and privatization, public–private partnerships may be seen by those who favour downsizing the public service as a way to get tasks which were formerly performed by public sector staff handed over to the staff of commercial or voluntary organizations
6 Power sharing	Partnerships may be seen as promoting more co-operative, 'horizontal', less authoritarian and hierarchical relationships

Another point to be taken from Table 3.1 is that the motives for partnership may not be particularly 'high-flown' at all, but actually rather 'base'. Governments may enter into partnerships not from any sincere wish to forge common purposes and share talents, but just to get someone else to bear a substantial share of the risks and costs of a project. Rosenau (2000) terms such arrangements 'minimalist' partnerships, and they may be rather common. For example, much of the rationale behind the UK's Private Finance Initiative (PFI) is to get private investment to substitute for public investment, through a series of public–private partnerships. Rowe and Devanney (2002: 1) quote a local partnership worker as saying that 'Partnership working consists of the temporary suppression of mutual loathing in the interests of mutual greed'.

There is one important reason why partnerships are formed which does not appear in Table 3.1. Partnerships are often formed because they are *required by some higher authority*. The European Commission, UK central government, and many other jurisdictions frequently make the existence of a partnership a qualification for bidding for certain types of finance or support. Bache (2001) describes how two different urban regeneration programmes in the same part of Sheffield, one run by the European Commission and the other by UK central government, both formally required partnerships. As he shows, this does not necessarily lead to an enthusiastic and full-blooded approach to the joys of participatory working. I have myself taken part in at least one research project financed by the EU, where a requirement was that the bid came from a partnership of institutions with their bases in at least three member states. Some aspects of this partnership were not so much 'minimalist' as 'sleeping' – in a two-and-a-half-year project one 'partner' never showed up at even a single meeting. His university was satisfied by having the project on his CV, while the rest of us (the 'active' partners) did not actually need his skills at all, and had only included him in the bid because we thought that the Commission would like to see a representative from that particular country on the sheet. As I recall, we did receive one message of good wishes from him at an early stage, but that was it.

Partnerships as a category

There are many quite different types of partnership – so different that it seems improbable that much that is useful and accurate can be said about partnerships *in general* (in this sense I have some sympathy with Bill Paisley). Consider, for example, the range of forms of PPPs shown in Table 3.2.

Thus, for example, British Columbia Online is a PPP in the buy–develop–operate category. Originally BC Online was government-run. It sold data from government databases to users – for example information about land claims to would-be property developers. A private sector company called MDA then bought BC Online for Canadian $55 million, although the databases remain the property of the government. Users of BC Online pay a fee, part of which goes to MDA and part of which is passed on to the government. All operational risks are carried by MDA. The economic risk (of unprofitability) is shared between the government and MDA according to a formula linked to transaction volumes.

Table 3.2 Forms of public–private partnerships (PPPs)

Type of partnership (private partner is responsible for . . .)	Degree of private sector involvement
Operations and maintenance	Low
Design–build	
Design–build–operate	
Wrap around addition	
Build–lease–operate	
Temporary privatization	
Lease/buy–develop–operate	
Build–transfer–operate	
Build–own–operate–transfer	
Build–own–operate	High

However, the classification in Table 3.2 mainly concerns projects involving the management of facilities and services and based upon some kind of commercial contract. It therefore understates the sheer variety of partnerships 'out there'. As we saw in the Middleton case, partnerships are also used for planning issues, for community development, for promotion of a locality, for educational campaigns, for joint working between health and social care agencies, or for any of a long list of other purposes (see, for example: Greer 2001; Rosenau 2000; Teisman and Klijn 2002). Public–private partnerships may be between public sector authorities and commercial companies (as in the BC Online example) or between public authorities and non-profit, voluntary associations, or between all three types of organization. Other partnerships may be public–public, such as those between central and local government or between housing authorities and the police, or between hospitals and social services departments. The topic of public–public partnerships shades off into that of 'joined-up government' (see the section, 'Joined-up government', p. 67).

Thus information-sharing may be useful, but the probability of this rises if the sharing takes place between projects with similar overall objectives, or which operate in a similar budgetary or legal environment. When Middleton chairperson Elizabeth Padgett asked her management team to come up with selected recommendations she was really asking them to puzzle out what were the crucial criteria of similarity and difference – a tough job, given the range of partnerships that were represented around the table.

As for the assumption that partnerships are normally egalitarian structures – partnerships of equals who come together voluntarily to share skills, information and resources – the literature cries out loud and clear that this happy state of affairs is the exception rather than the rule (Bache 2001; Lowndes and Skelcher 1998). More commonly than not, some partners are richer or more powerful than others, and can effectively veto ideas which do not appeal to them. If a local authority is working 'in partnership' with small local community groups, the disparity in organizing capacity and resources is likely to be huge. There is therefore nothing *automatically* 'horizontal' about partnerships, if by horizontal one means roughly equal in relevant resources, although procedural rules.can be devised which may help to limit the effects of resource disparities.

One simple lesson that can be drawn from this great variety is that just to say something is a 'partnership' tells one very little. One would need to know much more about the members, their goals, their resources and the rules of procedure before serious analysis or assessment could begin.

Gains from partnerships

Academic research does not indicate that the partnership form (or, more accurately, forms – see previous section) regularly produce(s) performance gains. In other words, we cannot assume that they usually 'work', in terms of delivering better programmes. A survey of the American partnership literature concluded that:

> Public–private partnerships improve short-term cost performance in several policy sectors studied here, but only to a very small degree. Long-term calculations are more complicated and could shift the balance in the other direction. Externalities could also easily overturn any savings. Quality performance is mixed on noneconomic performance variables.
>
> (Rosenau 2000: 233–4)

Meanwhile two of the most experienced partnership action-researchers in the UK summed up their findings as follows:

> Those involved in partnerships frequently comment that little is being achieved. We regularly hear people complain that they are forever attending meetings but that there is little in the way of material output. Where achievements are made they comment that the process of getting there has been slow and painful in the sense that the various parties have found it difficult to agree on actions, responsibilities and so on. It is not uncommon for people to argue that positive outputs have happened despite the partnership rather than because of it!
>
> (Huxham and Vangen 2000a: 294)

Conditions for successful partnerships

As one would expect from the preceding paragraphs, the specification of conditions is a complex matter in which one usually has to say something about what kind of partnership one is talking about, and what the success criteria are supposed to be, before a list of characteristics or factors can have much meaning.

I will briefly summarize two recent pieces of research which sought to identify the consequences of partnership and the conditions that influenced those consequences. These two sources are certainly not exhaustive, but they do give some flavour of the kinds of factors which current scholarship is focusing on.

The first piece is the concluding chapter of an edited American collection (Rosenau 2000). Pauline Rosenau poses and answers a series of questions about partnerships, basing her responses on an overview of 11 substantive chapters covering partnerships in areas such as technology research and development, nuclear power, transportation, infrastructure, environmental policy, education, health policy, welfare and prisons. Reduced to their essentials, her findings (for the USA) are roughly as follows:

- *What is the state of evaluation of PPPs?* Not much is known – 'politics and discourse seem to drive the process' (Rosenau 2000: 217).
- *What forms do PPPs take?* Several. Some involve little co-operation and may be *de facto* close to privatization (Rosenau 2000: 219).
- *What effects do partnerships have on costs and quality?* The evidence on costs is mixed. Generally it seems that partnership at least does not increase costs in the short term. Quality of service may also increase, though not by much. In some cases greater efficiency is achieved at the price of less of some other desirable quality, such as equity or accountability. External effects are very difficult to calculate and are usually not taken into account. They may well be negative (Rosenau 2000: 221).
- *What about equity, access and democracy?* Hard to generalize – the picture is complicated (Rosenau 2000: 222).
- *Can PPPs be trusted to deal with particularly vulnerable sections of the population such as the elderly or the mentally ill?* There are dangers, particularly where profit-oriented commercial companies are supplying services to the vulnerable in competitive markets (Rosenau 2000: 223).
- *Do PPPs increase public participation in the policy process?* There is evidence that sometimes PPPs have reduced public participation, but, on the other hand, in principle, PPPs can be structured so as to encourage participation (Rosenau 2000: 224).
- *Do partnerships decrease regulation?* Not necessarily (Rosenau 2000: 225).
- *Are PPPs sufficiently accountable?* There are no easy solutions here. Some are, some aren't. Again, much depends on how the partnerships are structured – is a clear set of rules for accountability written in from the outset? (Rosenau 2000: 228).
- *Can there be conflicts of interest in PPPs?* Sometimes there are. The definition of objectives is once more crucial here. 'Where tangible economic benefits accrue to both public (government) and private partners, the public interest is not always well served . . . when a coalition of businesses (in need of a ready supply of prisoners) and politicians (for whom prison projects give a tough-on-crime image that they believe will gain votes) find their interests aligned

. . . the total cost of incarceration may go up because of the greatly increased cost to the public of incarcerating people who do not need to be incarcerated' (Rosenau 2000: 229).

- *What are the conditions for success?* Key decisions need to be made at the beginning of a partnership, and set out in a concrete plan. Lines of responsibility must be clarified. Achievable goals should be identified and stated. Partners should be given some incentives to pursue the goals. The whole operation requires systematic monitoring (Rosenau 2000: 232–3).

Interestingly, these conclusions quite closely match those of an earlier Dutch analyst, Kouwenhoven (1993). Attention to the processes and organizational structures of partnerships is also seen as of key importance in Huxham and Vangen's (2000a) summary, 'What makes partnerships work?'.

The second study is of partnerships in the particularly difficult circumstances of Northern Ireland (Greer 2001). The author surveys a good deal of literature and comes to the conclusion that 'there is no one model for success' (Greer 2001: 35). He also makes the interesting point that, since we don't know enough to be confident about getting the design right at the start, it can be vital to set up procedures for learning from the early experiences of partnership, and adjusting to its different phases. This echoes the findings of English researchers Lowndes and Skelcher (1998). Finally, he warns of the dangers; 'too many partnership initiatives creates fragmentation, increases confusion among participants and limits strategic development' (Greer 2001: 247). A partial remedy may be the establishment of 'an overall framework in the form of an institutional or government structure . . . to oversee partnerships, particularly to ensure common policy development, allocate funding and provide advice and guidelines in management' (Greer 2001: 248). Greer is mainly concerned with relatively small scale, local partnerships, and believes they need a guiding governmental hand.

Partnerships are evidently therefore something of a slippery topic. Whether or not they are 'a good thing' would appear to depend on *what* the partnerships are for, *who* they are between, and *how* they are managed. Some guidelines are beginning to emerge, and certainly some theories and models are starting to appear in the literature (for some idea of the level of complexity of such proto theories, see Table 2.4 in Greer 2001: 46–7). The concept of 'partnership' certainly enjoys the favourable 'vibes' mentioned at the beginning of this chapter – it seems to be a more 'horizontal', equal form of relationship than a bureaucratic hierarchy. Thus it carries an apparent legitimacy that more authoritarian modes of managing are thought to have lost (I say 'apparent' because of multiple case study evidence that many partnerships are inegalitarian, and dominated by one or two key members). Ideas of 'horizontality' can be extended still further. Beyond partnerships lie other, even flatter and more flexible forms of relationship, which we can refer to collectively as 'networks'. They have attracted such widespread attention in the academic world that they deserve a section of their own.

Networks: forwards to the past?

In the mid-1990s Manuel Castells, a famous Spanish professor of sociology and planning who had worked in universities all over the world, published three ambitious volumes analysing contemporary global social and economic trends. Significantly, his first volume was entitled *The Rise of the Network Society*. Networks, he saw as central to a new era in which nation states became weakened and 'hollowed out' both by the development of *global* relationships and by the flourishing vigour of *local* political movements and identities. At the end of his second volume, he summed up the matter thus:

> Power . . . is no longer concentrated in institutions (the state), organizations (capitalist firms), or symbolic controllers (corporate media, churches). It is diffused in global networks of wealth, power, information and images, which circulate and transmute in a system of variable geometry and dematerialized geography.
>
> (Castells 1997: 359)

Castells thus provides the background for our much more humble concerns with networks as a factor in the work of public managers. How can his global vision be 'downloaded' into the public management debate? Well, a good start can be made by considering this quotation from a recent article in *Public Management Review* (Klijn 2002: 150–1):

> To overstate the image, one could say that the classic image of the state that organizes service delivery and policymaking with its own bureaucracy is being replaced by a state which only sets the conditions and tries to specify the products or policy aims it wants to achieve. Then other actors carry out the implementation . . . .
>
> But the hollow state is not only characterized by the fact that the implementation of politics is increasingly being done by autonomous actors. The hollow state is also characterized by the complexity of its decision making. Because policy cannot be controlled from the centre, decision making involves more actors and becomes more complex.

Klijn's perspective therefore takes us far beyond the 'contracting out' that was one of the key ingredients of the NPM. It takes us to a world where policy-making itself (not just implementation) is shared out across networks of institutions and groups. It also takes us to a world where policy-makers are frequently uncertain about the nature of the extremely complex problems which face them, about which organizations can or should be given responsibility for these problems, and about what strategies may be feasible and acceptable to the many interested parties involved.

It is easy to be persuaded by the literature on networks and partnerships. It is already huge and is still growing fast. It has many distinguished and thoughtful contributors, especially in Germany, the Netherlands, the UK and the USA. It has developed a technical language of its own (and that language sounds more modern and less threatening than traditional political and administrative language – 'inter-dependency', 'steering', 'interactive', 'complexity', 'diversity'). In some countries the network approach can boast that it has attracted the support of powerful politicians. And yet, on the whole, I find it unsatisfying, indeed, at times, frustrating. This is *not* because I deny the existence or sometimes importance of networks. On the contrary, it is hard to ignore them, and plenty of people talked about and acknowledged their significance long before the network theorists appropriated the concept. No, my disappointment with the network theory literature – and most of the political rhetoric on 'networked solutions' and 'partnerships' – derives from a number of (what I see as) serious weaknesses in the contemporary debate. The main ones are the following:

- The ahistorical assumption that networks and partnerships are somehow new. This slides in to many of the network writings by references which contrast networks with 'existing forms of neo-corporate decision-making' (Klijn and Koppenjan 2000: 368) or 'traditional forms of governing based on a top-down perspective and a rational central rule approach' (Kooiman 1993: 255). 'We live in a network society . . .' we are told, and therefore 'It is *no longer possible* for politicians to take authoritative, substantive decisions on the basis of ideology or representation of a clearly defined electorate' (Klijn and Koppenjan 2000: 383–4, my italics). The need for effective governance of . . . interactions, and therefore for *new* forms of public management such as network steering will increase . . .' (Kickert, Klijn and Koppenjan 1997: 190, my italics).

- The confident assertion that we have more networks now, and that they are more important. A number of authors quite cheerfully advance this point as though it were a fact. But, as far as I am aware, no-one has been able to count either the number of networks which existed in the past, or measure their importance in any reasonably robust way. In fact networks are rather difficult to define, and very hard to count. So we just can't know these things. What we do know is that networks have been around for decades, and that 'the centre' has frequently found it hard to steer them. To take just one historical case, Pemberton (2001) offers a carefully researched account of central government trying but failing to steer a network concerned with industrial training in the late 1950s and early 1960s. He concludes that 'the attempt to revolutionize British industrial training in the 1960s has revealed that British policy-making was already conducted within a polity characterized by fragmentation, inter-dependency and self-organizing policy networks and that the core executive already lacked the power to impose change' (Pemberton 2001: 18).

- The assumption (or, in some cases, open assertion) that networks somehow represent a more advanced form of democracy than traditional representative democracy. This is sometimes taken to the point of claiming that representative politicians should stand aside for networks and network-generated solutions to public problems. An example here would be Klijn and Koppenjan's discussion of attempts to bridge the gap between politicians and the electorate. In an article on networks and 'interactive policymaking' they say that such attempts 'can only be successful if they are based on a new interpretation of political primacy. This primacy is not so much based on the right to define the substance of government policy based on an *ex ante* interpretation of the general interest, but on the capacity to initiate and guide societal discourses aimed at the exploration of interests, the creation of solutions, and thus the *gradual discovery* of the common interest' (Klijn and Koppenjan 2000: 385, original italics). Klijn and Koppenjan are to be praised for stating the proposition so explicitly – in other texts the superior political legitimacy of network-engendered solutions is hinted at rather than openly declared. The problem, to my mind, is that this proposition is highly controversial, and I see little evidence that, in general, citizens find decisions taken by networks democratically superior to the same decisions taken by democratically elected politicians. There are so many issues to be discussed in this regard – What kind of decisions? Taken by what kind of networks (networks can be highly *un*democratic and *un*transparent)? Compared with what kind of traditional ministry-and-parliament arrangements? In any case, is it an either/or choice (traditional approach/network approach) or can there be a combination? If so, how can such a combination best be organized? Regrettably, few of the network theorists seem to venture far into this maze of problems.

- The methodological weaknesses of many (not all) books and articles on networks and partnerships. Too often, one or a few case studies are examined – frequently in a loosely descriptive way – and on this slim basis big generalizations are offered about networks or partnerships in general. For example, *Managing Complex Networks*, one of the best-known books on networks during the late 1990s, says hardly anything about the methodological problems of researching networks (Kickert, Klijn and Koppenjan 1997).

- The theoretical weaknesses of most books and articles on networks and partnerships. As Dowding (1995) has trenchantly argued, the main burden of network theory explanations is often placed on the resources, strategies (etc.) of individual actors in the network, not on the properties of networks as such. So the network concept serves more as a useful metaphor than as the real basis for the explanation. The latter is much more orthodox than it may at first appear, since it concerns the resources, interests and strategies of individual actors. In other words, in practice, network theorists explanations tend to use exactly the same building blocks as have been used by political scientists and public administrationists for decades.

- For the public manager, perhaps the biggest disappointment of all is the paucity of interesting and tested propositions for action coming from network theory. Some theorists fight shy of any general propositions at all. 'Because of the complex character of interaction, due to the variety in strategies and perceptions of different actors, we do not believe in the fruitfulness of suggesting a contingency scheme with regard to which strategy is appropriate in which situation' (Kickert, Klijn and Koppenjan 1997: 169). Others do offer general statements, but these tend to be highly abstract and hard to translate into specific actions in specific circumstances. For example, government organizations should take 'an external and interactive orientation', and government 'should try to disperse macro responsibilities to social actors' (Kooiman 1993: 261). The output of middle-range, context-nuanced generalizations seems rather modest (the partnership literature is probably more advanced on this score than the network literature – see previous section).

This is not to say that network theory has nothing to offer. Rather, I see it as just somewhat overblown. At its worst it offers a romantic vision of a whole new way of governing, pivoted on a disparate bunch of case studies, usually drawn from a limited number of sectors. At its best, though, it reminds us of the (longstanding) importance of informal relationships *between* organizations and groups, and how these interorganizational dynamics can set the context for more formal and specific processes of decision-making. Some of the literature also suggests ways of modelling or classifying different network structures and processes. For example, the distinction between network management and network restructuring (just playing the game, or seeking to change the rules of the game) is a useful one, as is the idea that it may be useful to appoint some trusted but fairly independent figure to the network management role (Kickert, Klijn and Koppenjan 1997: Chapter 10). Overall, however:

> What might be surprising to practitioners looking for new insights is just how few specific and practical 'tricks' are actually offered that are not at some level just common sense, or simply applications to the field of trust building, network steering or partnership building of much wider and more general good management practices.
>
> (6 *et al.* 2002: 128)

Joined-up government

'Joined-up government' (hereafter JUG) goes along with 'networks' and 'partnership' as one more theme in the current wave of interest in 'horizontal' approaches to governing and organizing. Indeed, it overlaps with ideas of partnership. It has an obvious and particular relevance for the public manager since it purports to be a new way of organizing what goes on in the public sector.

JUG has become one of the principal themes in the 'modernization' programme of Tony Blair's New Labour administration. Although it was not a prominent goal at the time of the 1997 General Election, it became so with the March 1999 white paper *Modernising Government* (Prime Minister and Minister for the Cabinet Office 1999). There have also been strong echoes of the JUG theme in some other countries, although sometimes under other names (6 *et al.* 2002; Hagen and Kubicek 2000; OECD 2001).

Despite this prominence, however, it is by no means entirely clear what, in concrete terms, JUG means. In the early UK literature on joined-up-ness explicit definitions were rare – for example, the foundational Cabinet Office paper *Wiring It Up* does not have one (Cabinet Office 2000). JUG has emerged as a fashionable term-of-art, rather than a precise scientific or technical concept.

JUG has at least four underlying goals. The first concerns the wish to eliminate contradictions and tensions between different policies, and is therefore aimed directly at increasing the effectiveness of policies. One case from the 1990s was the way in which a well-intentioned intensification of performance management in schools 'led to a dramatic rise in the exclusion of difficult pupils from school and a rise in criminality among young people' (DETR 2000: para. 1.7).

The second goal behind JUG is to make better use of resources, through the elimination and duplication and/or contradiction between different programmes. For example, it has frequently been observed that school buildings lie empty and unused for significant parts of the year – or week – and could perhaps be used for other community activities, saving the need to hire or build other accommodation for these. Sharing buildings, staff, information or equipment may lead to a more efficient use of resources.

The third goal is to improve the flow of good ideas and co-operation between different stakeholders in a particular policy sector, thus producing 'synergy' or smarter ways of working. On 'problem estates', for example, joint working between the police, local authority housing departments, schools, local shopkeepers and residents associations may generate new, innovative and more effective approaches.

The fourth goal is to produce a more integrated or 'seamless' set of services, from the point of view of the citizens who use them. Thus a 'one stop shop' may enable a resident to pay local taxes, get information about improvement grants, access local public health services and get advice from a Citizen's Advice Bureau, all at the same premises. Or a well-designed website will enable the citizens who use it easily to transfer their search to other websites belonging to other public agencies or services that may be of interest to them.

This fourfold classification is predominantly managerial. Clearly, however, JUG also has a strong *political* dimension. It can be presented as an approach which chimes, rhetorically and operationally, with the emerging theme of 'partnership'. It appears to be 'inclusive', and could be contrasted by New Labour with the alleged abrasiveness of the previous Conservative governments. It could also be used to differentiate New Labour from the fragmentizing, NPM-ish policies of its predecessors: 'An increasing separation between policy and delivery has acted as a barrier to involving in policy-making those people who are responsible for delivering results in the front line' (Prime Minister and Minister for the Cabinet Office 1999: 15). JUG was to be the answer to contemporary fears about the 'hollowing out' of British central government (Rhodes 1997). In short, it sounded good – catchy, inclusive, common-sensical and sufficiently different from the policies of the defeated Conservatives.

It should be noted that different aspects of JUG have manifested themselves under different labels. In the UK debate 'cross-cutting issues' has become a term of art. Similarly 'holistic government' has been used to denote a territory which very much includes JUG, although it sometimes carries the additional, almost spiritual, connotations of 'connexity'. A more pedestrian, but perhaps more immediately understandable term is 'service integration', which is in wide use in North America and some parts of Europe.

As a number of commentators have noted, 'joining up' only *seems* new. In fact it is the latest manifestation of one of the oldest preoccupations in the field of politics and public administration – the *co-ordination* of policy-making and administration (see: Kavanagh and Richards 2001: 3; Pollitt 2003). Recent scholarship suggests that it is particularly associated with centrist administrations (6 *et al.* 2002: 16–18).

Within the broad notion of JUG sketched above, lie some important distinctions and elaborations, including:

- The distinction between joined-up *policy-making* (such as a co-ordinated policy for the elderly or youth or transport) and joined-up *implementation* (such as the delivery of multiple services through One Stop Shops, or the synchronization of local bus, metro and tram timetables).
- Acknowledgement that the line between policy-making and implementation is often far from watertight. In so far as this is true, it becomes insufficient to think of joining up policy-making as simply a matter of joining up those individuals – mainly ministers and senior officials – whose roles are formally designated as being concerned with 'policy'. Implementation 'infects' policy-making – and *vice versa.*
- The Cabinet Office also make a distinction between 'broad over-arching themes used to pull together a range of policies and decisions to ensure that they add up to a coherent picture and, on the other hand, objectives used to bind together and provide a framework for the performance management of a cross-cutting programme' (Cabinet Office 2000: para. 4.10). The example they give of the first is checking the impact of policies on women, and the example they give of the second is setting a cross-cutting objective of 'reducing crime and fear of crime' for the whole of the criminal justice system. One might characterize this as concerning the *intensity* of joining up, ranging from looser forms of co-ordination (having some unit to 'keep an eye out' for contradictions) to progressively tighter systems, driven by common operational objectives, joint budgets or even agreed action protocols.
- The distinction between *horizontal* linkages (for example, when three or four ministries combine to formulate a single coherent policy on youth) and *vertical* linkages (where a ministry co-ordinates its actions 'upwards' with EU institutions and 'downwards' with local authorities).
- The distinction between different kinds of *target* for JUG – who or what is government being joined up *for*? For example, is the aim to develop joined-up policies for a *group* (older people; asylum seekers) or for a *region/locality* (the Lake District, post foot and mouth disease; New Labour's various 'action

zones') or for a *policy sector* (transport, health care) or for some other category (people who don't have internet access)? It could be that 'best practice' varies somewhat according to the type of target.

- The distinction between joined-up *government* (where different public sector bodies co-ordinate their actions) and the more ambitious joined-up *governance* (where public sector bodies co-operate not only with each other but also with for-profit firms and/or voluntary associations).

There may well be *trade-offs between risks and rewards*. The most ambitious forms of joined-up-ness (for example, including several levels of government, firms, voluntary associations and individual citizens) promise major benefits but also turn out to be more costly (through delays or higher transaction costs) and/or run higher risks of failure (because of complexity, irreconcilable disagreements, obscure accountability arrangements and so on). More modest forms of joining up may be safer, but yield less dramatic results.

Efforts at JUG tend to be more fragile than 'normal', single silo policy-making. The Cabinet Office's initial review of cross-cutting issues put it like this:

> By their nature, cross-cutting policies tend to have more stakeholders; be harder to monitor and evaluate; and run greater risks of failure and communications breakdown.
>
> (Cabinet Office 2000: para. 2.8)

The possible *costs* include:

- 'less clear lines of accountability for policy and service delivery';
- 'greater difficulty in measuring effectiveness and impact, because of the need to develop and maintain more sophisticated performance measurement systems';
- 'direct and opportunity costs of management and staff time spent establishing and sustaining cross-cutting working arrangements';
- 'organisational and transitional costs of introducing cross-cutting approaches and structures'.

> (all quotations from Cabinet Office 2000)

Finally, efforts at JUG must be careful not to throw the baby out with the bath water. The existence of well-defined organizational boundaries – both horizontal and vertical – should not be regarded purely as a symptom of obsolescent thinking:

> External boundaries define an organisation and give it shape; internal boundaries provide a way of organising work and helping people know what job they are supposed to do. Internal boundaries enable organisations to exploit the basic concepts of comparative advantage and division of labour – dividing an organisation into sections with defined responsibilities means that staff know what job they are expected to do, and can acquire the knowledge, skills and experience to do it.
>
> (Cabinet Office 2000: para. 8.7)

There is at least one other benefit associated with more traditional approaches to organizing by organizational 'silo'. Membership of, and loyalty to, a single organization and its activities has often provided a powerful focus for adhesion among public servants at all levels. Strong personal identification with more abstract cross-cutting objectives, or with a temporary multi-organizational team, may be more difficult to cultivate.

Some key issues affecting 'joining up'

A central message from both practitioner and academic sources is that 'structure alone cannot drive cultural change, as processes and attitudes also need addressing' (Centre for Management and Policy Studies 2000). 'Simply removing barriers to cross-cutting working is not enough: more needs to be done if cross-cutting policy initiatives are to hold their own against purely departmental objectives' (Cabinet Office 2000: executive summary). This insight carries strong implications for senior civil servants, for professional service deliverers, and for politicians themselves:

- *For politicians*: '. . . the signals which ministers give civil servants about the priority they wish to be given to cross-cutting approaches is the key to it all' (Cabinet Office 2000: executive summary). Kavanagh and Richards (2001: 16) quote a 'senior civil servant at the heart of the joined-up process': 'At the moment we have tried to join up government with Sellotape and bandages . . . . It will take serious incentives, and I do not mean just threats, something is going to have to happen to make officials and ministers working within departments realize that they are being judged on the outcome of the overall policy and not just their individual role or that of their department'.
- *For civil servants*: 'We want new style joined-up civil servants – but don't know who they are or how to pick them' (Cabinet Office 2000: annex A6). Civil servants must learn to communicate faster, earlier and with a wider range of stakeholders. They need to acquire new skills, and the systems which recruit, train, appraise, audit and reward them all require adjustment. The notion of leadership takes on new dimensions (Huxham and Vangen 2000b).
- *For professional service deliverers*: the different practice protocols and classification systems used by professional groupings can pose major barriers to effective and efficient joint working. For example, among children who leave care 'For those who develop mental health difficulties . . . there are major problems concerning different assessments of the nature of problems between social services, the health service and the juvenile justice system' (DETR 2000: para. 3.107). Such ingrained professional practices cannot be changed overnight – their harmonization or simplification is bound to require a long-term effort.

Other literature identifies additional obstacles which bar the path to JUG. Three in particular seem worthy of mention. The first is the tension between, on the one hand, JUG and, on the other, the past and continuing success of NPM-style performance management. Individuals and organizations have become ever more focused on meeting their own (individual, unit and departmental) performance targets. There has also been some fragmentation of organizational forms, for example, through the Next Steps programme of creating executive agencies (Rhodes 1997). Unless and until cross-cutting targets can be given equal status, JUG is likely to remain on the margins.

The second is that of accountability. It is widely acknowledged that public sector modernization (not just JUG) has unsettled traditional models of ministerial and political accountability. It is more specifically acknowledged that the management of cross-cutting issues, and the use of partnership and network forms of governance not infrequently encounter problems on clarifying lines of accountability (Cabinet Office 2000: box 4.3). The accountability literature appears to hold several lessons for JUG:

- Several commentators emphasize the importance of making a formal agreement, at or near the beginning of any co-ordinated effort or partnership, as to the respective responsibilities of the different parties and institutions involved (for example, Kouwenhoven 1993). It may also be wise to agree what the procedure should be for revising that agreement, should that become necessary in the light of later experiences.
- A formal agreement is necessary, but seldom sufficient. Those in partnership should seek to cultivate a culture that promotes and supports a sense of individual responsibility on the part of staff (see Bovens 1998: Chapter 8). Vertical accountability remains, but horizontal accountability grows in importance.
- There is also likely to be a need to adjust procedures for external oversight. Audit bodies, inspectorates and even legislatures themselves will need to adjust to the reality of joined-up operations (Cabinet Office 2000: paras 10.13–10.23).

(The topic of accountability is dealt with at greater length in Chapter 4.)

The final issue is the danger of going about JUG in a way that unintentionally creates a new set of organizational enclaves. For example, the idea of building cross-cutting policies around groups of clients rather than around functional silos seems a very attractive one. Instead of organizing by function (health care, housing, etc.) one could organize by major client groups (older persons, the socially excluded, etc. – Cabinet Office 2000 and OECD 2001: 2–3). Yet there is a hidden danger. It would not be difficult to slide into the worst of both worlds – a combination of traditional, 'vertical' organizations, still carrying the principal legal responsibilities and means of delivery, and an overlay of fashionable new units or teams, which cream off the most talented staff but lack either clear lines of accountability or the implementation capacity to get things done.

To conclude this section on JUG, it may be worth summarizing some of the actual instruments and tactics which are cited, in the literature, as being helpful in promoting a more co-ordinated approach (see Table 3.3).

JUG may well be a good idea, but it is not in any deep sense a new idea. Nor is it an easy idea to implement. While we have some promising craft-like

Table 3.3   Ways of promoting joined-up policy-making and implementation

A	Shifting to an outcome-and-effectiveness-focused mode of policy-making, where different organizations can be united in the pursuit of commonly defined, shared outcome targets (Cabinet Office 2000; DETR 2000: executive summary). Usually, only politicians can set overall objectives at this level.
B	Firmly lodging the strategic leadership of the joined-up initiative with one or more senior politicians.
C	Creating a top-level co-ordination device/steering group, with direct political participation (Cabinet Office 2000).
D	Appointing joint teams at operational (middle management) level (Bardach 1998).
E	Organizing one-stop or one-window delivery at street level.
F	Developing common budgets that can only be accessed ('unlocked') when all the key stakeholders agree (Cabinet Office 2000).
G	Developing incentives and rewards for success in cross-cutting working (Cabinet Office 2000: para. 8.20; Centre for Management and Policy Studies 2000).
H	Basing strategic planning for the stakeholder organizations on cross-cutting themes (Centre for Management and Policy Studies 2000).
I	Agreeing a formal partnership document which includes procedural rules specifying when mutual consultation is required and how it should be conducted. This should also set out the distribution of responsibilities. It may also need to include provisions relating to: veto points; withdrawal from the partnership; risk sharing (Kouwenhoven 1993).
J	Appointing a senior and trusted 'process manager' whose job it is creatively to manage relations between the principal participants, so as to maximize productive interactions (Bardach 1998: 36).
K	Organizing effective systems for the early consultation of key stakeholders, rather than the 'too little, too late, with too few' mode of consultation which the civil service is sometimes accused of (Cabinet Office 2000: annex 6).
L	Joint training and development of staff (Bardach 1998; DETR 2000: para. 3.15).
M	Specific development of cross-cutting skills among staff – acknowledging that this has wide implications for recruitment, training, appraisal and promotion (Cabinet Office 2000: annex A6).
N	Exchanging key staff between the different organizations involved (through secondment, etc.) (DETR 2000: para. 3.113).
O	Developing common IT systems so that everyone agrees to use and contribute to the same database (Bardach 1998). This does not necessarily mean using exactly the same software – a fully integrated system may be more trouble than it is worth (Homburg 2000).
P	Early involvement of outside experts (Cabinet Office 2000: paras 7.7–7.11).
Q	Agreeing to support joint research and information gathering, so that the main database for policy-making is developed and owned by the group, or at least by several members of it, rather than by just one of the participants (Homburg 2000).

suggestions for how to get started (Table 3.3), we are also aware that JUG has risks and costs, and that it requires some substantial changes in 'normal' behaviour by ministers and managers and professionals (at least in the British system, and almost certainly in most other governmental systems as well). Because cultures and behaviours have to change, and professionals have to undergo a somewhat different training, JUG will not be achieved overnight. Despite the difficulties, however, it could be argued that there are certain factors which increase the chances of success this time, as compared with earlier attempts at improved co-ordination. One such factor is simply the advance of management knowledge itself – we perhaps understand organizational life rather better now than 40, or even 20 years ago, and can therefore anticipate some of the problems and identify some of the likely costs. A second factor – seen as extremely important by some JUG advocates – is the improvement of information and communication technologies. These technologies are widely believed to open up the possibility of new kinds of organizational design, including feats of far-flung and rapid co-ordination that would have been unthinkable prior to the advent of the internet. So it is to computers that we finally turn.

The information age

The influence of modern information and communication technologies (ICTs) is so pervasive that almost any chapter in this book could have included a section with this heading. This is, however, arguably a particularly appropriate place for it, given that we have been discussing a variety of (allegedly) 'horizontal' modes of organization (partnerships, networks, JUG) and that many commentators see the internet as the ultimate 'horizontal' network. A Dutch post-modern public administration scholar celebrates this perspective in the following, sweeping terms:

> Boundaries will be trespassed. Horizontal communication and information structures will prevail over vertical lines of command and control.
>
> (Frissen 1998: 42)

(Notice, by the way, the usual stereotyping of the past as simply hierarchical bureaucracy – this was discussed in Chapter 2, in the section 'NPM as a triumph over bureaucracy'.)

Along with their 'horizontality' modern ICTs have frequently been seen as liberating technologies, which will lead to more information about government for citizens, more information about citizens for government, more participation, more speed and more flexibility in providing public services – even more democracy. Opinions differ, however, about the probability of these multiple benefits being realized. A few 'technological determinists' see them as virtually inevitable – the very existence of advanced computers and the internet will somehow *force* such liberating developments upon government. More see them as *possible* gains, contingent on a variety of factors and by no means certain of achievement. Some also envisage possible disbenefits, such as a 'big brother' state snooping indiscriminately on all its citizens' electronic transactions and communications, or, alternatively, a desperately weakened state that has lost control of its own fundamental technologies and is totally reliant on profit-focused multi-national electronic companies for the supply, maintenance and operation of all its basic systems.

Indeed, ICTs seem somehow to invite dramatic prophecies (of both good and bad varieties). 'E-government' is alternately portrayed as 'big brother' or 'soft sister' (Frissen 1998). One article purveys an electronic utopia, the next a computerized dystopia. Even post-modernists (who in theory should be resisting the temptation to make huge generalizations/'metanarratives') cannot help themselves – the generalizations just pop out. Here are a range of examples:

> To speak of a top and a basis – the ground structure of a pyramid – will be highly inadequate. The top will be de-centred and the primacy of politics infringed.
>
> Another important trait of Internet developments – de-territorialization – undermines the concept of the nation state as the representation of political and administrative integrity of a specific territory.
>
> (Frissen 1998: 44)

Or:

> The act of putting software in the public domain makes the technology self-propagating and prevents anybody from trying to establish exclusive owner-ship of the tools. It is the active participation of thousands upon thousands of communities in designing their own spaces on the Net that will sustain its rich potential for shared experience and its characteristics as the defining institution of an Information Society.
>
> (Graham 1994: unpaged, quoted in Bellamy and Taylor 1998: 110)

Or:

> [The] IM/IT revolution has allowed to imagine [sic] new ways of connecting citizens, or eliminating barriers of distance, and of giving a fuller, richer meaning to democracy.
>
> (Treasury Board of Canada 1995: 19)

Or:

> And yet . . . the Web era still holds out the promise of genuinely open government (backed by the power of rapid reaction, cost-sharing on-line communities) *at the same time* as more efficient government.
>
> (Dunleavy and Margetts 2000: 25, original italics)

All this is looking *forward*. If instead we look *back*, a rather different picture emerges. First, we notice that past prophecies of the development of ICTs were often erroneous. Many of you may remember the suggestion, in the early 1980s, that we were on the brink of the 'paperless office'. Second, it is clear that, in several countries, large scale public sector IT projects have rather frequently resulted in painful disappointments. In the UK, for example, 'the litany of failed and failing public sector IT projects makes for depressing reading' (Brown 2001: 363). The House of Commons became so concerned with the waste of public funds that it launched a special select committee investigation (Committee of Public Accounts 2000). To take just two examples (each of which deserves a much fuller telling than I can give it here):

- In the early 1980s the UK Department of Social Security launched a ten-year-plus 'Operational Strategy' to automate many of its processes. Fifteen years later the National Audit Office study, *Government on the Web*, commented that 'it did not achieve planned staff reductions or service quality improvements and was never fully completed' (National Audit Office 1999: 25).

- The UK Passports Agency, determined to cut costs, contracted out its 'non-core' operations to a private computer company, but the software did not work as well as forecast, the public heard of delays and then lost confidence and flooded the system with early applications. The Agency's phone and mail systems could not cope. During 1999 the whole affair became a national media event, with leading opposition MPs getting themselves filmed talking to discontented applicants queuing for hours to try to get their passports (Committee of Public Accounts 2000; Dunleavy and Margetts 2000: 19). It would be nice to think that lessons would have been learned but two years later the same company was involved in a situation with the Criminal Records Department in which serious backlogs and delays occurred in connection with the installation of a new computer system that was used to 'vet' couples who had applied to adopt children. These delays caused extensive heartache and concern for both would-be adoptive parents and babies and children who were waiting for adoption. A government minister, interviewed on the radio (BBC Radio 4, *Woman's Hour*, 10 July 2002), was quite unable to say either when the problems would finally be solved or whether the company concerned would suffer any penalty.

Three Dutch academics, reviewing central government policies towards ICT applications in Australia, Canada, the Netherlands and the UK, came to the conclusion that official statements quite frequently incorporate myths or unrealistic assumptions (Bekkers, Homburg and Smeekes 2002). One myth is that of technological inevitability – the notion that greater use of ICTs is inevitable, and that they will automatically engender higher quality services with greater citizen participation. Citizens are – or will soon become – empowered, intelligent users of the new technologies. ICTs will promote JUG and will break down the old barriers between different organizations. Such texts seldom give explicit consideration to some of the obvious question marks against this kind of 'vision' – that citizens may have no more motivation to participate electronically than in any other way; that substantial sections of the population may not want or be able to use the new technology; or that service quality can sometimes actually deteriorate if ICTs are not well managed (see the Passport Office and Criminal Records examples mentioned above.

Seeking a balanced picture

Thus, many prophecies are not fulfilled, and doubtful assumptions frequently creep in to public sector ICT strategies. This much is clear, but it is not enough to warrant general despair. Blanket cynicism is itself undermined by the many examples of real successes (which are naturally not always trouble-free) and by informed analysis that points to real potential not too far ahead. Dunleavy and Margetts tell of Companies House, the UK agency responsible for producing business information about companies. Before computerization it employed 700 staff and sent out 4.5 million paper forms each year. 'Fully digitalized' it can reduce staff by 40 per cent, improve data quality and speed up its service. Customers now use the web to notify the agency of their needs, and to pay for services received.

Many readers of this book may have used NHS Direct, the National Health Service website which affords citizens access to very extensive amounts of information about a wide range of illnesses and conditions and treatments, and which can put one directly in touch with a qualified nurse if necessary. Sitting in my office at Erasmus University Rotterdam, I can and occasionally do check my little collection of ailments out with the website. Several times I have found useful information which has either reassured (or worried!) me, or which has sharpened the questions I put to my primary care doctor when eventually I go to see him. On one occasion I downloaded several pages of guidance, originally intended for district nurses, and was able to use it to deduce (correctly, as it turned out) that my wife had been given a mistaken prescription by her doctor. This is a genuinely new type of public service which is low cost and accessible to anyone who has an internet connection. (Whether it decreases or increases the pressure on conventional, face-to-face health services is an interesting question.)

A third example comes from the Child Support Agency (CSA). The CSA deals with a notoriously complex and sensitive issue – the payment of financial support by separated parents. In the late 1990s its staff manual and guides ran to over 4000 pages, and amendments were issued every two weeks. Usually there was one manual per office, with a clerk spending about an hour per week updating it. Furthermore CSA had a 27 per cent annual staff turnover, so many staff worked part time or on temporary contracts – not ideal circumstances for settling down to read 4000 pages before dealing with the in-tray! By putting an interactive electronic version of all this guidance on the CSA intranet it is possible to save staff time and to provide case workers with algorithms and other tools that will guide them quickly to the material which is likely to be most relevant for their particular need of the moment (National Audit Office 1999: 31–2).

Such positive examples could easily be multiplied. They provide evidence not for utopia, but for the possibility of specific advances in speed, efficiency or convenience, both for staff and for citizens, in those many situations where a process of payment or calculation or classification or certification can be specified in a reasonably precise form.

Other effects of ICTs: information is power

One of the themes in the analytical literature on ICTs in the public sector is that they can act as catalysts either to reinforce or to change power relationships – both within public agencies and between these agencies and their users and suppliers.

The suggestion is not that any single effect is inevitable and constant, but that some effect is common, and that designers and implementers of ICT programmes should be aware of this dimension of their work. In short, changing ICTs is usually not just a technical matter, but also a means through which, consciously or otherwise, different stakeholders in the particular agency or programme will gain or lose influence.

All I can do in this limited account is give the briefest indication of the kinds of power effects which ICTs can help to bring about:

- *The 'big brother' effect.* This is a popular theme. The general idea is that governments' ability to 'snoop' on their citizens will be vastly enhanced, creating an Orwellian 'big brother' state–society relationship in which citizens rapidly lose all privacy. Each time we make a phone call, make a payment or get cash, drive our car on the roads or walk in public spaces (both increasingly heavily populated with surveillance cameras), we are monitored. All our multifarious transactions with government – which have previously been with separate departments and agencies and have been recorded in separate databases – are now linked together so that government can follow our every move. The fear, of course, is that such panoptic knowledge could as well be exploited by authoritarian undemocratic regimes as by liberal, open ones.

- *The empowerment effect.* Here the idea is almost the opposite of the big brother effect. Government becomes more transparent as ICTs are used to give citizens more rapid and deep access to the processes of public administration and decision-making, enabling the woman or man in the street to participate as often and as much as she or he wants to. Let us take two examples, one very narrow and functional, the other much broader and more in the tradition of 'deliberative democracy'. (The concept of deliberative democracy is discussed at greater length in Chapter 4.) For some years now, if one buys a book over the internet from Amazon.com, one can track the progress of one's order, because the company allows customers to look into their own internal processes. Similarly, it is perfectly possible to create ICT systems that would allow citizens to check the daily or hourly progress of their passport or driving licence or planning permission applications, to look through the rule book which the public officials are themselves using to decide the case, and to query or otherwise intervene in the process at any stage. The broader example might be Amsterdam Digital City. This system 'provides local community facilities, including direct links with political parties, election candidates, public officials and municipal information systems. It also offers a platform for a number of well-supported local discussion groups which have been formed on a wide range of local and general issues' (Bellamy and Taylor 1998: 112). Thus the state becomes a 'soft sister' that uses ICTs to provide functional and democratic tools for citizen empowerment.

- *Big Brother* and *Soft Sister?* Perhaps these two visions of the future, ICT-sophisticated state are not alternatives? Perhaps they go together. As Paul Frissen memorably put it: 'In order for the government to become a Soft

Sister it needs access to all the data gathered by Big Brother. Big Brother and Soft Sister are Siamese twins' (Frissen 1998: 35).

- *The 'two societies' effect.* One effect which has already been noticed with some ICT schemes is the way they can create (or reinforce) 'in-groups' and 'out-groups' (perhaps one should say 'on-line' and 'off-line'). The first have access to the ICT in question, and the skills and confidence to use it. The second do not, and therefore miss out on all the service improvements, or increased possibilities for democratic participation, which are on offer. To take a small scale example, in the mid-1990s a student I was supervising carried out research into a project run by a London borough to set up electronic public information kiosks. The idea was that these kiosks would give 'one window' information about the full range of council services, and could be developed to be interactive, so that they could be used for paying tax bills, etc. In practice, however, the kiosks were used mainly by young white males. They were little used by the elderly, and hardly at all by the (substantial) ethnic minority population. This latter failing may have been partly explained by the fact that it took the council a long time to get all the information translated into the various minority languages. Of course, there are things which can be done to lessen the potentially divisive effects of ICTs, but these cost time and money, and even then, some groups are very hard to reach.
- *The shift from street bureaucracy to screen bureaucracy and then to system bureaucracy.* ICTs can also shift relationships of power and dependency *within* public sector organizations. Many such organizations handle large numbers of routine transactions – tax and benefit offices, licence application offices, agencies dealing with parking fines or issuing passports. In these cases scholars Marc Bovens and Stavros Zouridis see a marked shift in the locus of discretion (Bovens and Zouridis 2002). In traditional, pre-computer times, the 'street-level bureaucrat' – the desk officer or inspector on the street – possessed considerable room for manoeuvre. There were written rules, of course, but the street-level personnel could look at each case as it arose, bending this way or that according to local circumstances. With the first wave of computerization, however, this began to change. 'Public servants can no longer freely take to the streets, but are always connected to the organization via the computer. Client data must be filled in, with the help of fixed templates, in electronic forms. Knowledge management systems and digital decision trees have strongly reduced the scope for administrative discretion' (Bovens and Zouridis 2002: 177). But there is a further shift to come. Now, 'Contacts with citizens no longer take place in the streets, in meeting rooms or from behind windows, but via cameras, modems and websites . . . . The process of issuing the decision is carried out – from virtually beginning to end – by computer systems' (Bovens and Zouridis 2002: 12). In these 'system level bureaucracies' the key players are those who design the computer systems. Such systems can bring huge advantages – not only higher speed and convenience but also more consistent and legally accurate decision-making. However, if badly

designed, they can also bring endlessly repeated difficulties or intrusions on citizen privacy. Therefore, argue Bovens and Zouridis, the new discretionary power of the system designers needs to be held to account. Transparency should be the operative principle. Citizens and their elected representatives must have the possibility of scrutinizing new systems before they are implemented. System designers must be dragged into the democratic spotlight. More generally, the implementation of ICT systems may lead to considerable changes – both intended and otherwise – in the formal structures of public sector organizations (Zouridis 1998).

• *Hollowed-out e-government?* In both this and the previous chapter I have made brief reference to the idea of 'hollowing out' – the notion that fragmentation of the traditional, big multi-purpose ministries, combined with contracting out and privatization, was creating a weak central state which now lacked the capacity and knowledge sensibly to steer itself, let alone guide broader social development (Rhodes 1997). The development and application of ICTs happens to be a field where these dangers can be seen at their most pronounced. More and more of the UK government's capacity to design and operate large-scale computer systems appears to have been contracted out during the 1980s and 1990s. There are concerns that 'these arrangements have put the few companies which are in a position to tender realistically for contracts of this size into a strategically powerful position in relation to information age government . . . . They also expose important issues about the control and exploitation of personal data on UK citizens which are now flowing into computer installations run by commercial companies' (Bellamy and Taylor 1998: 155). A shortage of government in-house IT expertise may mean that public sector organizations do not even have the capacity intelligently to assess the bids that are put to them by the big multi-national computer companies (Brown 2001). So the government ends up hiring external consultants from the industry to advise it about which bids to accept from the small number of large firms which are in a position to tender, and then further contracting out the operation and maintenance of the systems which are absolutely basic to the operation of the social security, health care, taxation and justice systems.

Improving the management of public ICTs

Computers are no longer new. Governments now have 30 years or more of experience with electronic ICTs. From what has been said above it is obvious that sometimes these ICTs facilitate the achievement of widely-supported goals and at other times they become 'part of the problem'. How can public managers make a difference – how can they raise the probability of sensible goals being set and achieved? The string of failures with big public sector computer projects has called forth a good deal of analysis and advice on this subject. Many of the most frequently recurring 'lessons' appear to be rather straightforward. For example, the UK Parliamentary Accounts Committee, after reviewing a number of major delays,

Table 3.4 Principles for the management of government IT projects (adapted from Brown (2001: 375) who summarizes Committee of Public Accounts 2000)

1	Key decisions about IT systems are business decisions not technical ones
2	The commitment of senior management is essential
3	Identifying end users and their needs is critical to the success of a project
4	Scale and complexity can easily lead to failure – consider breaking a project down into manageable sub-components
5	Management and oversight of a project by skilled and knowledgeable managers is essential
6	Project managers have to be imaginative and skilled in risk control as well as in project management
7	A high degree of professionalism is required in the definition, negotiation and management of IT contracts
8	Adequate training is essential for both system users and system operators
9	Contingency plans must be in place and they must provide adequate service levels
10	A post-implementation review of the project is essential for both monitoring the success of the project and for learning from it

cost over-runs and failures to meet technical specifications, suggested that more attention should be paid to the principles outlined in Table 3.4.

It is distressing that principles as obvious as, say, items 2, 3, 7 and 8 in Table 3.4 should have had to be re-stated at all. Yet failures on these points emerge again and again. Part of the problem is evidently the loss of in-house expertise referred to above. Another is the lack of understanding, or even interest, among politicians. In one of the recent wave of texts on 'IKM' (Information and Knowledge Management – a burgeoning field) Eileen Milner bewails the barriers and difficulties that seem to prevent the UK public sector from adopting a clear and progressive IKM strategy. One of her conclusions is that:

> Time and senior level commitment could, therefore, appear to be the two crucial ingredients in moving to a credible position of IKM-focused public sector management, and it is by no means certain that these inputs will always, or indeed often, be made available.
>
> (Milner 2000: 172)

Alternative futures: public sector use of ICTs

There are strong links between ICTs and the other themes of horizontality and participation which have been discussed earlier in this chapter. Dunleavy and Margetts make the interesting suggestion that governments can adopt a number of alternative strategies towards the potential of modern ICTs. In their scheme, one route would be to use ICTs mainly to support NPM-type reforms – to make public services faster, cheaper and more efficient. They call this the 'Digital NPM scenario' and it would result mainly in standardized, low-cost services, many of which would be contracted out to the private sector (Dunleavy and Margetts 2000: 14). Another (the one they obviously favour) is the 'Digital State paradigm'. Here ICT-facilitated change replaces NPM as a new paradigm 'entailing agency staff really trying to get close to customers and to use their feedback to re-engineer public services' (Dunleavy and Margetts 2000: 18). This would use 'Web-based changes to dramatically enhance citizen competences and radically to cut policy complexity' (Dunleavy and Margetts 2000: 19). Finally there would be a 'State Residualization scenario' in which government fails to adapt to the new ICTs and becomes a backwater, reinforcing existing prejudices to the effect that government is inefficient and out of touch.

Of course, this is not the only way of classifying alternative ICT-influenced futures, but it is a provocative taxonomy, and one which reminds us that there *are* choices, and that ICTs can serve a number of different strategic priorities.

Guide to further reading

For partnerships Rosenau (2000) is a reasonably interesting American collection, although (like so many edited collections) of mixed quality. Several of the many publications by Chris Huxham provide a fresh, no-nonsense, action-research perspective from the UK – I would recommend both her articles with Vangen (Huxham and Vangen (2000a; 2000b). For contrasting English and Dutch case studies of partnerships you could try Lowndes and Skelcher (1998) and Teisman and Klijn (2002). The IPPR's (2001) *Building Better Partnerships* was a very useful overview of the arguments for and against.

On networks, despite my criticisms, you should definitely read Kickert, Klijn and Koppenjaan's (1997) *Managing Complex Networks*. If you would like to look back at an influential early example of the pro-network club, Kooiman's (1993) *Modern Governance* is a good choice. But for a strong theoretical critique, try Dowding's (1995) article. Concerning joined-up government, the original Cabinet Office (2000) paper, *Wiring It Up*, gives an authentic flavour of the practitioner approach, while 6 *et al.* (2002) *Towards Holistic Governance* offers a more academic (but still fairly enthusiastic) overview. My own article (Pollitt 2003) provides a more cautious commentary.

New books and articles on the information age seem to appear almost by the minute, so anything I say here may be dated by the time you read it. Several volumes were published by a group of Dutch and other 'informatics' scholars, and you might want to sample their *magnum opus*, *Public Administration in an Information Age* (Snellen and van de Donk 1998). A solid, sensible overview is also provided by Christine Bellamy and John Taylor (1998) in their *Governing in the Information Age*, but you should also look for more recent material – I am confident there will be lots of it!

4

Politicians, accountability, citizens and participation – public managers facing every which way?

Introduction

'Democracy' has multiple definitions, and debating these has kept many scholars busy for many years (Held 1987; Held and Pollitt 1986). If, however, we strip off all the complications and the subtleties, most of the modern versions of the concept are centrally concerned with the relationship between the citizens and the state power – and particularly that part of that power which is exercised by governments. Confronted with state power, what rights, duties, entitlements or other kinds of levers and incentives, are possessed by the individual citizen (and by organized groups)?

It would be easy to think that high-flown debates about citizens' rights are positioned at some distance from the humdrum business of everyday public management. Or, at least, that worries about democracy are largely confined to the more intrusive of the state's activities, such as controlling demonstrations or arresting people or censoring the media. But no, a few moments cogitation should convince that issues concerning the nature of democracy are actually present throughout public administration – in the payment of pensions as well as the arrest of suspects, in the development of town plans as well as the conduct of elections.

Indeed, in some ways the past 20 or so years have seen politicians and citizens closing in on public managers from two sides. Although the NPM discourse (Chapter 2) includes loud noises about letting the manager manage, it has become entwined with at least two other discourses – alternative logics which actually seem to restrict and encumber public managers rather than liberating them. I refer, first, to the concern about public accountability and the 'primacy of politics' and, second, to the widespread demands for greater public participation in the design, provision and evaluation of public services of many kinds. So the 'message' for public managers can easily seem rather contradictory:

- behave more entrepreneurially, take risks, be creative, exercise your new managerial freedoms;
- but at the same time, be more responsive to the current government's new policy desires – bureaucratic inertia is supposed to belong to the 'bad old days';

- and, by the way, make sure you are more transparent, more measured, more audited, more quality-checked than ever before;
- and don't take any significant decisions which will affect particular groups of citizens without getting their participation or, at the very least, thoroughly consulting them beforehand.

In this chapter I will explore this seeming contradiction – that public managers are being given greater autonomy, yet at the same time their roles often seem to be more politicized – at least in a broad sense – than ever before.

Before plunging into the details of the topic, it is helpful to acknowledge a very deep contrast that runs down the middle of democratic theory. It is the contrast between those thinkers who regard democracy as essentially a kind of *market*, in which votes and interests are traded, and those who see democracy as a *forum*, in which debates perpetually proceed, and from which (provisional) decisions occasionally emerge. These two perspectives tend to lead to different perceptions of problems, different reform agendas and, ultimately, different implications for the work of public managers.

From the *market perspective* people are seen as having well-defined interests (as an elderly person, as a Roman Catholic, as a pregnant woman, as a nature-lover, etc.) which they attempt to provide for both through the market (jobs and shopping) and through the political process. The more transparently and efficiently the political system registers these interests and communicates information about the interests of others (so that deals and compromises can be arrived at) the more we can define the political process as 'democratic'. The political system aggregates (adds up) interests and the task of political leaders is to form these many interests into coherent packages and then deliver on the promises they have made to their supporters. A strong system of democratic accountability allows citizens to see how far the political leadership has responded to their interests – what they have done with the authority and resources with which they have been entrusted. If they have done a poor job then the citizens who voted for them last time will take their votes elsewhere – to a new team that seems likely to try harder to realize their interests. A bad deal in the political marketplace leads to a transfer of voting power to a new product. To be effective the political consumer (citizen) needs reliable information about what products (policies) are on offer, information about how much they are going to cost (taxation, and any other negative effects), and the existence of strong competition (political parties) to ensure that there will always be choice. This is, therefore, primarily a *process* view of democracy – get the processes right and the balance of interests in society will be accurately reflected on the face of public policies.

From the *forum perspective* the job of the political process is somewhat different. Here the essence of democracy is *deliberation* – informed reflection and discussion between equals. The process of deliberation is not simply one in which the goodies (hospitals, schools, roads, tax cuts) get handed out to the majority interests, because it is assumed that *interests, instead of being absolutely known and fixed, are themselves constantly reshaped by the process of debate itself*. Indeed, not only interests but, ultimately, identities themselves are discovered through deliberation. When (and if) the Catholics and Protestants in Northern Ireland, or the Israelis and Palestinians in the occupied territories sit down round the table they begin to discover that perhaps they have incomplete or inaccurate pictures of each other and that, indeed, they may have some *common* interests which they had never noticed before (or, at least, which they had never seen as *shared*). From this forum perspective, processes are certainly of great importance (especially those intended to promote free, fair and equal participation in deliberation) but democracy is also seen as a *substantive* phenomenon, in the sense that it is a set of political arrangements which allows and encourages the emergence of collective interests and identities and, ultimately, fosters some common sense of humanity.

This is not a text on political theory, so it would be inappropriate to go much further into the (huge) body of thought which has been built up around these issues. As we will see, however, the different perspectives set different contexts for the practice of public management. For example, consider the local council which is developing a plan for the regeneration of a run-down area near the centre of town. 'We need to consult the local residents' say the local politicians. Since it is most unlikely that the politicians would be able to (or even want to) undertake all this consultation themselves, much of the work will fall to their public managers. (Indeed, in many cases the politicians would call for advice from managers about how and when consultation should be carried out.) But which model of democracy do the local politicians have in mind? If it is the market model, then an opinion survey may be perfectly satisfactory. Design a questionnaire that sets out two or three options for the regeneration project (including implications for local taxation), then take a count of citizen preferences. The result is 56 per cent for scheme A, 31 per cent for scheme B, 5 per cent for scheme C and 8 per cent don't knows – fine, the council goes for scheme A, and the requirements of marketplace democracy are satisfied.

But what if it is the forum model which local councillors are thinking about? Then an opinion survey would hardly suffice. *Deliberation* would require the creation of some forum or fora in which citizens could develop their arguments and refine their understandings of the issues. Such deliberative devices would themselves need rules to promote, as nearly as possible, an *equal* exchange – so that those with softer voices, or fewer experts, or a different mother tongue, or more pressures on their availability (for example, full-time carers) were not effectively excluded. Effort would need to be put into identifying and communicating with any sections of the community who were not participating in the debate. Why were they not able or not interested in taking part? *Time* would have to be made available, so that citizens could reach new understandings of their interdependencies, new definitions of self-interest and community interest. What is more, it is entirely possible that, in such deliberative fora, citizens might develop their own views of the nature of the issues – substantially different from those originally put forward by the council. Ultimately the councillors might lose control of the agenda, and be faced with demands for a fundamental re-conceptualization of the original problem.

I will come back to the challenges of citizen participation further on in this chapter. For the moment, however, I turn to a more conventional, and limited issue – that of the relationship between politicians and managers or, to put it more precisely, between politics and management.

Politics and management

Politicians are very often highly dependent on public managers to get their wishes/policies realized. Politicians frequently form very close and mutually trusting relationships with these officials. But, quite often, they also find an element of frustration in the relationship. The American President Franklin D. Roosevelt was extremely skilful at getting what he wanted out of the US federal government machine, but, even so, he sometimes ended up blocked:

> The Treasury is so large and far-flung and ingrained in its practices that I find it is almost impossible to get the action and results I want . . . . But the Treasury is not to be compared with the State Department. You should go through the experience of trying to get any changes in the thinking, policy, and action of career diplomats and then you'd know what a real problem was. But the Treasury and the State Department put together are nothing compared with the Na-a-vy . . . . To change anything in the Na-a-vy is like punching a feather bed. You punch it with your right and you punch it with your left until you are finally exhausted and then you find the damn bed just as it was before you started punching.
>
> (Franklin Roosevelt, quoted in Eccles 1951: 336 and reproduced in
> Allison and Zelikow 1999: 174)

The Roosevelt quotation reminds us of the stereotype of bureaucracy which was discussed in Chapter 2. Roosevelt was one of a long line of American Presidents who found it politically advantageous to attack their own civil servants by accusing them of inertia and inefficiency (Carter, Reagan, Clinton and G.W. Bush – the first President to hold an MBA – all did more or less the same at some point or other in their careers). This is a slightly less popular sport in the UK, but, there, too, various ministers and Prime Ministers have taken the opportunity to criticize the immobility of the civil service (from Margaret Thatcher on the right through Tony Blair in the middle to Tony Benn on the left). But is this criticism true and fair, and what can be done about it if it is?

Here are some of the main possibilities:

- Civil servants *do* obstruct the wishes of their political leaders, because they have agendas of their own (the '*conspiracy theory*').
- Civil servants *do* block the wishes of their political leaders, not because they want to, but because they are trapped in bureaucratic routines which make them slow and unresponsive (the '*bureaucracy theory*').
- Civil servants *appear* to block the wishes of their political leaders but that is because what they are actually doing is pointing out real and substantial

obstacles to or flaws in the politicians' plans, problems which the politicians had been too ignorant or ideologically committed to see for themselves (the '*wise counsellors theory*'). When politicians blame their civil servants they are really (and unfairly) shooting the messenger because they don't like the message.

- Civil servants *don't* block the wishes of political leaders. The latter make up negative stories about bureaucracy to excuse their own failings, because civil servants are in no position to answer back ('*the scapegoat theory*').

As noted in Chapter 2, the bureaucracy theory has proved quite popular, both in the UK and internationally, over the past 20 years or so. Conspiracy theory also occasionally grabs the headlines – conspiracies, real or supposed, make good copy. Scapegoat theory is frequently resorted to by political oppositions, keen to undermine the reputations of ministers and make them appear weak. It is perhaps the wise counsellors theory that the public hear least of, partly because it is less dramatic than the others, but partly also because civil servants are usually constrained from rehearsing these issues in public. Recently, however, there have been some notable examples. Here, for instance, is a senior UK civil servant describing how, under the New Labour government of Tony Blair, civil servants were progressively downgraded as givers of policy advice, because their advice was too often that what ministers proposed had serious difficulties:

> Ministers are no longer prepared to regard chief civil servants as the real, albeit shadowy, rulers of the land. A rash of political advisers has appeared in Whitehall. They seem to have taken over the Prime Minister's office and they largely run the Treasury . . . . Ministers now seem to find it easier, when they put forward ideas, to have the uncritical support of young enthusiasts than face a sober appraisal of their workability by an experienced official.
>
> (Denman 2002: 254–5)

The same theory is echoed by no less a person than the recently retired Permanent Secretary of the Office of the Public Service:

> What is much more worrying than politicization of the people in the Civil Service is the way the Service itself is being sidelined . . . . This government has used specialist advisers far more intensively than its predecessors in press communication, in side-stepping the official machine . . . . At the heart of government the position of special advisers is becoming more powerful and potentially dangerous, particularly in Number 10, the Cabinet Office and the Treasury.
>
> (Mountfield 2002: 4)

Clearly, there are at least two important questions about all this. First, which theory is the correct one? Second, what should be done about it?

As to the first question, it is, of course, possible that more than one of the theories is right for some of the time. Indeed, *prima facie*, in some situations it seems quite likely that civil servants will have their own agendas. One example would be when politicians want radically to downsize the civil service. Another would be when civil servants themselves are likely to have political careers, as happens in some systems where top civil service posts and political roles are intertwined, as in France or the USA. In other situations it is equally likely that civil servants will find themselves acting as wise counsellors/unwelcome messengers. After all, civil servants may have many years of experience of working in a particular policy sector, whereas a minister may be totally new to the subject and/or quite without experience of the management of complex organizations (and therefore rather naïve about the problems of implementing his or her pet ideas).

So I doubt whether one universal answer can be given to the question of which theory is right. One needs a case-by-case analysis, and in some instances there may be several elements present in different degrees at the same time. Perhaps the minister was inexperienced, and just a touch naïve, *and* his or her civil servants somewhat bureaucratically defensive, *and then*, frustrated, the minister was tempted into blaming the situation on a conspiracy against himself or herself instead of admitting that his or her original idea would not work, and then seeking a variant of it that would stand a better chance of success.

Coming to the second question, in general terms the remedies for each version of the problem appear fairly obvious (though not necessarily easy to implement):

- *Conspiracy theory*: there are two courses of action, either or both of which could be pursued. The first would be to acquire alternative advisers whose interests were more closely aligned with those of the political leadership (for example, political sympathizers). But note that this is precisely what the advocates of the wise counsellors perspective are complaining about! The second would be to find organizational arrangements which restrained the ability of civil servants to act in their own interests where these were contrary to politicians' wishes. Much of the 'New Institutional Economics' is devoted to suggesting organizational arrangements through which 'principals' (in this case political leaders) can exercise more effective control of 'agents' (in this case civil servants). A basic assumption in principal agent theory is that the agent will begin with superior information about the work actually being done (information asymmetry) so that the principal will need to take steps to reduce this disadvantage (see Douma and Schreuder 1998, for a simple, formal treatment). Competition is hypothesized to be one important way of lessening the agent's advantage – if they have to compete with others then they will be pushed towards higher levels of efficiency and compliance in meeting the principal's demands. (There is a further, boxed discussion of the principal–agent model in the section on motivation in Chapter 6.)
- *Bureaucracy theory*: one remedy would be to find alternative organizational forms (that is, non-bureaucracies) so that responsiveness would be improved. To some extent that is what the NPM was supposed to be about (see Chapter 2). Another remedy would be, as with conspiracy theory, to find an alternative set of more responsive advisers.

- *Wise counsellor theory*: since the problem here is with the failings of ministers, the remedies will concern the protection of civil servants (for example, through strong forms of tenure) and the re-shaping of political careers (for example, so that candidates for ministerial positions are obliged to undergo some kind of training before being put in charge of a department).
- *Scapegoat theory*: again the problem is with the politicians, so civil servants need protection and politicians need stronger deterrents to blame-shifting (examples would include strong freedom of information legislation, or special procedures through which civil servants can report unreasonable manipulation by their political bosses – such as the so-called 'whistleblowers' arrangements which a number of countries have introduced – see Bovens 1998: Part 3 for a menu of ideas about how such problems can be addressed.

Accountability

Almost everyone, it seems, is agreed that 'accountability' is 'a good thing', that it is fundamental to liberal democracy, and that we need more of it. Some, however, believe that, with the advent of the NPM (see Chapter 2) and various other developments, we are actually getting *less* of it than before. Others believe that we need more of one *kind* (accountability for results) but less of other kinds (accountability for the processes by which the results are arrived at – see Behn 2001).

There is a pretty large and diverse literature on accountability. Definitions vary, but probably most of them include, as a central notion, the idea that accountability is a relationship in which one party, the *accountor*, recognizes an *obligation to explain and justify their conduct* to another, the *accountee*. Not necessarily all their conduct – that depends on what is defined as within the scope of the accountable relationship and what is outside. A civil servant, for instance, must account to her superior for the way she has spent her budget, but not for the way she brings up her children.

Slightly more controversially, the idea of accountability usually incorporates some sense of a *superior/subordinate relationship*, and of *sanctions*. The accountor is rendering their account to someone/something that is, for the purposes of this particular relationship at least, their superior – in the sense that it is for the accountee to pass judgement. In passing that judgement it is frequently, but not always, the case that the accountee has access to some sort of sanction over the accountor. If the President of the United States cannot adequately account to Congress for either his co-operation with judicial investigations ('Watergate') or his sexual conduct in the Oval Office ('Monicagate'), he may be impeached. The sanctioning aspect can easily come to overshadow accountability relations so that, instead of being a means to foster learning and improvement, they become the focus for elaborately precautionary and defensive behaviour. Public managers opt for procedurally constipated, rule-bound decision-making rather than a creative, results-oriented approach. As one American put it 'rule-obsessed organizations turn the timid into cowards and the bold into outlaws' (Zegans 1997: 115). This observation ushers in an important sub-theme in the accountability debate – accountability may be 'a good thing', but it also has costs. It may stifle creative decision-making. It may also prove very costly in terms of time and energy – public managers may spend more and more of their time preparing reports and accounts of their actions, and less actually doing the job (remember the complaint of Jeremy, the primary school headteacher in Chapters 1 and 2 – 'I went into education to teach kids, not to fill in forms for the Ministry'). Acknowledging that accountability has costs leads swiftly to the question of 'how much accountability is enough?' At what point is there a reasonable balance between discretion (room for manoeuvre) and accountability? When does the cost of an accountability system become more than the benefits?

While this is an important question, it is also one that is never likely to have a single, stable and universally agreed answer. That is in part because individuals will always disagree on what a little bit more or less accountability is 'worth'. For some, procedural fairness is all-important, and the slightest injustice must be relentlessly tracked down and vigorously repaired. If this means long, legalistic procedures and heavy supervision, so be it. This point of view can usually be supported by heart-rending tales of individuals who have suffered at the hands of insensitive and seemingly arbitrary public officials. For others, however, the benefits of a rapid, simple procedure for all outweigh the occasional mistake. The heart-rending case becomes a statistical abnormality, something that requires redress, certainly, but a very narrow and misleading foundation on which to build an entire policy. Furthermore, the advocates of discretion will argue, the best way to get loyal and responsible public servants to do their best is to trust them with considerable freedom of action, within a broad framework. What kind of person will the public service be able to recruit and retain if staff are constantly enmeshed in red tape and report forms?

Box 4.1   Accountability: individuals and systems

When a US Air Force F-15 crashed in Germany on May 30, 1995, killing the pilot, an investigation revealed that the two mechanics had installed flight control rods incorrectly and that this mistake had caused the fatal crash. But the error was not only quite easy to make, it was common, having been made many times in the previous decade. Moreover, senior officers knew about the problem, yet they failed to correct it. Indeed, air force safety officers had recommended specific solutions, but higher officers had ignored them. Who should have been held accountable? Predictably, the air force accused the two mechanics of negligent homicide. On the day that the court martial was to begin, one of the mechanics killed himself.

(Behn 2001: 72)

Thus the answer to the question of 'how much accountability?' rests partly on the trade-offs between different values (fairness, effectiveness, efficiency, etc.), and therefore cannot have a final, indisputable solution. However, it is not *only* a question of values. It is also a question of probabilities – how *likely* is it that various outcomes (both good and bad) will occur? And that is an *empirical* question, the answer to which depends on getting good information about how the system works and how often certain types of mistake or error are likely to occur. If one applicant in a million for social security is likely to be incorrectly rejected (and if there are accessible appeal mechanisms in place) then the system may be judged adequate. But if evidence shows that one in ten is being incorrectly rejected then we want to know much more about what is going on – we want tighter accountability. From this part of the analysis it follows that one of the responsibilities of public managers is to introduce and maintain information systems which will tell them (and their political masters, if the latter want to know) what kinds of errors occur, how often and under what circumstances. In the case of the US Air Force F-15 it seems that the error was a common one, and on these grounds Behn implies that the higher officers – the guardians of the *system* – also bore some responsibility, because they had done little to reduce the *probability* of recurrence.

Nevertheless, as indicated above, our *valuation* of the consequences also plays a part here. For most of us an unfair rejection of a driving licence application is regrettable, but not earth-shattering. An unfair rejection of a social security application is more important, because it threatens someone's basic livelihood. The incorrect installation of a vital part in an aircraft is more important still, because lives rather than livelihoods are immediately and directly at stake. The general message, therefore, is that accountability systems need to be designed with *both the probabilities and the values* attaching to various possible events in mind (see Hammond 1996 for an extended application of this crucial distinction to decision-making in social policy). Ignoring either ingredient in the mixture is a recipe for trouble.

Accountability may already seem a complicated enough issue. Unfortunately, however, thus far I have only scratched its surface. The discussion has proceeded on the basis of a number of assumptions which, for many public managers, either never applied or, at least, no longer fully hold. These assumptions are the following:

- the criteria for judging the accountor's performance are (a) reasonably clear and (b) agreed in advance by all those concerned;
- accountability is dyadic – a relationship between two parties;
- accountability is essentially hierarchical – a line relationship between some kind of subordinate and some kind of boss.

In the real world of public management none of these assumptions can be consistently relied upon. Each deserves further discussion.

Criteria for judgement

Accountability is founded on *expectations*. What does the accountee expect from the accountor? If there is either disagreement or ambiguity over this, then either or both parties may easily be surprised or even outraged at what happens. In the real world, however, there are many reasons why disagreement and/or ambiguity may occur. Politicians, for example, are frequently masters of ambiguity. Building the political coalition necessary to get a policy over the various executive and legislative hurdles may require a certain amount of fudging, a claim that the policy can simultaneously serve many goals (and therefore many constituencies). Are prisons for punishment or rehabilitation? (Both!) Are social benefits low enough to discourage 'scrounging' but high enough to permit recipients to live a dignified life? (Both!) Are safety-at-work regulations strict enough to catch unscrupulous employers who put the welfare of their workers at risk, but light enough not to be a burden on business and profitability? (Yes!) And so on. Public managers are left 'holding the can' for ambiguous policies, and they can be caught out when politicians shift emphasis within an existing policy (from being tough on 'scroungers' to encouraging more people to apply for benefits, for example, or *vice versa*).

It is worth recalling the case of Derek Lewis, already mentioned in Chapter 2. The minister of the day dismissed him from his post as the Director of the Prison Service. Yet he had achieved almost all the performance targets set out in his contract. He had therefore satisfied the expectations expressed by the minister only a relatively short time before. So what was going on? In effect the minister had decided – in the aftermath of a prison escape by IRA terrorists – to change the criteria, and to add a new requirement, 'thou shalt not allow *any* politically sensitive escapes' (Lewis 1997). One might say that Derek Lewis was a victim of 'aftermath accountability' where the accountee says, in effect: 'oh, I didn't think of that but, now it has happened, someone is going to be punished, and isn't going to be me!'.

But public managers are not always the victims: they can sometimes be the initiators of actions which confuse or obscure accountability. In 1991 the UK parliament, in response to a series of highly-publicized dog attacks, passed a new Dangerous Dogs Act. But in 1992, when the Metropolitan Police found the new legislation was difficult to implement, they 'made a conscious decision not to be pro-active in enforcing the Act' (Hood, Rothstein and Baldwin 2001). This was at least understandable, in the sense that it was an operationally rational decision openly taken by a police force. Much less accountable was the case of the poor West German Minister of Home Affairs, Hans Maihofer. Pressed on the issue of whether a prominent physicist was being bugged by the security services, he sought the advice of his civil servants, and was able to go to the German parliament with a clear denial. Unfortunately, the civil servants were lying to their minister and, even more unfortunately (for him), the truth subsequently got out. He resigned (Bovens 1998: 87).

Dyadic accountability and multiple accountability

As Chapter 3 acknowledged, the public sector does not run, and never has run, entirely on the basis of simple 'twosomes' in which one person or institution gives the orders and the other carries them out. This may happen occasionally, but very often the way things are done is much more complex, with partnerships, networks and attempts to 'join up' organizations of different types on different levels in order to achieve better co-ordination and higher effectiveness. But how does the dyadic, accountor and accountee model of accountability apply to these more multi-dimensional situations? The short answer, as many commentators have noticed, is 'with great difficulty, if at all'.

In partnerships and networks it is frequently the case that different partners are responsible for different things, and perhaps accountability should follow that pattern also. Thus there are multiple accountors, instead of one. One partner may be responsible for providing the finance, another for supplying the skilled staff to carry out a project, and a third for legal advice. So if the legal advice is faulty, the third partner should account for it, whereas if there is a financial shortfall it is the first partner that has to explain and justify. This *could* work, but notice that, if it is to do so, there are various requirements – and some drawbacks. One requirement seems to be that the pattern of accountability needs to be spelled out at an early stage, and in a fairly formal way (Kouwenhoven 1993). When things go wrong it is too late to begin discussing who is going to answer for what. One drawback is that it is hard for outsiders, including the public, to understand the system of accountability, because of its complexity. For all its limitations, traditional ministerial responsibility has the virtue of simplicity – if something happens in the ministry then the minister must answer for it (though only *answer*, which is not the same as accepting *culpability*, as many would-be bringers-down of ministers have discovered – Bovens 1998: 87–8).

Even within ministries, however, (and certainly in other parts of the public sector) ministerial accountability is not the only form of accountability with which the public manager has to reckon. Public managers must do what their ministers ask them to do, but they must also obey the law, and, in many cases, they have professional or bureaucratic codes to respect. In short, the norm is for public managers to be multiply accountable, *even if they are working within one institution and not in a partnership or contractual relationship*. This is illustrated in Table 4.1.

Table 4.1   A typology of accountability (extensively adapted from Behn 2001: 59)

Political accountability	Accountability to elected representatives. In systems with ministerial responsibility (most obviously in the 'Westminster model') accountability to the minister is usually the biggest influence on the public servant's work. But there are other accountable relationships with politicians too, for example, public managers may have to appear before parliamentary committees to answer questions
Legal accountability	Accountability to the courts. Public managers must not break the law, any more than any other citizen. Depending on the system of law, this may mean accountability to specialized administrative courts and/or accountability to the general court system (for example, civil servants must not steal or commit assaults on their superiors/subordinates)
Bureaucratic accountability	Accountability to codes and norms within the bureaucratic context. For example, many civil services now have codes of conduct or codes of ethics (see Chapter 6 for more on this)
Professional accountability	Accountability to the standards laid down by one's professional body. For example, doctors, nurses and teachers all have various kinds of codes of practice, and usually there is a professional oversight body that considers alleged breaches of these rules

Depending on the precise position of the public manager, one or other of these systems of accountability may assume the dominant influence. If you are a doctor in a public hospital then the main day-to-day influences will be professional accountability (you must act in the patient's best interest, preserve patient confidentiality, etc.) and bureaucratic accountability (if the hospital has a policy that only the director of finance and the chief executive should speak to the press about budgetary issues, then you should not go moaning to the local newspaper about the cutbacks in paediatrics). You are liable to be disciplined for breaches of either set of rules. Political accountability is not likely to loom very large.

By contrast, as the head of health policy division in the ministry, political accountability will be an everyday fact of life, and professional accountability will be less prominent (in the UK, at least, there is no professional institute of civil servants that maintains codes of practice and sanctions members for falling short of the expected standards). Bureaucratic accountability will also be important – if your permanent secretary asks you to come and explain some advice you offered the minister yesterday, you go! If, on the other hand, you are working in contracts division, then legal accountability may be more to the fore. The correct legal procedures for letting contracts must be followed and, if they are not, you may be in trouble not only with domestic courts, but also with the European Union.

To summarize the story so far, there are two sets of reasons why a simple, single accountor and single accountee model of accountability is an inadequate description of reality. First, many public managers find themselves working in partnerships or contractual relationships, where different parties are accountable for different aspects of a joint activity (*multiple accountors*). Second, even where a public manager is working within a single institution they will often have several lines of accountability – political, legal, professional, bureaucratic (*multiple accountees*). Both these sets of reasons complicate the concept of 'accountable actions'. They mean that most public managers, in most circumstances, need to think about satisfying several different potential accountees, with several different criteria of appropriate behaviour, simultaneously. This is one of the daily, unsung achievements of the public manager.

Hierarchical accountability and '360 degree accountability'

The above might sound complex enough, but there is still more to come. Some contemporary commentators have borrowed the idea of '360 degree accountability' from the business world (a practice, one may add, which may be more often written about than actually undertaken!). Behn (2001: 199) puts it like this:

> Now people are not just accountable to their boss. They are accountable to their subordinates, peers, team members, customers and suppliers.

Behn (a visiting professor at Harvard) goes on to advocate a shift away from what he sees as a dominant emphasis on hierarchical, essentially punitive accountability, that is mainly concerned with following the rules, to a more collective form of accountability, that lays greater emphasis on achieving results. He proclaims that:

> [W]e need a new mental model of accountability: we need to shift from the implicit conception of linear, hierarchical, uni-directional, holder–holdee accountability to an explicit recognition that we need mutual and collective accountability. And we need . . . to shift our accountability emphasis from finances and fairness to finances, fairness and performance . . . .
>
> (Behn 2001: 211)

I must confess to a little spurt of weary scepticism when I read this. While I accept many of the points that Behn makes (for example, about the punitive nature of much accountability in the public sector, and the tendency just to add more rules and regulations every time something goes wrong) I can detect little public (or, indeed, political) sentiment in favour of mutual, non-punitive accountability for public programmes. I can therefore see little reason to expect the kind of change that Behn is advocating, however attractive and egalitarian it may seem in theory. It would be nice to be proved wrong, but I cannot see where the 'push' for this kind of paradigm shift is going to come from, on either side of the Atlantic. On the contrary, the tendency (amplified by the mass media) seems to be to *intensify* the transparency and hierarchical accountability of both ministers and public managers. And this may not be an entirely bad thing. In the not too distant past it seemed that ministers and senior public servants were rather easily able to conceal and cover up incompetence and wrong-doing, as the long litany of public policy fiascos, disasters and frauds in an uncomfortably large number of countries bears witness. A stronger spotlight, backed up by codes of practice, ethical awareness training and more hawkish courts may not be such an unmitigated disaster, even if, as would no doubt be the case, it proved less than 100 per cent effective.

Furthermore, the preferred alternative of 'webs of mutual responsibilities' (Behn 2001: 213) sounds dangerously vague to me. It might work well in circumstances where there is stability of staff, an equally stable task, and a firm and shared politico-administrative culture. Unfortunately, though, these are precisely the circumstances which are becoming rarer and rarer in many parts of the public sector. Additionally, there is the point raised earlier about the *costs* of accountability systems. In a situation where everyone is accountable to everyone else, how high are the transaction costs? One is put in mind of those stories from the hippy communes of the 1970s where the whole evening was spent sitting in a circle democratically discussing who might be responsible for the washing-up, while the dirty dishes remained in the sink. However, this is only my opinion (jaundiced, as you can tell). To get a more 'progressive' view you should read Behn's (2001) *Re-thinking Democratic Accountability.*

An alternative approach: personal responsibility?

A Dutch academic, who has studied issues of accountability and responsibility in both public and private sector organizations, comes to a very different kind of conclusion from that of Robert Behn (Bovens 1998). Situating his text in the 'world of complex organizations' he begins by identifying and analysing the 'problem of many hands' – the difficulty (especially for outsiders, but also for insiders) of finding one individual who is clearly responsible for what has gone wrong. Remember the fatal crash of the F-15? Was it the two maintenance men, or the senior officers who knew that this error had happened before, or was it perhaps the safety inspectors, or the base commander, or the designers of the plane, or even someone else? So many different people could be said to have had a hand in this, as in most organizational failures. In his book *The Quest for Responsibility* Marc Bovens (1998) produces an impressive (and depressing) list of adverse events for which it proved extremely difficult to pin down responsibility – bank collapses, financial frauds, chemical plant explosions, sinking ships, river pollution, the fatal fire on the US space shuttle, *Challenger*, and so on. He then considers four possible approaches to addressing what appears to be a massive and repetitive failure in the accountability systems of complex organizations. Interestingly, one of these possibilities is '*collective accountability*' – 'a personal accountability on the part of all individual members of the collective for the conduct of the whole' (Bovens 1998: 96). In some ways this sounds quite close to Behn's solution ('mutual and collective accountability' – see above), but Bovens finds it seriously inadequate. It may work, in certain defined circumstances, he allows, but it is not a general solution for the problems of encouraging responsible behaviour in complex organizations. Too often there will be a 'collective action problem', that is 'If the chances of being held accountable are approximately equal for everybody, but are not too great, then it becomes less attractive for members to stick their necks out . . .' (Bovens 1998: 102). This will be particularly true in the kind of temporary, shifting teams which are supposed to be more and more frequent in both public and private sector organizations.

Bovens also finds problems with his second and third approaches, which he calls 'corporate accountability' and 'hierarchical accountability'. In corporate accountability the whole organization is treated as if it were a single person. The basic idea is that when something goes wrong one should not waste time trying to sort out the inevitably complex details of exactly which individuals were responsible, one should simply hold the organization as a whole responsible. However, Bovens is unhappy with this principle in practice (and cites a number of cases where it seems to have failed). He argues that it tends to be weak in *ex ante* (before the event) responsibility, and offer a too-limited role to external scrutiny. Finally, Bovens criticizes notions of collective responsibility for lacking the (in his view) vital ingredient of personal moral conscience. 'In so far as the corporate model results in a situation in which no-one can be held to account for the conduct of complex organizations, then it must be said to fail in moral respect' (Bovens 1998: 73).

'Hierarchical accountability', the third approach, includes, but is not confined to, ministerial responsibility. Bovens produces a careful analysis of the components and track record of ministerial responsibility (1998: 85–9). His final remark is that:

there is a tendency to restrict accountability to that business of which the minister has had personal knowledge and that he was in a position actually to influence.

(Bovens 1998: 89)

This means that ministerial responsibility alone, though important, is an insufficient instrument for keeping tabs on the large, complex organizations that most ministries are. More generally, and after reviewing a number of prominent cases, Bovens concludes that trying to hold individuals responsible by using hierarchical accountability as the sole principle is:

sometimes a little like trying to grab hold of a piece of soap in a bathtub; whenever you think you have found someone, first at the top and then a little lower down, who meets all the necessary criteria, he once again slips through your fingers.

(Bovens 1998: 89)

Finally, Bovens turns to 'active, individual accountability'. This he sees as crucial – not on its own, but as a foundation for various combinations of the other forms of accountability (collective, corporate and hierarchical). 'In this concept of responsibility, the emphasis lies on the beliefs and personal values of the civil servant or employee. When a functionary finds that an assignment is irresponsible, loyalty to his own conscience and to his own identity should in the long run be the decisive factor' (Bovens 1998: 157). However, this emphasis on personal values should not be construed as an invitation to 'anything goes'. The individual employee (in our case, public manager) may exercise autonomy from organizational or hierarchical imperatives only under certain circumstances and for certain 'civic' reasons. Thus, resistance, refusal and/or 'whistleblowing' may be justified if democratic procedures are under threat (for example, if a minister is blatantly lying to parliament) or constitutionally illegal actions are about to be undertaken (for example, a prime minister or president is illegally planning to put electronic 'bugs' in the house of the leader of the opposition, or to manipulate voting procedures at election time). Resistance to actions which are deeply wasteful of public resources may also qualify, although Bovens does not think such cases are quite as forceful as the two previous categories (Bovens 1998: 170). Certainly if waste and illegality are combined (for example, if a public contract is let to a firm owned by the minister's brother, despite being one of the poorer bids on price/quality grounds) then 'autonomous action' by the public managers concerned would be appropriate.

Bovens is quite clear that such individual autonomy cannot, in practice, be left up to heroic individuals alone. He is equally firm that the existence of real discretion/room for manoeuvre is an essential pre-condition for active, individual accountability. If, as citizens of a democratic state, we want our public employees to behave in this conscience-directed way, then we need to create organizational rules and opportunities which enable them to do so. There could, for example, be some carefully-framed general provision which recognized the right of employees to resist illegal and anti-democratic actions, or even indemnified them for any punishments

they might suffer because of their refusal to co-operate. There can be special channels created for internal dissent ('whistleblowers hotlines' to the top, or to some
independent arbitrator). And so on, the list is long and each particular instrument
requires very careful design, and has its own particular limitations.

Bovens and Behn are not totally in disagreement with each other. They share
a common recognition of some elements of 'the problem' (or, to be more accurate,
the various problems). They also agree about at least some of the weaknesses of
the traditional remedies. Both admit the difficulties, and neither claims to have a
complete solution. However, their preferred directions of travel are sharply different.
For my money, Bovens is a broader scope treatment, and a more scholarly and
thoughtful one. It is also more intricate and nuanced; Bovens' recommendations
emerge in a more qualified and subtle manner than those of Behn. But if accountability is a topic that interests you, it would be a good idea to read both works, and
make your own comparisons.

To conclude, the notion of accountability plays a fairly central role in the
set of ideas that make up the model of liberal democracy. Recent changes in
most public sectors – the kinds of changes described in Chapters 2 and 3 – have
challenged the adequacy of traditional concepts of hierarchical accountability
and led to an international debate about how traditional mechanisms can be
supplemented (not replaced) by other forms. This debate has become intricate, and
there is as yet (and may well never be) any single model of what new arrangements
would be most appropriate. Public managers can and do contribute to this debate,
but they are not (and should not be) the only voices. Meanwhile, piecemeal reforms
proceed in many jurisdictions, and help to make what was already a complex,
multiple set of accountability relationships for public managers to work within
steadily more complex. As accountors, most public managers may not yet be facing
'360 degree accountability' but they are certainly being expected to face in several
directions at once.

Customers, citizens and communities

Now I turn from accountability to action. In this section I want to begin to look at a
more routine, less disaster-and-scandal-dominated aspect of the public manager's
existence: that of dealing with the public. Involving the public, in one way or
another, is certainly in fashion, at least in the Anglophone world. The previous
chapter touched on one aspect of it when partnerships with community groups and
voluntary sector organizations were discussed. Now I will broaden that discussion
to look across a variety of other forms of connection.

Involving the public *in one way or another* – the words were deliberately
chosen, because there are many different ways, with different implications for both
public managers and politicians. To begin with there is a useful distinction between:

- *Informing the public* (which can be active communication or passive production of information which is then simply available for those who seek it out).
  This is mainly a one-way relationship: the public body informs the citizens.

- *Consulting the public.* This is a two-way process, but the public body has defined the agenda in advance. 'We want your views about X.'
- *Public participation.* The most active form of relationship, where citizens are directly engaged with the decision-making process. Thus it is a two-way process, usually with more scope for influencing the agenda (for example, by developing new options) than consultation (this typology adapted from OECD 2001: 2). In genuine participation power is shared between the public authority and the participating citizens.

These distinctions concern the level (intensity) of interaction, and the distribution of power between the state and the citizens. Each step requires more from the citizens – from passive receiving of information, through the giving of opinions and suggestions, to active participation in agenda-setting, information gathering and decision-making.

Another relevant set of distinctions concerns the identity of those who are receiving information/being consulted/participating in decision-making. Thus far I have referred to them, vaguely, as 'citizens' or 'the public', but the public manager needs to get much more precise than that. For example, if a consultation exercise is being planned concerning a proposed change in the opening hours of a public facility, who is to be consulted? It could be:

- The current users ('customers') of the facility, on the grounds that they are those with the strongest interest in the change.
- All the citizens in the district, on the grounds that their taxes are going to pay for any extension to existing opening hours – and also that there may be citizens out there who do not currently use the facility, but would if it were open at different times.
- All the residents in the district. This is a somewhat different group from the citizens, because it will include various non-citizens (for example, foreigners) who live in the area and may well use services, but who do not have a vote and do not pay (at least some) of the taxes.

Steve Martin and Annette Boaz, researchers at Warwick University, have developed a useful diagram which combines the intensity dimension with the identity dimension (Martin and Boaz 2000: 50). Somewhat adapted, I reproduce it here as Figure 4.1.

At this point I want to refer back to the distinction between 'market' and 'forum' models of democracy which was introduced in the first section of this chapter. As one moves from left to right on Figure 4.1 one is moving more and more into the 'forum' zone. In the co-production/participation column one is concerned with deliberative democracy, where service users, citizens and communities play an active and influential part in discussing how the authority and resources of the state should be deployed. Furthermore, as one moves up the left-hand column, from bottom to top, one moves from an individualistic conception of participation (individual service users playing a part in determining how a particular service should be provided) to a more collective identity – the 'community'.

Intensity of interaction

←——— LESS   MORE ———→

		Information	Consultation	Participation
Identity of audience	Communities	Public relations	Community planning	Community leadership
	Citizens	Information for citizens	Citizen surveys Citizen focus groups	Citizen centred governance
	Users/ customers	Customer relations	User panels User surveys	User-led services (co-production)

Figure 4.1 Modes of citizen–state interaction (considerably adapted from Martin and Boaz (2000))

Participation 1

Most governments say they are in favour of participation, but many of them do very little of it. According to the OECD, active participation is 'undertaken on a pilot basis only and confined to a very few OECD countries' (OECD 2001: 1). Where it *is* practised it is not always successful, either in the eyes of governments or those of the citizens who are supposed to participate:

> Governments may seek to inform, consult and engage citizens in order to enhance the quality, credibility and legitimacy of their policy decisions . . . only to produce the opposite effect if citizens discover that their efforts to stay informed, provide feedback and actively participate are ignored, have no impact at all on the decisions reached or remain unaccounted for.
> (OECD 2001: 1. Notice that this is the cautious, intergovernmental OECD speaking, not some radical democrat!)

This quotation from the OECD lists some of the motives for governments to engage with participation. To enhance the quality of services (if service users participate, then surely they will know best what they want?). To increase the credibility of policy decisions ('this is not just our "political" decision, it is yours too, because you participated in it'). To raise the legitimacy of government ('you can trust us because you know we are open to your views and always listen to your points').

Many of the arguments for greater public participation grow out of one very powerful observation, which is that the classic form of representative democracy – elections every few years – is by itself a very crude and inadequate way of guiding state power and holding it to account. You cannot (usually) use your vote in a general election to indicate that you want better rural bus services, or that the local authority planning office is slow and inefficient or that the local hospital has made inadequate provision for persons in wheelchairs. In order to have any direct influence on these and a host of other specific issues the public needs to have other, more precise and targeted means of participating in decisions, above and beyond using a vote to elect a government. In terms of potential instruments for participation the list is long, and grows longer as our communication and decision technologies continue to improve. The following are only a sample:

- *National or local referenda on specific issues* (should the UK join the euro-zone? Should the town council allow a new supermarket development at the edge of the town park?). Referenda can be held using the traditional ballot papers or by a variety of electronic means.
- *Local meetings which are given some specific decision-making authority* (that is, not just talking shops).
- *Boards or panels of citizens, or of the users of a particular facility or service* (a local school or community centre or refuse collection service) which debate issues and can make a direct input to the management of the facility or service.

Is the interest shown by (some) governments new? By now you will probably be able to predict my answer to this question. Just like performance measurement, networking and joined-up government, the idea of greater public participation is a re-cycled idea that is far from novel. In general terms it has a long history, but even in more specific, modern terms the enthusiasm for participation since the late 1990s strikingly echoes some of the debates of an earlier wave of participation-itis, during the 1960s. Consider this, from a UK government report (published in 1969):

> It may be that the evolution of the structures of representative government which has concerned western nations for the last century and a half is now entering a new phase. There is a growing demand by many groups for more opportunity to contribute, and for more say in the working out of policies which affect people not merely at election time, but continuously as proposals are being hammered out and, certainly, as they are being implemented.
> (Ministry of Housing and Local Government 1969
> (The Skeffington Report): 3)

Similarly, in the USA, the 1960s 'War on Poverty' included huge efforts to get underprivileged local people to participate in the development of programmes aimed at bettering their circumstances. Kramer's (1969) book, *Participation of the Poor: Comparative Case Studies in the War on Poverty*, makes sobering reading for the participationists of the twenty-first century.

And just as today there are sceptics about the degree of public interest in 'participation', so too were there sceptics during that earlier phase. Anthony Crosland, a Labour Party intellectual and cabinet minister, put it like this:

. . . experience shows that only a small minority of the population wish to participate in this way [that is, directly in decision-making] . . . the majority prefer to lead a full family life and cultivate their gardens. And a good thing too. For if we believe in socialism as a means of increasing personal freedom and the range of choice, we do not necessarily want a busy, bustling society in which everyone is politically active, and fussing around in an interfering and responsible manner, and herding us all into participating groups. The threat to privacy and freedom would be intolerable . . . .

(Crosland 1970: 12–13)

Listening to the people

The tea ladies had done the meeting proud. At the back of the hall a couple of trestle tables groaned under the weight of a row of gleaming metal tea and coffee urns, flanked by plates of biscuits, including both bourbons and chocolate digestives – varieties seldom seen at normal meetings within the hospital.

When Kate and the members of the Project Team arrived the only other occupant of the room was an elderly lady, sitting in the back row of seats, ignoring the biscuits and munching away instead at what appeared to be a gigantic home-made sandwich. Soon, however, other people began to file in – mostly women and mostly elderly. About a dozen had arrived by the 11.00am scheduled start time of the meeting, so Kate announced that she would delay proceedings by a few minutes to give others time to arrive. By ten past the audience had risen to nearly 20, which, at a conservative estimate, worked out at ten cups of coffee or tea and about 20 biscuits per person. The Project Team had been hoping for 150, and the 'central estimate' had been 100. An advertising mail shot of nearly 6000 had been made a couple of weeks earlier, including more than 20 community groups and residents' associations, as well as the usual 'friends of the hospital'-type groups. Posters had gone up and advertisements had appeared in the hospital newsletter, two local newspapers and other places.

'Welcome to St Mark's, everyone' began Kate. 'My name is Kate Trevelyan, and I am Director of the hospital's Customers First Project Team. As you may know, Customers First is a radical reform aimed at greatly improving the hospital's services to you, its customers. As part of this reform we need to find out which aspects of the hospital's present service most need to be changed, and to do that we need to hear your views. Yours are the needs we are seeking to meet, so your wishes and experiences are the ones we have to learn more about. St Mark's is a major London teaching hospital and a centre for medical research. But we are very conscious that, for many of you, it is also simply your local hospital, on which you rely for basic services. So we must try hard to get the balance right between our specialist services and our general services, and we must do this in a way that satisfies a very varied group of customers with a wide range of needs and expectations.'

'We have already carried out a questionnaire survey of customers' needs, and I will say a little bit about that in a moment, but a questionnaire alone is not enough. We need to hear first hand what people think, and why they hold the views that they do. That is why we have called a series of open meetings, of which this is the first. The other meetings will be held at different times on different days so as to give access to the widest possible range of local people. At this meeting you are welcome to raise any issue which you think is important. We will be recording the proceedings so that we can have a full record of your suggestions. I can assure you that the Project Team, in developing its proposals for improving customer service, will pay great attention to your suggestions and comments. We believe in a participative approach to change.'

'Many interesting things came out of our survey.' (She shows a couple of slides with issues and percentages.) As you can see, the most frequently mentioned item was long waits in Accident and Emergency before being seen by a doctor, closely followed by the practice of customers being placed on trollies in the corridors while we arranged admission to the appropriate ward. In third place was communication with doctors – more than 40 per cent of you indicated that you felt you did not have a long enough or full enough discussion with the specialist, when you saw him or her. There are many other points, but we can pick up on these later.'

'Finally, before we get to the discussion, let me introduce my colleagues on the Project Team. This is Dr Charles Tibbins, a consultant paediatrician. On his left is Dr Sunethra Dyasena, a consultant geriatrician. Sally Holmes is a sister in Accident and Emergency. Duncan Mackenzie is Deputy Director of the Coronary Care Unit, which is to say he is a manager, and I, as I said, am Kate Trevelyan, Director of the Customers First Project Team.'

'So now the floor is yours. What are the things we need to improve at St Arthur's, and why?'

A lengthy silence followed. Dr Tibbins eventually broke it by saying 'I know it can be hard to be the first to speak up, but unless you tell us what you want, we will be working in the dark. We really do need your comments.' At this a bulky man in the front row held up his hand. 'Yes, please' said Kate, pointing at him.

'Well, I think your survey is right' began the man. 'My wife had to wait nearly ten hours on a trolley before they could find her a bed. It was humiliating, being treated like a spare package like that. She was very upset. But this isn't new, is it? It's been going on for years, so what's supposed to be different this time?'

'What is new is that we are tackling the problem in a new way' said Kate. 'For Accident and Emergency to work well a number of different parts of the hospital have to co-operate closely. In the past that didn't always happen. But the Customers First Project covers the whole hospital – it is a holistic approach, not a departmental approach. It has the full backing of the Trust Board and the Chief

Executive, and it is focused on the wishes of our customers, not on the convenience of doctors and nurses.'

'OK' responded a rather fierce-looking, red-haired woman in the middle of the room, 'that's all very well, but a lot of this is down to money. Does your project actually have more money to spend. Will the hospital get more beds, reversing the cuts of the last ten years, so that waiting in corridors isn't necessary any more?'

'Good morning Mrs Riley' said Dr Dyansena (recognizing the red-head as the ex-Chairperson of the Community Health Council, and a 'regular' at hospital public meetings of all kinds). 'Actually there *is* some more money, but money isn't the answer to everything. We can achieve a lot of improvements just by using what we have in a more efficient way. For example, we are installing a new computerized patient information system, integrated with the bed management system, and this will make communications between A&E and the wards much quicker and more accurate.'

'What about the food?' suddenly called out the woman with the monster sandwich. 'When my sister Dolly was in for her stomach in February doctor said she 'ad to 'ave a special diet, but every day they just brought her the usual – same as everyone else on the ward – meat and two veg. She tried to tell 'em but they didn't listen. And some of it – well, I saw it – I wouldn't 'ave fed it to our cat.'

Kate nodded at Duncan Mackenzie. 'Yes, food has sometimes been a problem' he said. 'And there is no excuse for the kind of thing you are talking about. But the worst part of your story, if I may say so, is that you say the staff didn't listen when your sister complained. That is very much the kind of thing we hope this project will tackle. So your point is well taken, and we will pay attention to it.'

Woman with sandwich: When?

Kate: We report this meeting to the Steering Group next Thursday. The project will produce its final recommendations in about two months' time. We are looking for rapid implementation.

Woman with sandwich: Well Dolly's due back in the week after next, so I s'pose that means she'll 'ave the same problem again.

Kate: No – if you will be kind enough to give me your sister's details at the end of this meeting, I will do my best to see that her dietary needs are fully met when she comes in.

Red-haired woman: What about the proposed merger with the Westminster Hospital? What effect will that have on patient care? Is it true that Accident and Emergency will disappear from this site, and be centralized at the Westminster?

Kate: The merger isn't really on the agenda for our project. And, as you will know, nothing final has been decided. In fact we are months away from any decision, so I don't think we can say much about that today.

Red-haired woman: You started by saying that we could talk about anything we liked. And if the merger goes through it is bound to have a huge effect on the availability of services and on patient care. So why can't we talk about it? And why is your project not supposed to pay attention to it?

Kate: Well, of course we *can* talk about it, Mrs Riley – in fact we *are* talking about it. But all I'm saying is that this probably isn't the best place or time to do so. The main aim of this meeting is to find out what aspects of our service our customers most want improving. There will be plenty of opportunity later to discuss the merger – if and when it becomes a firm proposal.

Red-haired woman: When the whole thing is signed and sealed you mean.

[*At this point a young child that is with one of the women near the front sets up a tremendous wail.*]

Young man at the back, speaking rather loud in order to be heard over the child's protestations: My name is Jungi Lilongo, and I want to say that I think all this 'customers' stuff is a mistake. Customer this, customer that. I'm not your customer, I'm your *patient.* I want to be treated like a patient not like someone wandering around a supermarket. I want to be treated *better* than a customer, and I want to feel I can trust the doctors and nurses much more than I would trust most shopkeepers.

Kate: I understand your feeling like that. None of these words – customer, patient, client, service user – pleases everyone. But for better or worse we chose Customers First as the title for our project, so there we are. Maybe I could ask you to concentrate on the *second* word in our title – the word 'first'. How can we make you as a patient feel that we are putting your interests first?

Young man: By talking to me as an equal. Not as a customer who has to be kept happy. And not as a perforated ulcer or the heart case in bed 6. I have a name. When I was here with kidney trouble the doctor hardly even looked at me. The few sentences he spoke were in a kind of sing-song voice, as though he was talking to a child. Maybe he thought 'young, black – not worth trying to explain', I don't know. But I felt patronized – it was just rude, if you ask me.

Dr Dyasena: Of course I can't comment on your particular experience, but . . .

At this point Dr Tibbin's pager began to buzz. He answered it in low tones while Dr Dyasena continued her reply to Mr Lilongo. Then he whispered something to Kate Trevelyan, stood up and tiptoed out of the room. When Dr Dyasena finished, Kate broke in: 'Dr Tibbins asked me to apologize to the meeting but he has been called back to the ward to deal with an emergency'. 'But that's typical, isn't it?' responded Mr Lilongo, 'the doctors are always too busy to stay and talk. So how are you going to change that? You can't give orders to doctors, and they *are* busy, so how can your Customers First Team do anything about it?'

At this point Kate was beginning to look slightly fazed. Sally Holmes took the question: 'You are right, doctors are often extremely pressed for time. As a nurse I see that every day – often we nurses feel the doctors don't talk enough to us either. But things are changing already. It is partly a generational thing. Nowadays the training for doctors includes quite a lot on communicating with patients, which it used not to. And the hospital can also develop its own policies – which is what we are trying to do with Customers First. If the Trust Board and the senior medical staff all put emphasis on the importance of talking with patients and involving them in their treatment, then the younger doctors soon take note.'

The meeting proceeded in this fashion for about 90 minutes, after which everyone except Mrs Riley ran out of steam, and the audience began to leave. Kate took the opportunity to sum up and close. She thanked the audience for their time and their suggestions and pointed out that there would be at least two more such meetings over the next three weeks.

Two weeks later the Customers First Steering Group (with the Chief Executive of St Mark's in the chair) considered the monthly activity report from the Project Team. Item 7, para. 7.2 read as follows:

> On April 7 the first open meeting in the Customer Participation series was held. Approximately 25 members of the public attended. A wide variety of points were put to members of the Project Team. In the main these reinforced the pattern of responses already seen in our customer survey. All suggestions have been recorded and are being fed into the on-going work of the Project Team. Two further such meetings are planned.

This item was noted, without further discussion.

(The meeting at St Mark's represents an amalgam of public meetings which I and colleagues I have been working with have attended. In this, admittedly limited, sample a large surplus of tea and biscuits was commonplace. All the arguments used in this sketch were made by hospital patients at one or other of these meetings.)

Participation 2

The meeting at St Mark's exemplified some of the difficulties (or 'challenges' if you prefer) of the involvement of public managers in exercises in citizen participation.

As you probably noticed, there were a number of awkward features to the meeting, including the following:

- A poor turn-out (low numbers) for a public meeting.
- A turn-out that was probably unrepresentative of the whole population of users of the hospital (those present were mainly older women, and mainly from the ethnic majority).
- A general difficulty in getting any 'overview' of public concerns – such meetings tend to become a succession of unrelated points, some big and general, some small and personal. On the other hand, if the people running the meeting attempt to impose an agenda then they are easily accused of having their own interests and conducting a 'rigged' exercise in consultation.
- A related difficulty in that items may come up which the managers concerned cannot really say anything about because they are too 'political'. In this case Mrs Riley was quite right to point out that a merger with another hospital could affect services in a fundamental way, but Kate Trevelyan and her team were in no position to discuss that issue.
- Members of the public not infrequently want specific, concrete answers to their questions, and often the managers cannot realistically give answers in that form (for example, can you promise that the doctors will talk to us more? When will the management of the hospital food service be improved?). When managers refer to 'taking views into account' or to future meetings of boards or committees this can easily sound like bureaucratic obfuscation by the management (and it may sometimes *be* bureaucratic obfuscation by the management!).
- More generally, there is often an uncomfortable vagueness about the underlying power relationships at such meetings. Kate began by saying that her Project Team was engaged in a 'participative approach' and that those attending were welcome to raise any issue they pleased. But in fact it sounded like an exercise in consultation rather than participation – the audience had no authority to make decisions about anything, and the meeting itself had been timetabled, designed and arranged by the hospital management, not by the citizens who used the hospital. Neither the Project Team nor the top management of the hospital was in any way bound by what was said at the meeting – they could take it or leave it. According to the definitions advanced in the section on 'Customers, citizens and communities' (page 98) this is consultation, not participation.

One of the underlying reasons why participation is such a tricky business is that many politicians themselves are highly ambivalent about it. They are part of a representative democratic system, in which their special position and power derive from their status as *elected representatives* of some defined population. So the idea that some power is going to be handed over to an unelected and possibly unpredictable group of citizens makes for anxiety. Could it lead not to an enhancement of the legitimacy of the council (or government) but rather to a *loss* of authority by the formal decision-makers (themselves – the politicians) and a gain by this (quite possibly unrepresentative) group of 'amateurs'? This is bad enough, but, in so far as public *managers* are involved in organizing participation, a further threat to politicians may be feared. If (as was discussed earlier) politicians are sometimes concerned at the superior knowledge or suspected alternative agendas of their advisers and managers, how much more will they worry when these managers are in regular, direct contact with citizens – contacts of a kind in which citizens are encouraged to develop new ideas and even take decisions for themselves? Participation may become a way in which officials make themselves even stronger in their dealings with elected politicians. 'Well, Councillor Smith, your suggestion is a very attractive one, but I am afraid we cannot go in that direction because in our participation exercise it became clear that the residents in Oakthorpe Ward are totally opposed to it. You will see that their decision to exclude that option is recorded in the minutes of the most recent Community Planning Council meeting.'

The development of modern information and communication technologies has, if anything, made this tension between managers and their political bosses worse. Now even more information about citizen preferences streams in, by more capacious, more numerous and more interactive channels. Politicians cannot possibly attend to all this information: they are obliged to delegate more and more of its collection, sifting and summarizing to their advisers. All of which brings us round full circle, back to the alternative interpretations of politico-management relations discussed in the section 'Politics and management' (pages 86–7). In a low trust, conspiracy theory environment, exercises in public participation can become a nightmare. Only when relationships of mutual understanding and trust can be built between politicians and their officials can large-scale modern exercises in public participation hope to bear fruit.

Concluding remarks: is 'progress' possible?

This chapter has taken the reader through a number of complex issues which, separately and together, defy single, simple solutions. Each issue – relations between managers and politicians, accountability, participation – drifts in and out of media attention. Each periodically assumes new forms and new jargon, but the novelties usually mark out a struggle with some much older, underlying issues. Public managers can and do make significant contributions to these on-going debates, and to the shaping of whatever may be the currently fashionable solutions. But managers certainly cannot 'solve' these issues – or even determine where, for a time, to balance the trade-offs – by themselves. Politics, accountability, participation – these are activities which mark the boundaries of management – they are where the public managers face their various 'audiences', where they receive their instructions, search for knowledge and authority which they themselves do not have, offer their explanations, make their excuses.

The theme of recurrence – of problems that return, of trade-offs that from time-to-time are re-balanced – is one which has already appeared in earlier chapters. It will itself recur in some of the chapters which are yet to come. Some of the academic disciplines which contribute to public administration and public management offer explanations for such 'cycles' or 'returns' of issues such as the accountability of civil servants or the participation of citizens. Anthropology, for example, offers an overarching view of cultural cycles in which public management tends to lurch between alternative but ultimately incompatible sets of values. Today we are enthusiastic about getting more participation, and including the voices of every stakeholder group in public decisions. Tomorrow, becoming uncomfortable with the slowness and messiness of this style of decision-making, we lurch towards a more hierarchical style, which (we hope) will give us greater speed and decisiveness, clearer-cut responsibilities and greater transparency about what is going on. 'In other words, cultural dynamics work by mutual antagonism among opposites seeking to blame adherents of alternative ways of life for the social ills they are held to create' (Hood 1998: 11). Decision theory – to take another discipline – conceptualizes many aspects of public policy as choices between different kinds of error or injustice. To correct the injustice of poverty, social security benefit levels are raised, and eligibility categories relaxed. That goes some way towards solving the original problem, but it also creates a new one – the growth of 'scrounging' – people who are capable of paid employment but would rather live on benefits, laughing in the faces of those 'saps' who work hard to pay the taxes that support state generosity. 'Although policy makers will set, or try to set, the decision criterion at a point that satisfies their sense of justice, that point will provide only an uneasy truce between each form of injustice: each constituency will remain convinced that it is being unjustly treated' (Hammond 1996: 56).

Do these views of recurrence and alternation between different value positions mean that everything just goes round in circles – that we must abandon any 'modernist' ideas of 'progress'? Not necessarily. While acknowledging the tendency for management reforms to oscillate between different criteria, there remains a difference between the drunk who weaves from side to side as he staggers home and the even drunker drunk who weaves from side to side as he wanders round in circles. It may well be that public management reforms usually produce unforeseen effects, and that some of these effects are negative (from a particular value standpoint). The early impacts of reform, in particular, may have a disorienting effect on staff and citizens alike – they both have to learn a new game (Dunleavy and Margetts 2000: 4–7). But in the longer term, as processes of learning take place, the negative effects may be reduced and the positives maximized – if the original reform was well-designed and appropriate for the particular organizational and cultural context. Not everything is a dilemma or a 50:50 trade-off. Paradoxically, it may be the most politically sensitive systems which act like the drunker drunk – at the first sign of trouble they weave violently to the other side and end up going round in circles. Those systems where the political or administrative leadership has greater authority and/or commands more trust can wobble to left and right but nevertheless 'hang on' with a particular line of reform for longer, and allow learning processes to come to the fore. (Indeed, part of the design of a clever reform is precisely to encourage and support learning processes.) Unfortunately, of course, the same conditions – strong authority or high trust – also permit governments to persist with badly thought-out reforms, and thereby increase the general misery. Thinking back to the 1980s, it strikes me as unlikely that in a less centralized and majoritarian political system than the UK's the Poll Tax (Community Charge) would ever have got as far as the statute book. So many people, always excepting Mrs Thatcher, could see what a disaster it was going to be.

Public managers are given the daunting task of administering the complex programmes which are supposed to embody these shifting mixtures of values, norms and technologies. They need to keep their ears to the cultural ground, but also to make their own contributions to the debate – to do their best to identify and assess both what will hopefully be gained *and* what will probably be lost with each turn of the wheel or stagger to the left or right. They can also strongly contribute to refining the instruments by which opinion and experience is gathered and aggregated and judged. Some methods are more precise or more reliable than others, and it is part of the job of officials to be able to advise and act on the basis of knowledge of the available instrumentalities. Public managers can no more than anyone else face in all directions at once, but their experiences can help the rest of us understand more clearly what the full consequences of any particular stance are likely to be.

Further reading

Those of you who are interested in the ideas of cycles and trade-offs (just discussed in the previous section) should certainly read Christopher Hood's (1998) ingenious book *The Art of the State: Culture, Rhetoric and Public Management*. An earlier work, *Administrative Argument* (Hood and Jackson 1991) is also worth searching for, as it contains a beautifully symmetric enumeration of all the key arguments and counter-arguments around which so much debate about public management has long revolved. For a more hard-edged, psychology-based approach to dilemmas and choices in public policy, I hope you will find Kenneth Hammond's (1996) *Human Judgement and Social Policy* as wise and fascinating as I did.

On the relationships between politics and management, a number of useful sources spring to mind. You might like to try a couple of biographies – one by an unusually managerially-minded politician and the other by a quite politically-minded civil servant. The first is Michael Heseltine's (1987) *Where There's a Will*, which also gives a good flavour of the heady, early days of the NPM under Mrs Thatcher's Conservative administration. The second is Roy Denman's (2002) *The Mandarin's Tale*, in which the author takes us through half a century of changes in the British civil service, with the added spice of many international assignments where cultural differences between the British civil servants and civil servants from other countries can be commented upon. Among more academic works, Chapter 5 of Christensen and Lægreid (2001) gives useful insights, Chapter 6 of Pollitt and Bouckaert (2000) also addresses the issue, and Hal Rainey (1997) takes a general look at the factors which might make public management special, including the overt presence of politics. None of these, however, use quite the fourfold set of competing theories (conspiracy/bureaucracy/wise counsellor/scapegoat) which I have employed above, although variations on this are present.

As far as accountability is concerned, I have already made my recommendations, and will only repeat here that Robert Behn's (2001) *Rethinking Democratic Accountability* and Marc Bovens' (1998) *The Quest for Responsibility* make a very good pair of contrasting analyses.

Many works deal with consultation and participation. Ranson and Stewart's (1994) *Management in the Public Domain* provides a good introduction to the background arguments concerning the relationship between the governors and the citizenry. The pair of articles by Lowndes, Pratchett and Stoker (2001a, 2001b) which appeared in the first and second issues of *Public Administration* for that year add some sobering empirical realism. Martin and Boaz (2000) also merits a visit. Finally, Kramer's (1969) study of the attempts at participation during the US 'War on Poverty' is still well worth reading, if you can get hold of it from a library.

5

Evaluation – how do we measure success?

Europe evaluates

It is 7pm on a cold, dark February evening in Brussels. Joanna is an English 'A' grade member of staff in the Agriculture Directorate General of the European Commission – what the frequently Europhobic and misinformed British press sometimes call a Eurocrat. She is a Grade 4, so she is fairly senior, but not yet a 'head of unit' (these distinctions matter in a classic hierarchical bureaucracy such as the Commission). Already tired from a long day of multi-lingual meetings, she now stares alternately at a fat document on her desk and at the screen of her desktop. The document bears the title *Evaluation of the School Milk Measure: Final Report.*

[Note to the reader: Joanna, Xavier and some of the incidental details of this story, are entirely fictional. But the evaluation report, and most of the subsequent events, are fact. Recent EU evaluation reports may be viewed on the EU Commission website, http://europa.eu.int/index_en.htm (accessed 24 January 2003).]

Joanna has already read the report, and knows that, in carefully coded language, it contains damning criticisms of both the design and the execution of a pro-gramme for which her Directorate is responsible. This is why her Director General's assistant, a sharp-faced, sharp-tongued and immaculate young Frenchman, has asked her to provide the DG with a brief by tomorrow morning. Soon the contents of the evaluation will reach the public domain. Euro MPs know that it has been completed. And the Commission's policy is, after all, to put all evalu-ations on the website. So, for several reasons, between now and her evening meal, a convincing defensive brief has to be composed on that accusingly blank screen in front of her.

Usually, a policy advisory division such as hers could be expected to resist any call for one of its programmes to be shut down (as this evaluation recommends). However, on this occasion, some special considerations apply. First, the evaluation in the report is clearly competent – hard to argue against. Second, the Agriculture

Directorate has for some time been criticized within the Commission – and more widely – for its slowness in embracing the new pro-evaluation culture. Although the largest spending DG in the whole of the EU Commission (because of the huge volume of funds going through the Common Agricultural Policy) DG Agriculture has not carried out many evaluations, especially compared with the second largest spending DG – DG Regions. DG Regions has a policy of mandatory evaluations for all its programmes, and has made a great fuss of developing its own evaluation unit and its own evaluation methods. One of its show-piece publications – a glossy six-volume boxed set of books, *Evaluating Socio-economic Programmes*, is currently lying, in self-satisfied prominence, on one corner of her piled-high side table. In short, DG Agriculture is suspected of reactionary resistance to a proper evaluation of its presumed-to-be-inefficient programmes. So to be able to show willing – to accept a critical evaluation report and take decisive action to meet its recommendations – could be a very useful move. It would be a shrewd bit of bureaucratic politics.

Joanna re-reads the key sections of the 171-page report:

Overall, the scheme's efficiency and effectiveness in reaching its target population is poor.

(CEAS Consultants 1999: vii)

. . . the main delivery mechanism of the School Milk Measure (price subsidy) is targeted at a factor of minor influence in determining consumption of milk and milk products.

(CEAS Consultants 1999: viii)

Judged purely against the current, stated documented objectives of the measure (maintaining and increasing consumption of milk products), the measure has had a marginal, positive impact and represents poor value for money. This suggests that the Commission should give serious consideration to withdrawing the measure.

(CEAS Consultants 1999: x)

The plain fact was that this was a useless, itsy-bitsy price subsidy, with no evidence that it met its own main objective ('to help expand the market for milk products'). The Commission, always hard-pressed for funds, was throwing away more than 100 million euros per annum on something that didn't work. These dismal outcomes had long been suspected, and the consultants' evaluation had merely confirmed them. Mind you, the School Milk Scheme was not the only such dubious activity. The Common Agricultural Policy was a veritable Jurassic Park of programmes left over from an earlier era. It contained other suspect measures, and the whole thing was so phenomenally complicated that frequently the Commission's right hand didn't really know what its left hand was doing. Nevertheless, the political forces defending the CAP were hugely powerful – taken as a whole it was one of the political foundation stones of the entire EU, and even a tiny chip off the block might be seen as dangerous by some.

Joanna began to tap at her keyboard. 'Let's go for it!', she thought, or, more pragmatically, 'let's get it done so I can go and eat'. Two hours later her brief for the Director General was finished. She recommended going along with the Report's recommendations, killing the School Milk Scheme, taking the maximum credit for having a keen, modern concern for efficiency and effectiveness, and proposing a further study of possible new schemes for using the funds more effectively.

The meeting with the DG took place two days later. Some voices were raised against giving such weight to a mere evaluation report, and various arguments about the irrelevance of the evaluation to 'real life' were put forward (mainly, Joanna noted, in terms that made it clear that the speakers had either not read the evaluation report, not understood it, or were chronically intellectually dishonest). However, it soon became clear that the DG himself was minded to go along with the recommendation to terminate the programme. Joanna was quietly delighted – her advice was being accepted. The sharp-jawed French assistant deigned to give her a nod of encouragement – maybe he wasn't such a pig after all?

However, the Commission could not just decide to do this by itself. In the dense institutional maze that was the EU, it had to secure the agreement of at least two other bodies – the European Parliament and the Council of Ministers. Some of the people around the table foresaw difficulties here – milk producers' lobbies pressing their governments and Euro MPs to keep their little subsidy, however useless it might be in terms of the overall objectives of the CAP. But the Commission would do its best. For once, at least, it would be fighting on the side of reason and efficiency.

Over the months that followed, the saga of the School Milk Measure rolled slowly forwards. The European Parliament, it seemed, was prepared to accept the Commission's recommendation to terminate the programme. But then came the discussion in the Council of Ministers. At this point the train of reason and good sense began to come off the rails. After hearing a slightly bizarre pot pourri of arguments from the ministers of the member states, the Council agreed that:

> The Ministers of Agriculture take the view that the consumption of milk is of great importance in view of its high nutrition value, particularly for children and young people. They therefore consider it appropriate to reflect further on how such consumption can be encouraged in a cost-efficient way, taking overall account of the overall availability of budgetary resources.
>
> (June 1999 'Agriculture' Council)

Back in her office, Joanna read this with a wry smile. The Council was stressing nutritional benefits – but this side-stepped several pertinent facts. First, health benefits were not the objective of the original policy, or of the CAP in general. The objective had been to promote the production and sale of milk products, which the evaluation showed it did not achieve. Second, changing medical opinion was anyway now beginning to cast doubt on the health benefits of higher milk consumption – the creamy white stuff had some dangers as well as benefits. The little kiddies might be better off with orange juice. Third, most milk (more than 99 per cent) was consumed outside school anyway, so even if there were health benefits they were, not to put too fine a point on it, a drop in the milky ocean.

Anyway, the Commission responded by proposing a modified scheme, in which member states contributed 50 per cent of the costs of a modernized subsidy system – what in EU jargon is called 'co-financing'. In crude terms this response could be construed as saying 'if you want it, you pay for it – or at least half of it'. The Council met again seven months later (quite quickly by EU standards). Unsurprisingly, the majority of member states were vigorously opposed to co-financing. Pleas for a simplification of the administration of the scheme were put forward. Suggestions for making milk products magic-ally more attractive to coke-swilling youngsters were earnestly debated. Further political to-ings and fro-ings took place. Fifteen months after the original evaluation came in, a new Council Regulation was finally adopted. The milk subsidy was retained, indeed, expanded to cover low-fat products such as skimmed and semi-skimmed milks and low-fat yoghurts. The Commission was instructed to find ways of simplifying the administration of the subsidy.

One evening, shortly after this resolution, Joanna went out with the DG's French assistant and shared a bottle of excellent gewurtztraminer. 'By the way', he said at one point, his fine jaw bones more sculpted than ever, 'you know who the key supporter of the scheme was? Your British Ministry of Agriculture! What is it with you Brits? You come to Council and lecture the Commission about our inefficiencies – and particularly about the in-equities of the CAP. Mr Blair gets onto his pulpit about "evidence-based policy-making" and the importance of identifying "what works". Then, when we finally find a gold-plated example of a useless programme, you rush in to rescue it?' 'Don't look at me', replied Joanna, extending her empty glass, 'I was born in Yorkshire'. For once, but only momentarily, Xavier looked puzzled.

Comment

Evaluation – the systematic assessment of public policies, programmes and projects – at first appears a devastatingly obvious activity. Surely, it is in everyone's interests – politicians, civil servants, the general public – to get the best possible information about whether government programmes (or in this case an EU programme) are working properly? Are they achieving their objectives? Are they being imple-mented efficiently? Is money being wasted? Are there better ways of achieving the same goals?

These are indeed important questions. In practice, however, there are both motivational and methodological hurdles which would-be evaluators have to overcome.

Motivationally, it is not in everyone's interest to have such questions vigorously pursued. Some people benefit from a programme even if it is inefficient – they receive a grant or a price subsidy, or whatever. They will not be overjoyed at proposals to cut it back. Others have made their reputation by launching the programme, or have found their employment by working for it. All these groups benefit from the programme, even if it is not very efficient, and even if it does not achieve its formal goals.

Methodologically, it can often be very hard to decide what the best way to study a programme may be. How should one decide whether a school is providing a good education? Just by looking at exam results? Or by asking children how happy they are? Or by observing how well the teachers teach? Furthermore, it may be impossible (for reasons of time, cost or access) to collect all the necessary evidence. Some preventative health programmes (for example, persuading teenagers not to smoke, putting fluoride in the water to help preserve people's teeth) may not have their full impact for years or even decades.

Both motivational and methodological issues can be seen in the tale of the School Milk Measure. Methodologically, for example, the evaluators found it very hard to estimate the precise effect of the subsidy on milk production. It was one small variable in a large and complex market for milk and milk products. Motivationally, just as DG Agriculture had a motive for wanting to appear open to evaluation, so certain politicians in the Council of Agriculture Ministers had motives for not wanting the Commission to end this subsidy – whether or not it was terribly effective.

Furthermore, the story brings out the point that evaluation is always conducted in an *institutional* environment. Evaluators are not white-coated scientists reporting the results of precise experiments to the respectful and expectant masses. They are economists and operational researchers and organizational analysts and other kinds of experts producing reports for particular institutions, which have commissioned these reports with a definite aim or objective in mind. Usually, these commissioning institutions are not able to act entirely alone. They are part of some wider policy community or network which contains other 'stakeholders' – other divisions of a ministry, other levels of government, pressure groups and so forth. In the EU context this institutional network is especially complex, but it exists in national and local settings also.

Another example may help to deepen understanding of the kind of activity which evaluation is. This time we can look at an evaluation of a public management reform. A big hospital decides to launch a huge 're-engineering project' (this illustration is based on a real UK case from the mid-1990s). The hospital – let's call it 'St Swithins' – spent millions of pounds bringing management consultants in over a two-year period in order to examine its core processes and redesign them for greater efficiency and effectiveness. It attempted to transform its accident and emergency department, its cancer care unit, its cardiac care facilities and so on.

They were re-organized, re-trained, and to some extent re-staffed. Patients were consulted. Local general practitioners and community health organizations were asked for their views. The hospital committed itself to a 'patient perspective' in the design and running of its services.

To his/her credit, the Chief Executive decided to ask for an independent external evaluation of the project. Various evaluation teams bid for the contract, and one – a university-based team – eventually won the competition. It began to work. It was supposed to look for evidence of the success and/or failure of the re-engineering effort. It decided to go for a mixture of 'hard' and 'soft' measures. On the hard side it wanted to look at whether the proportion of patients undergoing major surgery for certain conditions who survived a given length of time after their treatment increased once reforms had been put in place. Then these survival rates could be compared with those which prevailed before the reforms (what is known in evaluation as a 'before and after' study). On the softer side, it wanted to know what staff and patients thought of the changes – did they consider that things had improved?

The evaluators also wanted to compare developments in the hospital with what was happening in other hospitals – both those with re-engineering projects and those without. In this way it might have been possible to get a clearer idea of which changes were due mainly to re-engineering and which ones were happening in many hospitals anyway. But the St Swithins management ruled out parallel studies of other hospitals – they seemed quite nervous about any such comparisons.

The university team now set about collecting the data. This turned out to be a major effort. The quality of much of the data collected by the hospital itself was poor, but for the evaluation team to collect all its own data would have been both time-consuming and very expensive (the evaluation budget was fixed, and allowed for so many days of academic time, and no more – although in the end the academics concerned ended up spending considerably more time on the project than they were paid for). Repeatedly, data was firmly promised for a particular date, but then did not turn up. (Some of it never did.) It soon dawned on the evaluators that the staff in the hospital frequently saw the daily care of patients as their priority (who can blame them?) and the collection of data – especially for management purposes – as much lower down the list of things to do. However, after many meetings and negotiations one particularly important set of clinical outcome data (outcomes – what actually happens to the health status of patients who are treated) was eventually secured.

Interviews carried out by the evaluators revealed a sharply divided picture – some hospital staff were very enthusiastic about the re-engineering project but quite a few were deeply sceptical. Some started out full of hopes (perhaps too high) and subsequently became disillusioned by the rather bombastic terms in which the first stage of the re-engineering project had been proclaimed, and by its apparent failure to lead directly to big changes. While many managers were keen (they almost had to be – the programme was high-profile and led by their Chief Executive) relatively few doctors were deeply involved. This was significant, because doctors enjoyed a good deal of clinical freedom and in these areas could not be ordered around by managers, however senior. As for the public, despite noble efforts by the hospital to involve them, only a few turned up to the meetings, and they often had quite individual points to pursue ('When my husband George was in for his heart operation, they never gave him the food he asked for', etc.).

So it turns out to be rather a messy evaluation, and, furthermore, one which is gradually overtaken by events. After a high profile start, the re-engineering programme seems to slip down the list of management priorities, and its dedicated staff and resources begin to shrink quite fast. The Chief Executive himself leaves St Swithins for another job. Many of the key staff on the re-engineering project itself are redeployed to other tasks. New issues move up to the top positions on the NHS hospitals' agenda.

Nevertheless, the evaluators burn the midnight oil in order to get their report written by the agreed date. The main findings are not particularly uplifting. There is no real evidence of the radical transformation of the hospital that had been talked about so much at the beginning of the re-engineering project. The measures of clinical outcome, which had been so hard to get hold of, actually show some *worsening* of patient outcomes on one of the services which was at the heart of the re-engineering effort. On the other hand, some benefits are identifiable – speeded-up procedures, better liaison between different parts of the hospital, and so on. Yet one would expect *something* to improve, after all, many talented people had spent a lot of time on the project and several millions of the taxpayers' pounds had been consumed. So, overall, the results of the evaluation will presumably be seen as disappointing.

What happened next can best be summarized as deafening silence. Months go by and the evaluators hear nothing from the hospital. Eventually, a puzzling message arrives at the university. It says that the last invoice the evaluation team sent in will not be paid until the evaluation report is delivered. The evaluation team contact St Swithins and point out that the report was submitted a long time ago. After a period of confusion the report is found at the bottom of a cupboard in the hospital – surely a definitive sign that the agenda really *has* moved on.

Although the report was retrieved, the evaluation team heard no more from St Swithins. Their offer of seminars for staff, explaining their findings, was never taken up. The report was never published or placed in the public domain – metaphorically, at least, it remained at the bottom of the cupboard. The evaluators never heard of any action being taken by the hospital management in the light of their recommendations.

This (95 per cent true) story of St Swithins contains further examples of the difficulties facing evaluators. To begin with, the hospital management wanted an 'independent' evaluation, but in practice they wanted to be able to influence how it was carried out (for example, they didn't want explicit comparisons with other hospitals). They were always ambiguous about whether the evaluation was intended to be *formative* (that is, it was to help management improve its performance) or *summative* (that is, a definitive judgement on how well or badly the programme had worked, intended for a wider audience). In the event there was no sign that it was used much, either formatively or summatively. Data problems were endless – much of the kind of information needed for an evaluation of efficiency or effectiveness either did not exist, or existed but was very hard to get hold of, or existed and was unreliable. Many staff were very helpful, but some were suspicious of the evaluators, or were so busy that it was hard to get to see them, or (in a few cases) just refused to reply to requests for interviews. All this was very time consuming, so that the evaluation team could not cover the ground nearly as quickly as it had originally hoped.

Even more fundamentally, perhaps, it became increasingly difficult to decide what was a result of the re-engineering programme and what was not. This is a familiar problem in many evaluations – particularly of organizational change – and is called the problem of *attribution*. To begin with, the re-engineering programme itself was made up of many different actions in many different departments of the hospital. So it wasn't one, simple thing, but many things, opening up the distinct possibility that some of these elements worked well and others did not. In addition, however, there were many other changes taking place in the hospital that were not part of the re-engineering programme. For example, there was a major rebuilding programme going on, and the clinical practice in various departments was being changed all the time as a result of new developments in medicine, new protocols issued by the institutions of the medical and nursing professions, and so on.

So even if a 'result' (for example, faster average time completing a particular type of diagnostic test; improved patient satisfaction ratings in the back pain clinic) was found, it was often very difficult indeed to be sure what had caused it. Was it the re-engineering project's re-organization of the process of sending and returning samples? Or was it a new piece of equipment which the pathology laboratory had purchased as a normal step in modernization (not part of re-engineering)? Or was it the appointment of a keen young consultant who was anxious to tighten up efficiency in the department? Or the nice new waiting room that had been provided through the rebuilding programme? Or some combination of all these things? And, finally, had the improvement in the speed of this particular test, or the satisfaction of the back pain patients, been achieved at the cost of a slowing down or reduction of service somewhere else?

What general conclusion might one draw from these cases? It is sometimes tempting to throw up one's hands in despair and say, in effect, 'it's all too difficult – evaluation can seldom be done properly, and even if it is, it will probably be ignored. So there is no point even trying'. My argument here, however, will be a different one. I would make just three points.

First, if evaluation is abandoned, how *will* we be able to check whether public programmes are working? Just by casual impressions? Or by the statements of politicians, most/all of whom have some axe to grind? Or by the claims of senior managers, who will usually bend over backwards to put the best possible face on whatever has happened (defending their own institution is, after all, part of their job).

Second, it is naïve to think of evaluation as an activity which provides definite answers which will then immediately be implemented by eager politicians and public managers. As the two cases described above make very clear, evaluation is just one ingredient in the debate over policies and programmes. It may have an influence, but so do other factors, including political commitments, the preservation of institutional relationships, public opinion and so on.

Third, evaluation may often be difficult (and may sometimes be impossible) but that doesn't mean that it is not worth trying. Over the past 40 years evaluators have worked out many ways of minimizing problems – both motivational and methodological. That is what most books on evaluation are all about. And alongside the many cases of disappointment and 'back-of-the-cupboard-ism', there are also examples of influence and success. This section concludes with one such example.

In the early 1990s the Australian Bureau of Transport and Communications Economics (BTCE) was commissioned to carry out an evaluation of the Australian Federal Government's 'Black Spot' Program. This was a programme of road improvements (for example, new traffic lights, new road markings) intended to reduce the number and severity of road accidents at a number of 'black spots' where accidents had taken place in the past. In a cost-cutting climate the programme was under pressure to 'show results' or suffer downsizing or even termination.

The BCTE selected 254 specific local projects out of a total of 3176 in the whole programme. They conducted a cost benefit analysis of these projects. For each, they estimated how many accidents (and of what severity) had been avoided by the installation of the road improvements. (They could do this by looking at before and after statistics for road accidents.) Then they estimated how much these 'avoided' accidents would have cost (for example, the value of lost output due to injuries plus the costs of vehicle damage and of ambulance and police services, etc.). Then they compared these 'benefits' (avoided costs) against the actual cost of the black spot improvement programme. The conclusion was that:

> the entire Black Spot program has delivered net benefits to the Australian community of at least $800 million, generating returns of around $4 for each dollar of expenditure. The results of the evaluation strongly suggest that the Program has achieved its aim of improving locations with a history of crashes involving death or serious injury.
>
> (Bureau of Transport and Communications Studies 1995: xxix)

It is not sensible here to go through all the methodological details of the evaluation, but suffice it to say that it was very thorough and convincing, and went far beyond what could have been guessed at just by looking at a few road traffic accident statistics alone. Most importantly, policy-makers were impressed with the evaluation, and the decision was taken to continue the programme.

Beyond the stories: some useful background and ideas

Since the early 1990s, 'evaluation' has been an activity which many governments and the EU Commission) have said is important (Pollitt 1998). Evaluation was also fashionable in a number of countries in the late 1960s and 1970s, so the recent resurgence of interest has been a kind of 'second coming'.

In an informal sense, governments have always 'evaluated'. That is to say, governments have always tried to foresee the effects of different possible courses of action, and they have always needed to be aware of the successes or failures of chosen actions which are already underway. However, over the past 30 years – and especially during the past decade – many governments have developed a more systematic and professional set of approaches to this process, and have termed this new field 'evaluation'.

Thus evaluation is essentially concerned with the *systematic analysis of public policies, programmes and projects*. It is to do with both the testing of existing knowledge and the creation of new knowledge. Within this broad concept there exist many different definitions of evaluation. Some definitions are focused on the particular analytical *methods* which are used – for there is a great range of these (see, for example, Shadish, Cook and Leviton 1991). Some are more concerned with the type of *object* which is under scrutiny – hence 'policy evaluation', 'programme evaluation', 'project evaluation', and so on. Some are built around the issues of *who participates in evaluations and to whom they are addressed* – hence 'partenarial evaluation', 'democratic evaluation' and 'managerial evaluation' (see Pollitt 1999).

So how can one evaluate a policy or programme? A *policy* is usually thought of as having a set of basic elements. There are *policy-makers*, who make *decisions*. They have *objectives* – states of the world they hope to achieve because they value them (such as less crime, better public health, safer public transportation, etc.). They use various *resources* as *inputs* to the policy – staff, money, equipment, buildings, etc. These inputs are combined into *programmes* of activity. The programmes produce *outputs* – police patrols, vaccination programmes, new railtrack, etc. These outputs it is hoped lead to the desired *outcomes* (sometimes called *impacts*) – less crime, etc. In a perfect policy the outcomes exactly match the original objectives. The main elements are therefore:

- Objectives
- Inputs
- Programmes of activity (processes)
- Outputs
- Outcomes/impacts

So how can a policy be evaluated? Isn't that simple? Surely, one simply examines the outcomes and sees how well they match the original objectives. If they match well it was a good policy, if they don't match at all, it was a bad policy.

Unfortunately, however, things aren't usually nearly as simple as that! To understand evaluation in practice it is necessary to look at some of the factors which can so easily complicate the idea of a straightforward comparison of outcomes with intentions. In the remainder of this section I will take a brief glance at some of these.

Why, who for, when?

Evaluations can be undertaken for very different purposes. For example, one purpose is to look back on a policy and decide whether it worked well enough to continue it, or improve it, or whether it should be dropped. This is sometimes called a *summative* evaluation – it sums up the impacts and costs of a policy so that decision-makers can say 'yes' or 'no' to the policy (or something like it) continuing. Like a customer at the end of a meal deciding whether to eat again at a particular restaurant. So the evaluation has to be undertaken after the policy has been in force for long enough for the outcomes/impacts to be detectable (it will be *ex post*, retrospective). With some policies (for example, a new education policy or health policy) it can easily be five years or more before enough impact information is available. That is a long time for politicians – and citizens – to wait for answers.

A different purpose is to help the management of an existing programme improve the way they implement it. Like a maintenance check on a car. This type of evaluation is usually called a *formative* evaluation. It is like the cook in a restaurant tasting what his staff have produced to see how to make it taste better. Like the first type (above) it necessarily has to be *ex post* (or, at least, *during* the running of the programme).

A third possibility is to have an evaluation of a policy proposal (or set of proposals) before they are implemented – in order to decide whether to choose a particular policy or not. This is an *ex ante* evaluation, and is necessarily more theoretical and speculative than *ex post* evaluations (like a cook looking at recipes, before the dish is actually made).

There can also be very different *audiences* for evaluations. An evaluation might be done for *the managers of a programme*, or for the *ministers who decide whether a policy should go ahead*, or for *the parliament*, to enable them to assess how well a government's policy was working, or even for *the general public*. Experience in many countries indicates that different types of evaluation are usually required for these different audiences. For example, programme managers probably want detailed technical information about how implementation is being carried out, whereas the general public may simply want to know whether, in broad, non-technical terms, the programme is achieving its objectives or not.

The evaluation of the school milk subsidy, for example, was an *ex post*, summative evaluation carried out in order to assist the politicians in the EU Commission and member states in deciding whether or not they should continue with the programme.

Criteria

No evaluation can be made without some *criteria*. What is a 'good' policy or programme? What is a 'success' or a 'failure'? Running 100 metres in 13 seconds would be a tremendous success for many people but a big failure for a professional athlete.

The number of possible criteria is quite large – in theory there are as many or even more criteria as there are relevant values and norms. However, it is easy to list some of the criteria which are most frequently used in evaluations:

- *Effectiveness*: how far were the original objectives actually achieved? Did the outcomes match the objectives?

- *Cost effectiveness*: not just the extent to which objectives were achieved, but also the costs of achieving those objectives. Two different policies may both achieve the same objectives, but one may do so at a lower cost than the other.
- *Overall impacts*: what were the total impacts of a policy? This includes the extent to which it achieved objectives (effectiveness – see above) but also looks at any *other* impacts which it may have had – intended or unintended. There may have been 'side effects', either positive or negative (for example, when stricter inspection of schools, intended to raise standards, actually causes more and more teachers to leave the profession because they feel they are not trusted, leading to a staffing crisis). This kind of criterion has sometimes been referred to as 'goal free' evaluation, because it tries to look at *all* outcomes, whether they are anything to do with the policy objectives or not.
- *Efficiency*: were the outputs the maximum that could be achieved for the given inputs, that is, was the input:output ratio as high as possible? Were as many licences issued per member of staff as possible, or were there inefficiencies?
- *Economy*: were the inputs purchased for the minimum possible prices, or was money wasted? For example, were staff paid more than was necessary? Was the equipment used too lavish or sophisticated?
- *Responsiveness*: was the programme formulated and implemented in full consultation with the other stakeholders? Was it sensitive to the needs of different groups affected by it?
- *Procedural correctness*: was the programme carried out according to the regulations and laws? Were all the requirements laid down properly observed? Was the programme free of corruption?

Clearly, a policy or programme may be very successful when evaluated against one of these criteria, yet fairly weak when evaluated against another one. So the selection of evaluative criteria is fundamental to any evaluation, and is one reason why so much attention is often given to the terms of reference for evaluations.

Policy-making in the real world – challenges for evaluators

Typically, many problems face evaluators in the real world. Some of the most common ones are:

- *Political and/or managerial sensitivity and resistance to evaluation*: independent evaluation can be threatening to the politicians and managers associated with a programme. They can often find ways of resisting evaluation, or of 'disarming' it by insisting on narrow terms of reference. Managers can also limit evaluators' access, or even supply them with unrepresentative or unreliable data (for example, when one is evaluating an overseas aid project and one is taken only to the 'model village', not the other ones where the programme has failed).
- *Vague and/or conflicting objectives*: many policies are formulated in fairly vague terms (indeed, this may be politically necessary in order to maintain maximum support for the policy). But if objectives are vague or conflicting

(for example, is the priority for the prison service to punish criminals or to rehabilitate them?) then it is going to be hard to measure effectiveness. Also, the objectives of a policy frequently shift over time, sometimes without this being fully recorded or acknowledged. Notice how, in the EU school milk story, politicians began to talk about the health benefits of the programme, although this was not its original objective.

- *Lack of independence*: much of the evaluation literature stresses the need for the evaluator to be independent of those he or she evaluates. However, some of the literature also stresses the need to get close to stakeholders in the policy, and to understand the values and perspectives of all the major players. But there are also considerable dangers for an evaluation in getting 'close' to powerful players (especially when policy disasters are being investigated). It can easily compromise independence or result in a 'compromise' analysis that states everybody's point of view but fails to come to a set of specific conclusions and recommendations of its own (Pollitt 1999).

- *Lack of crucial data*: if a programme does not routinely monitor its own outputs and outcomes in a systematic and reliable way, then it can be very difficult (and/or expensive) for evaluators to measure these things.

- *The importance of contexts*: it is quite common for the same government programme to work quite well in some places but much less well in others. This is often because the specific context influences effectiveness. So there is a challenge for evaluators to be able to classify key success factors which occur in some contexts but not in others (Pawson and Tilley 1997). For example, a new teaching technique may work well in schools which are strongly led by a sympathetic headteacher, but poorly in schools where the head is more consensus-oriented or passive.

- *Timing problems*: politicians frequently want evaluators to produce their reports quickly. But measuring outcomes properly may take years and years. So many evaluations end up concentrating mainly on efficiency and responsiveness rather than on effectiveness. Alternatively, if evaluators wait until all the evidence is available, they may be too late to influence the political decisions about the future of the programme.

- *Hindsight bias*: with *ex post* evaluations it is hard to avoid judging programmes according to what is known now, rather than what was known at the time when the decisions were actually taken. This is particularly dangerous when assessing events a long time ago, where we now know much more about consequences than anyone could have done at the time.

- *What kind of evidence to look at*: one's discipline (economist, political scientist, sociologist) and theoretical perspective tends to influence the evidence one seeks out. This is as true for evaluators as for other kinds of analyst and academic. If evaluators follow 'rational actor' assumptions, they may concentrate on interviewing top decision-makers, to try to clarify their objectives and to establish what information was available to them. But if, instead, they prefer an organizational behaviour approach, they may want to examine the standard operating procedures of the various organizations involved in delivering a particular programme, and how these fit together or fail to fit together (Allison and Zelikow 1999); and so on. With a programme of any complexity, it is usually impossible for an evaluator to examine *all* the evidence. Decisions will have to be taken about what kind of evidence is likely to be most relevant and reliable, and that is where theoretical assumptions may have their influence.

There is a close connection between evaluation and the theme of performance management which was discussed in Chapter 2. In practical terms evaluation becomes much less difficult if an organization is already strongly performance-oriented and is therefore already collecting reliable data about key aspects of its activities and impacts. If, however, an organization is mainly oriented to following complex legal and bureaucratic rules and processes, and collects little data on how efficient or effective it is, then the evaluator is left to start from almost nothing, and faces a huge (and usually impossible) data collection task.

There is also an increasingly close connection between evaluation and *audit*. In a number of countries various types of *performance audit* have developed which go far beyond traditional financial audit. These new types of audit attempt to examine the efficiency and effectiveness of public programmes, as well as how well managed they have been (Pollitt *et al.* 1999). This has brought some state audit offices onto the borders of evaluation-like activities. It has also led to some debate as to whether evaluation is an appropriate activity for audit offices (see, for example, Pollitt and Summa 1998). This, in turn, is part of an even broader controversy about the growth and diversification of audit activities, especially in the UK. One prominent expert has argued that we are witnessing the growth of an 'audit society' in which the checking of management systems has developed a rather unhealthy momentum of its own (Power 1997, 2000).

Guide to key sources

There is a big literature on programme and policy evaluation, the majority of it American. One classic is Michael Quinn Patton's (1997) *Utilisation-focused Evaluation*. Patton is full of examples and the book is quite amusingly written – something which not many evaluation textbooks can be accused of. If you want a detailed theoretical and methodological history, then Shadish, Cook and Leviton (1991) *Foundations of Program Evaluation: Theories of Practice* is worth trying.

One lively and challenging European contribution is Pawson and Tilley's (1997) *Realistic Evaluation*, which provides both a potted history of fashions in evaluation and some detailed examples of actual evaluation studies. (Like Quinn Patton, Pawson and Tilley's book is also entertainingly written, though the humour is more 'dry English' than Patton's 'folksy/philosophical'). Less theoretically, Davies *et al.* (2000) *What Works?* looks at the origins and sector-by-sector practices of the 'evidence-based policy' (EBP) movement in the UK. The 'New Labour' government that came to power in 1997 was strongly committed both to evaluation and to an outcomes-based approach. Walker (2001) provides a sobering and detailed analysis of why these laudable objectives proved very hard to attain. Turning to development aid – a field which has attracted much evaluation activity from the World Bank, the European Commission and national donor states – a comprehensive guide has recently been published by one experienced evaluator: you should read Basil Cracknell's (2000) *Evaluating Development Aid*.

Many governments also produce guides or handbooks on this subject. The European Commission (1997) published *Evaluation of EU Expenditure Programmes: A Guide*, and HM Treasury (1997) produced *Appraisal and Evaluation in Central Government*. The French Conseil Scientifique de l'Evaluation (1996) published a *Petit guide de l'evaluation des politiques publiques*. Indeed, the 1990s was a period of boom (or at least a bubble) in European evaluation (Pollitt 1998). Evaluation societies were set up in France, Germany, Italy, Switzerland and the UK. A European Evaluation Society appeared in 1994, and has held conferences in Den Haag, Stockholm, Rome, Lausanne and Seville. You can find its website at www.europeanevaluation.org. In the USA evaluation had been more firmly institutionalized at an earlier stage. The procedural and methodological standards the Americans set have had a wide international influence (see Joint Committee on Standards for Educational Evaluation 1994).

6

Values, ethics and motives – what makes public managers tick?

An awkward customer

No-one in the school really liked Donald Snail. Several generations of students, and not a few of his fellow staff had recited the inevitable 'Snail by name, slimey by nature' – or worse. But mere unpopularity had not previously provoked a crisis. Now it was different: more serious, more dangerous, more important for all concerned. Snail, the long-standing head of the history department at Dulston Comprehensive School, had clashed, and clashed bloodily, with the new school head, Mary Minton. The school governors and the National Union of Teachers were involved, parents were beginning to gossip, and among the rest of the staff there was talk of little else.

Mary Minton was more worried than she cared to admit. There had been nothing strategic, or considered, about the way the conflict had started. She had slipped into the situation without realizing that a full-scale war was about to begin. One Thursday afternoon a group of seven or eight or so anxious-looking 16-year-olds had turned up at her office door. Once admitted to the head's inner sanctum, they had timidly explained that they wanted to complain about Mr Snail's lower-sixth history classes. Mr Snail wasn't covering the syllabus, they said, but rather was concentrating on topics that he himself was interested in, ignoring the other topics the students would be expected to know about when the exams came round. What is more, his manner in the classroom was unsympathetic. If you asked a question he usually made fun of you, and often in a nasty, sarcastic way. He would also make uncomplimentary remarks about 'you students of today' and 'declining standards'. They had tried to raise these issues with him, but he had become even more irritable, had pointed out that he was the historian, not them, and had suggested that the complaints tended to come from people who were getting poor results because they hadn't worked hard enough. Finally, Mr Snail often 'looked at them in a funny way', which made them feel uncomfortable. In short, they were very unhappy in his class.

Mary had asked a few questions. How long had they felt like this? What did the rest of the class think? Which parts of the syllabus did they feel were being neglected, and how could they be sure of this, since the term still had several weeks to run? The answers were reasonable enough: they had known Mr Snail for years, and it had always been like this, more or less. The rest of the class was effectively unanimous – they themselves were an informal deputation on behalf of everyone. And, yes, it was true that there were three weeks of classes left, but, by their calculations, less than half the curriculum had been covered.

Mary's initial reaction was that this was a tiff that could fairly quickly be resolved. She was an experienced teacher and had seen things like this before. Maybe Snail – something of an awkward character, she had already realized – had been a bit too harsh in his language. Sixteen-year-olds could be very sensitive, and anyway, perhaps they were exaggerating. Probably the whole thing could be resolved quickly and informally, by having an off-the-record word with Snail, and persuading him to show the class his softer side during the run-in to the mock exams at the end of term.

With studied casualness, therefore, she chose her moment and asked Snail if he would mind popping into her office for five minutes at the end of the school day. Mary knew she was good at this kind of thing – the informal handling of day-to-day frictions – it was one of the reasons why she had achieved a headship fairly young, and was now head of a big, 1800 student secondary school. When Snail was in her office she laid on the charm. A small problem had blown up, she knew how touchy 16-year-olds could be, she was sure he could sort it out, etc., etc. During this speech Snail's pale, slab-like face showed no emotion whatsoever. When Mary had finished there was a silence. Eventually she filled it with 'Well, Donald, what do you think?'. 'Do I understand correctly', he began 'that you talked to students about my teaching performance behind my back? And do I now further understand that you are accepting the fantasies of a small bunch of adolescent trouble-makers rather than the word of one of your most experienced senior teachers?' From here the exchange had gone from bad to worse. By the time Snail stalked out of her office he had already said he would no longer discuss any of these issues with her without the presence of an officer of the union, and he had demanded a written record of the accusations that had been made, together with the names of the students who had made them. He had also suggested that she had been prejudiced against him since her arrival at the school, and had warned her that he would be taking up the whole matter with his solicitor. Throughout, his facial expression had never changed, and his eyes had stared unwaveringly directly into hers. Mary suddenly felt simultaneously shallow, threatened and extremely angry.

In the next few days she consulted a number of other people. The deputy director of the local educational authority had begun with a harsh laugh. 'Snail!', he said, 'you should see the files on him. You aren't the first you know – but nobody has ever been able to pin him down. Can be vicious – you need to watch out. My advice would be not to take it any further unless you have a really watertight case, chapter and verse'.

Hanif Patel, her Deputy Head, had been gentler, but equally cautious. 'Most of the rest of the staff hate him, but that doesn't necessarily mean they would back an attempt to sack him. When that kind of process is applied to a longstanding, senior member of staff, everyone feels a bit vulnerable. Will I be next? – that sort of idea. One issue for you to think about, Mary, is 'Why now?'. Snail has been a pain for years. He hasn't changed. There have been complaints about him before, but he's also cunning – there never seems to be anything quite big enough or definite enough to form a basis for disciplinary action. Just lots of little crimes – he doesn't do his admin. work well, he constantly criticizes his junior staff in the history department, which tends to demoralize them, he often dodges staff meetings, he never plays any part in extra-curricular activities, he's constantly bad-tempered with the kids, so that fewer and fewer are choosing to take history in the sixth form, and so on. There have been a couple of incidents where girls have said that they feel embarrassed by the way he stares at them, but there's nothing solid there – he is just a man who has an unsettling stare, which he seems to apply to all sorts and conditions, not just the girls. So, all in all, he's a disagreeable underperformer, and a combative colleague, but he's not Adolf Hitler'. 'It's a good question', replied Mary, 'but I have another one, which is – if he has been a consistent underperformer for so long, why *not* now?'

Two days later Mary's secretary handed her an envelope as she arrived in the morning. She immediately recognized Snail's (excellent) handwriting. She opened it to find a 12-page letter, accusing her of all manner of crimes – victimizing Snail, showing favouritism to women staff, stirring up students to complain against him. It was a rant, an obsessively detailed but wholly fantasized picture of a sustained campaign to discredit him. Points were numbered (there were nine in all) and subdivided, and the whole thing smacked of a poisonous late night drafting session. The letter concluded with the statement that, until she publicly apologized, he would boycott all staff meetings and refuse to undertake his administrative duties.

After a few moments of rage and panic, Mary was able to think clearly. This was a direct challenge to her authority. Clearly she could not make a public apology – and certainly not for things she had never done or even thought of doing. But neither could she accept Snail's unilateral withdrawal from his non-teaching duties. This had suddenly become a disciplinary case. And that meant she needed to move quickly and carefully. Snail's letter had not made further mention of his solicitor, and neither had it referred to the formal grievance procedure. If he started a grievance procedure against her that could complicate any disciplinary process she might bring against him. So if she *was* going to discipline him, she had better get the process launched straightaway. It would involve, she knew, a long drawn out sequence of formal written warnings, careful investigations, interviews and other time-consuming tasks. She could rely on Snail (and the union representative he would presumably bring in to support him) to seize upon any divergence from the exact procedures laid down in the Governing Body's regulations and use it as a reason for halting proceedings. She groaned at the prospect of having to get on top of all the minutiae of the Governing Body's disciplinary rules and the Local Education Authority's accompanying guidance. Mary went over to her bookshelf and reached for the fat file of LEA circulars.

Years later, looking back on the Snail affair, Mary could never be entirely sure that she had done the right thing. Or, at least, that she had done it in the best possible way. In a sense she had 'won' – they had got rid of Snail – but the cost of this 'victory' had been heavy indeed. Eighteen months of agony, during which she had had to endure several interrogations at the hands of the union representative, who had crawled over every tiny action she had taken (and some she had not taken) in great detail, trying to build the case that *she* had acted precipitately and with disproportionate force. Snail's wife had even phoned her at home, late one evening, to accuse her of victimizing her husband (Mary had quickly hit the record button on her telephone, and when she told Mrs Snail that she was recording the conversation, the latter's wild accusations were quickly terminated). After missing the first two, Snail himself had attended every staff meeting. He would sit silently at the back, taking notes and obviously looking for the slightest slip-up on her part – on any or every aspect of running the school. He had questioned, in writing and at length, almost every decision she had made. He had occasionally repeated his threat of legal action, but never put it into effect (though the threat alone caused Mary to consult her own solicitor, so as to clarify what her position might be in the event of a libel case). Mysteriously, he had never initiated a grievance procedure, although the union representative would undoubtedly have drawn his attention to that as a possibility.

Despite the huge amount of time she had spent on the disciplinary procedure, it had never been completed. Before they could reach the finishing line Snail took early retirement on the grounds of ill health. Mary was deeply suspicious as to whether the ill health was real, but at least this got rid of the man without further agonies or risks. Snail went quietly, with a generous financial settlement. Many members of staff rushed to congratulate her. The Director of Education, and the Chairman of the School Governing Body both turned up in her office and quaffed a glass of celebratory dry sherry. Suddenly she had a reputation as a determined and decisive head who 'could not be messed with' (a reputation she was able to turn to good effect once or twice later in her career).

Yet Mary herself was far from convinced that it had been a 'victory'. She felt exhausted. She felt acutely conscious that many of those who were now congratulating her and emptying her bottle of Dry Sack had kept their heads well down during the process itself, and, if things had gone the other way, would probably now be nodding sagely over her foolish impetuosity. She was also painfully aware of the 'opportunity cost' of the process – the numerous hours that had been spent on one errant member of staff and therefore had not been available for the children, parents or other members of staff. She had even had a minor row with her oldest friend over the matter. After two hours of fevered speculation about Snail's true motives, Mary had exploded when her friend had gently suggested that she was perhaps getting slightly obsessed with the whole thing. Finally, and most acutely, she felt 'soiled' by the whole affair – stained by the horrible accusations and implications which Snail had aimed at her personally. Her rational self could see these as the rantings of a weak man – a bully whose bluff had finally been called. But there was another part of her that wondered, from time to time, if there was not some morsel of truth in his slanders – were her motives really so pure, or was she caught up in the same ruthless and competitive game?

Discussion of the case

Mary Minton had a difficult balancing act to perform. On the one hand, as headteacher, she had to protect her staff and follow the correct procedures. On the other, she felt she had an over-riding duty to seek the best interests of the students in her care. (Interestingly enough, the 2001 edition of Teachers' Pay and Conditions, which contains a list of headteachers' statutory duties, makes no mention of a head's duties to his or her students! It refers to many things – liaison with staff unions, appraisal of staff, relations with parents, etc. – but does not make any direct reference to protecting pupils. In practice, however, for many heads, this is a paramount concern.)

Also, Mary believed she had to protect the reputation of the school – if she 'did the right thing', but the result was that the school's name was besmirched in the media, this would damage both the interests of her staff and the interests of the students. Last, but not least, she had her own reputation and career to think of. If she tried, but failed, to get rid of Donald Snail, her own standing in the school would be reduced, her reputation for good judgement in the local education authority would be tarnished, and, worst of all, she would have to face her failure in the corridor every day, glowering at her with what she imagined would be even deeper resent-ment than in the past. Protecting staff, furthering the children's best interests, respecting procedures, safeguarding the school's reputation and her own – these were all *values* for Mary. They formed part – but not all – of her *motives* for taking the actions which she did.

What is more (as is often the case in the public sector) all this balancing of values had to be done within a fairly heavy and elaborate set of procedural rules – teachers, civil servants, doctors and university lecturers cannot just be sacked when they incur the displeasure of the boss, as sometimes seems to happen to staff in private sector employment. There are carefully worked out procedures, and if these are broken the 'case for the prosecution' will probably collapse. So it is not surprising that the decision in cases like this is often to 'let sleeping dogs lie', to 'paper over the cracks', to 'reach an accommodation'.

In the Snail case (an amalgam of several real cases) the complexity of 'ethics in the real world' is plain to see. While, at a first reading, it may seem that good and right was all on the side of Mary Minton, and that Snail was 'all bad', closer inspection indicates a more mixed assessment. Mary herself was conscious that, by launching the disciplinary procedure, she was, in effect, depriving students, parents and staff of a substantial portion of her attention over quite a long period (the 'opportunity cost' point made in the last paragraph of the story). Was the case worth this distraction?

Furthermore, once the procedure was in progress, Mary felt obliged to be less than fully open with a number of people. So long as Snail continued to teach, she had to pretend to the parents of students in his classes that she thought he was competent, and that all was well. Also, she began actively to conceal small things she did from Snail's knowledge, simply because she didn't want to give him anything he might be able to use as ammunition. She certainly no longer took him into her confidence as a senior professional colleague, and, in general, she minimized her relationship with him. Her actions definitely put him under pressure, even if they were fair and in accordance with the rule books. Who can say whether this pressure made him worse, or brought on his ill health (if the latter was genuine)? Thus the whole process *may* have had a negative effect on the running of the history department, and therefore on the 'best interests' of the students. In situations like this it is not unusual that there is, in effect, some trade-off between the interests of staff and students *now* and the interests of staff and students in the *future*. A hoped-for future improvement (Snail retired and a keen new teacher was brought in to head the history department) has to be paid for by stress and unpleasantness in the present.

There were other issues too. Mary had suspected that Snail's medical condition was wholly or partly 'manufactured'. She thought that he had probably persuaded his family doctor to take the easiest course and sign the letter which declared him to be suffering from acute stress. But she had no standing to challenge that – it was strictly a matter between Snail and the Teachers' Pensions Agency. Although she had done nothing wrong, Mary felt faintly ashamed of herself for being so relieved that Snail was now being generously supported by the 'Great British taxpayer', for a condition that he probably didn't have or, at the least, was exaggerating.

In English schools the business of retirement on grounds of ill health is currently one between the teacher, the Teachers' Pensions Agency and their respective medical advisers. However, in other parts of the public sector, the temptation to 'buy out' awkward members of staff rather than confront them with a disciplinary procedure may be greater. The following extract is from a report of the House of Commons Committee of Public Accounts:

West Midlands Regional Health Authority
The Director of Regionally Managed Services of the West Midlands Regional Health Authority was allowed to leave on redundancy terms after five years' service with Authority, with an immediate pension of 6,462 pounds a year and lump sums totalling 81,837 pounds. The Authority and the NHS Management Executive told us that he should have been dismissed not

made redundant. The Authority's explanation that they did not have the full facts until later was evidence of their failure to know about and control what their senior staff were doing in their name.

(Committee of Public Accounts 1994: xi)

Finally, Mary Minton had talked the case over privately with her oldest friend. While it was true that she absolutely trusted her friend not to pass the details on to anyone else, those conversations had, nevertheless, constituted a breach of professional confidence. She should not have discussed Snail's details with any 'outsider'.

Ethics and values: a brief analysis

Motives, ethics and values are all difficult things to pin down. They all exist 'in the mind', 'in the heart', or in some mixture of these (and other) organs. They are psychological or philosophical constructs, not things which can easily be observed, weighed or counted. That makes them easy to write about (because it is easy to form and express personal 'impressions') but hard to write about well.

It may be useful to make a few preliminary clarifications. First, what are the relationships between these three concepts, and what is the relationship between any of them and what people actually *do*? As usual, different academics have defined and used the terms in different ways, but the way I will use the terms here (and I believe this will be a fairly mainstream usage) is as follows:

- *Values*: a value is 'an enduring belief that a specific mode of conduct or end-state of existence is personally or socially preferable to an opposite or converse mode of conduct or end state of existence' (Rokeach 1973: 5). Thus, for example 'honesty' (a specific mode of conduct) is a value, and so is 'the greatest happiness for the greatest number' (an end state of existence which is held to be socially preferable).
- *Ethics*: ethics are rules of conduct and behaviour. They are, in a sense, a particular sub-class of values – those which relate to questions of right or wrong, good and evil. So some values (for example, honesty) are ethical values while other values (for example, an intense belief in the importance of elegance) are not.
- *Motives*: motives are what move people to behave in particular ways. Motives are psychological constructs used to answer the question '*why* did she/he/they do that?' Different psychological theories have advanced different models of motivation, for example that people mainly act to maximize their pleasure and avoid pain, or that, once basic needs (food, shelter) are satisfied people seek ever higher states, such as love and 'self-actualization'. Professional success (for example, being promoted to Permanent Secretary at a young age) could certainly be seen as a form of self-actualization (most Permanent Secretaries having already sorted out the problems of their food and shelter).

Now we can consider what the relations between these various concepts can be. Fairly obviously, values can play an important part in motivation. If I have a deep belief in the ethical value of honesty, then I will try very hard to avoid ever telling lies. If I am a civil servant and my minister suggests that I should draft a statement which contains facts I strongly believe to be inaccurate, or sentences which I judge to be deliberately misleading, I will argue against his or her wishes, and, if the statement goes forward anyway, may even consider 'whistleblowing'. But if my leading values are loyalty to 'my minister', and eagerness to advance my career, then I may go ahead and draft the statement just as the minister wants. (For a lively treatment of an actual case of this kind, see Ponting 1985.)

However, the linkages between a particular value (honesty, loyalty) and an actual piece of behaviour may be long and complicated, for several reasons. To begin with, most of us hold a considerable number of values, and there is no guarantee that these are all mutually consistent. On the contrary, it is highly likely that tensions will arise as to which particular values should have preference. Take the case of Mary Minton and Donald Snail. The values of openness and transparency would suggest that Mary should have told Donald everything she did and said about his case. However, once Mary had decided that it was best for the children and the school if Donald was removed, and once she fully understood what a cunning and determined opponent her head of history was, then she became cautious about giving him extra 'ammunition' for delay and counter-attack. So she did informally consult about the case with a number of people without telling Donald. In effect, she was deciding that the value of protecting the students and the school's reputation came higher than 100 per cent adherence to the values of openness and transparency.

A second complication in the chain linking values to actions is that many other ingredients go into motivation apart from ethical values. Fear, dislike, admiration, fatigue, shortage of resources, time constraints and sheer lack of information – all these and more may influence what happens. One important ingredient – often confused with values, but conceptually rather different – is *norms*. Sir Geoffrey Vickers, a noted English public administration writer in the 1960s and 1970s, argued that norms played an absolutely central role in public policy-making, but that whereas values were usually explicit and general ('fairness', 'democracy', 'honesty'), norms tended to be tacit and particular ('all children should be taught how to read and write', 'every household is entitled to a supply of clean running water and proper sanitation') (Vickers 1973). Public policy decisions, Vickers claimed, were frequently prompted by the discovery that a norm was being broken, for example that 12 per cent of 10-year-olds could not read or 6 per cent of households were still not connected to the public water supply and sewerage. Norms and values interacted to drive policy-making, but they were different kinds of animal.

In short, ethical values may play an important role in managerial decision-making, but they may themselves contain tensions and contradictions, and, in any case, in the real world they are almost always only one influence among a mixture of influences (see Figure 6.1).

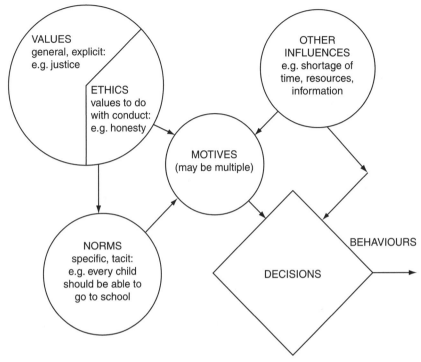

Figure 6.1 Values, motives and behaviour

One final conceptual distinction may be helpful. Ethical values can themselves be subdivided in various ways. One approach is to distinguish between the
following (Report of the Task Force on Public Service Values and Ethics 1996:
53–8):

- *Democratic values*, such as serving the common good rather than sectional
  interests, promoting public accountability, supporting elected representatives,
  always observing the law.
- *Professional values*, such as promotion by merit, continuous improvement,
  impartiality, effectiveness, creativity, loyalty to professional colleagues, putting
  the client's interests first.
- *General ethical values*, such as integrity, honesty, equity, probity.
- *People values*, such as reasonableness, civility, respect for differences, kindness.

There is some overlap between the subdivisions (for example, integrity could
appear under the second, third or fourth) but at the same time this classification
helps us to discuss the different domains of ethics that may be involved in the day-
to-day work of the public manager. For example, it helps us understand how and
why value conflicts can occur. Thus the professional value of client confidentiality
may conflict with the democratic value of public accountability, or, where the

temptation is to tell a friend a 'white lie', the 'people value' of kindness may be in tension with the general ethical value of honesty.

Are public service ethics being undermined by the new public management?

Now we can turn to some of the current ethical issues that are being most ener-getically debated in the academic and practitioner communities. The foremost of these are the questions of whether there is a special set of 'public service ethics', whether (if there are) these are changing, and whether the alleged changes are a good or bad thing? Here are some opinions:

> Local authorities are dedicated to helping the community rather than helping their own pockets, like commercial organisations.

> Public service ethos? The quicker it goes, the better for the customer. It means 'we do it when we feel good about it, but we don't do it all the time'.

> We are reliant on the morals of the government of the day (for example, if the Raving Loony Party got in and ordered us to pay weird benefits, I'd do it).

> > (The above three quotations are from interviews with managers
> > in Goodwin 2000: 9–23)

> We see them [ministers] warts and all. Often selfish, vain, ambitious, un-reasonable and sometimes personally unpleasant: but at the same time conscientious, honourable and courageous. I would apply these last three adjectives to every minister I have worked with.
> > (Cubbon 1993: 9. Sir Brian Cubbon, a widely experienced senior
> > civil servant, who completed his career as Permanent Secretary
> > at the Home Office)

> 'Public service' is a concept, an attitude, a sense of duty – yes, even a sense of public morality.
> > (Staats 1988. Elmer B. Staats was the Controller General of the
> > US General Accounting Office)

> Staff shall always act objectively and impartially, in the Community interest and for the public good. They shall act independently within the framework of the policy fixed by the Commission and their conduct shall never be guided by personal or national interest or political pressure.
> > (European Commission 2000)

One popular line of argument has been that the advent of New Public Management (NPM) thinking has, to greater or lesser degree, undermined a previously existing public service ethic or public service ethos. (For readers who are skipping over sections of this book, Chapter 2 has already dealt with the nature of the NPM.) This basic accusation has been framed in somewhat different ways by different writers. For example, in a widely quoted article, Hood (1991) suggested that the NPM emphasized values such as efficiency and having clear goals, and that this central thrust might be in tension with some of the more traditional values like honesty and fair dealing, as well as with stability-oriented values such as security and resilience. A Canadian federal government report on public service values and ethics, the investigating team wrote that:

> We spoke to public servants who told us that in their daily work they are experiencing the tension between ... the emphasis on results and the emphasis on rules. They are pulled in one direction by the 'entrepreneurial' outlook with its emphasis on innovation, risk-taking and results before process. They are pulled in another direction by the traditional public service culture with its emphasis on prudence and probity, on due process, on political accountability, and on the primacy of law and regulation.
>
> (Report of the Task Force on Public Service Values and Ethics 1996: 41)

Two respected British academics, writing of the way a 'beleaguered' public sector was under attack after 15 years of pro-market Conservative government, argued that:

> The primary focus of the criticisms is less the internal working of public organizations than a challenge to the objectives of the public organization itself. It is the publicness of public organizations, or even the very conception of publicness, which have been brought into question. Thus the values of the private sector have in recent times come to dominate thinking about every type of organization.
>
> (Ranson and Stewart 1994: 4)

A Danish and an American academic have studied cases of contracting out in their two countries and concluded that there is a risk to public values such as equal treatment, political accountability, the rule of law, transparency, etc. because:

> There is no public sector equivalent of cost reduction, pricing efficiency, or outcomes measured in monetary units. In a sense, public values are fragile, both in their expression and enactment. This fragility may make it relatively easy to set them aside in favour of the more concrete and consensual issues of price and efficiency.
>
> (Jørgenson and Bozeman 2002: 65–6)

A Norwegian researcher, Anne Marie Berg, has noted that:

> The concept of value has become more and more widely used in public sector discourse. Value added, value creation, value (based) management, best value, value for money, value-in-use, social value, political value, intangible values, value statements, value accounts, are uses of the term which have entered the public sector reform language over the past 20 years.
>
> (Berg 2001)

Berg goes on to argue that the concept of value is highly ambiguous and multi-dimensional, and that part of what has happened during the past decade or so is a process of semantic 'invasion and conquest' through which economic terms such as efficiency and value added have spread their influence deep into the public sector, somewhat displacing 'intangible' values such as trust, impartiality, etc.

One might term the above commentators members of the 'undermining' school. That is, they assert, with varying degrees of qualification and certainty, that the NPM tends to undermine traditional public service values of fairness, equity, continuity and due process. In the mid-1990s even the House of Commons seemed to lean towards this position when the Public Accounts Committee produced a report which, although supporting the 'drive for economy and efficiency', asserted that:

> In recent years we have seen and reported on a number of serious failures in administrative and financial systems and controls within departments and other public bodies, which have led to money being wasted or otherwise improperly spent. These failings represent a departure from the standards of public conduct which have mainly been established during the past 140 years.
>
> (Committee of Public Accounts 1994: v)

Other commentators, however, have rejected this critique – on various grounds. One, quite fundamental counter-attack has been to claim that there never was a 'public service ethic', or a uniform 'public service culture' in which values of stability, honesty and fair dealing held sway. In the UK this point has been advanced by the senior Treasury civil servant who Mrs Thatcher appointed to lead the process of creating 'Next Steps' executive agencies. Kemp wrote that:

> In fact there is no such thing as a single 'public service ethos'. Different parts of the service and different agencies and units have their own ethos which will vary according to their function . . . .
>
> (Kemp 1993: 33)

Similarly, Pratchett and Wingfield (1994: 32), surveying local government officers, concluded that there was no ' "universal" ethos, clearly articulated and defined'.

A second, more methodological point is that, since it is very hard to measure unethical behaviour (or corruption), it is very difficult to know whether the total amount of it is rising, falling or about the same. There have always been occasional scandals and isolated incidents of unethical behaviour by politicians and/or civil servants. For example, during the 1980s the Conservative leader of Westminster Borough Council, Dame Shirley Porter, instituted a policy of selling council houses in a way that was intended to boost her party's electoral strength within the Borough, and she also took steps to conceal the true nature of that policy. Subsequently, the House of Lords found her guilty of corruption (Waugh 2001). But this had little to do with the NPM – this was old-fashioned political 'gerry-mandering' (to use the term chosen by one of the Law Lords), and it had been exposed by old-fashioned means: a complaint to the district auditor. (Dame Shirley was fined £26.5 million, but at the time of writing it seems likely she would be able to evade most of that fine since she had already moved her assets abroad.) Similarly, in 2000, following some serious scandals involving senior civil servants, the Japanese government felt bound to introduce a National Public Service Ethics Act. But this had little to do with the NPM – indeed, Japan had ignored most of the fuss about Anglo-Saxon-style NPM, at least until the late 1990s. Like the Westminster/Porter case these Japanese incidents had been examples of a more traditional kind of 'bad behaviour'.

A third counter argument to the 'undermining' school has been to seek to minimize the clash between traditional and NPM values. Those taking this position may concede that there can be tensions under certain specific circumstances, but claim that, in the main, the new values sit comfortably alongside the old, and do not contradict them. Furthermore, the NPM values bring something extra – they add highly desirable values such as good customer service to the public service repertoire. For example, Brereton and Temple (1999: 471) claim that 'The move from public sector ethos to public service ethos might thus be understood as a move from seeing the public as a client/supplicant to one of seeing them as a consumer/purchaser' (there are also some sections of Goodwin 2000 which support this point). Brereton and Temple (1999: 458) also attack the idea of a former 'golden age of ethics':

> The belief that integrity has markedly declined confuses the official rhetoric of previous ages with the often sordid reality; a severe code of official secrecy and media deference meant that politicians and officials were able to hide misdemeanours in a way that is largely unthinkable now.

Or again, Goodwin, who was concerned to test the popular idea that ethical standards were slipping, investigated two local authorities, a water company, a bank, an accountancy firm, an airline, a trade union and concluded that:

> . . . the participants in the study exhibited a strong sense of personal responsibility and were willing to accept vicarious responsibility for the work of their staff . . . my research suggests that there was no slippage of moral standards or moral relativism among the participants in this research and that the organisations themselves were endeavouring to transact ethically most of the time.
>
> (Goodwin 2000: 2)

Faced with such apparently contradictory evidence, what can one say? First, up to a point, all the above commentators could be correct. The public service does indeed have many different types of organization, with quite different subcultures and – probably – values. Compare, for example, the heart surgery department of a top London teaching hospital with the local social security office in Hartlepool and then with the Driving and Vehicle Licensing Agency in Swansea. Some ethical principles may be very general (honesty, for example) but other values may be more or less appropriate and important, according to the type of function one is looking at. 'Professional values' are presumably most important in highly professionalized services, such as health care and education. 'People values' are most necessary where a service deals face-to-face with many citizens; and so on. In other words, what we might normatively think of as the appropriate mix of general and particular values changes according to context – and (perhaps) actual held values vary in a similar way.

Second, it seems almost self-evident that, as Brereton and Temple say, some of the 'new', NPM-ish values are valuable additions (if they really are additions – which is another point to be debated). In most public service contexts, for example, it is hard to see why most of us would not want customer-responsiveness and efficiency *as well as* the traditional virtues of impartiality and equity.

Third, present concerns probably *are* magnified by the far more aggressive behaviour of the modern mass media, and by the higher standards of openness and transparency towards which at least some governments have moved. So perhaps much more *was* concealed in the past – although it is almost impossible to know that. It may also be that the ruling elite used to be somewhat more homogenous than it has become, so that it could formerly rely on a system of widely shared values and norms of conduct, whereas today different groups bring a somewhat varied set of standards into the corridors of power. Chapman (1993: 160) puts the matter as follows:

> This unprecedented public attention is not because comparable cases did not exist before modern times; of course they did. The difference is that in earlier times citizens generally may have been less interested; the values of society may have been different; the requirements of national and international law may have been less sensitive to the human rights of citizens and officials; in many cases less openness in government meant that details were never published; modern technologies which both involve the media and are used in administrative practice were not available; and in some instances individuals (or their friends or supporters) were less connected with or aware of publicity as a facet of democracy.

Nevertheless, even if there was no golden age of ethical purity, and even if some diversification of membership of the elite is highly desirable on other grounds, these are not reasons to be complacent about the risks of unethical behaviours today.

Fourth, therefore, the concerns of what I perhaps unfairly dubbed the 'underminers' school can be re-formulated in a more 'targeted' fashion. Instead of projecting a general decline of standards, one might say that the spread of NPM values can lead to amplified tensions within new mixtures of values, especially in certain specific contexts. These might include, for example, Public Private Partnerships (PPPs) and/or the competitive tendering of public services, in both of which public servants may find themselves working in daily proximity to the staff of for-profit corporations (Goodwin 2000: 41; Report of the Task Force on Public Service Values and Ethics 1996: 41). Another important type of context is that in which public servants are dealing with very vulnerable members of society – the poor, the frail elderly, the mentally ill, and so on. Goodwin (who is otherwise fairly positive about the ethical standards of the private sector) makes a particular point about this group:

Customers who are not in any real sense customers, like benefits claimants, or who cannot help being customers, like water users, are vulnerable people because they are *powerless* people. When the public sector supplies such people with essential services the fact that the services are not run for profit protects them against exploitation; the public service ethos also safeguards their interests. If privatisation or marketisation threaten the [public service ethos], they reduce the protection for captive customers and particularly for the vulnerable.

(Goodwin 2000: 144, original italics)

In short, the particular mixture of leading values appears to vary somewhat from one context to another, and to develop dynamically over time, even if some values are fairly widespread and durable (such as honesty or impartiality). There may even be some oscillation between contrasting poles – a period when the values of fairness, equity and due process are given prominence being followed by a period during which efficiency and flexibility of process are stressed, followed in turn by a swing back towards a rule-bound approach. The grass on the other side of ethical trade-offs often looks greener, so political leaders wobble from one emphasis to another. Hood (1998:11) argues that this takes place on a grand historical scale, and between four basic systems of values and institutional types: 'cultural dynamics work by mutual antagonism among opposites seeking to blame adherents of alternative ways of life for the social ills they are held to create' (Hood's argument is too subtle and complex for me to be able to summarize it here; there is no simple alternative to reading the book itself). Whether any given shift or adjustment is a good or bad thing depends, of course, on the judge's own leading values. Certainly, however, it would be hard to grant credulity to either extreme in the NPM debate – that is, *either* to the proposition that the 'new' values of efficiency and entrepreneurialism could be adopted right across the public sector without any loss of other desirable values, *or* to the counter claim that traditional bureaucracy was universally infused with a fine public service ethic that could only be damaged by the NPM barbarians, with their quest for efficiency and customer responsiveness. The truth seems much more likely to lie between these two poles, and can only be further clarified with the aid of considerably more context-specific empirical research into values and value change than has yet been undertaken.

Motives: a brief analysis

Many different social science disciplines have made use of the concept of *motives*, and a number of fundamentally different approaches exist. In this small space it is impossible to do justice to these, so all that will be attempted is a short sketch of some of the principal ways in which the concept has been applied within the study of public administration.

One major divide is that between, on the one hand, economists and, on the other, psychologists, sociologists and many political scientists. This split to some extent parallels the divide already referred to between 'economic' values and 'intangible' values. On the one hand, economists tend to use an individualistic, basically utilitarian model in which individual civil servants – like all other people – strive to maximize their utility. Thus Dunleavy, who (although himself a political scientist) has developed one of the most sophisticated economistic models of bureaucratic behaviour, begins by saying plainly that:

> I assume that bureaucrats maximize self-regarding and hard-edged utilities in making official decisions. A bureau's overall policy is set by some combination of individual decisions made by its officials, and by interactions with a sponsor body.

(Dunleavy 1991: 174)

By 'self-regarding and hard-edged utilities' Dunleavy means that officials seek promotion, upward job re-grading, improvements in working conditions (including lower workloads) and pay increases. These are their principal individual motivations.

Many critics (the present author included) have accused economists of working with over-simplified (sometimes called 'under-socialized') models of motivation. It should be acknowledged, however, that this simplicity brings considerable advantages. It permits neo-classical economists to construct extensive and elegant theories, and to generate behavioural predictions with a precision and specificity that usually elude their counterparts in other social science disciplines. One type of economic theory that was particularly influential on public sector organizations during the last two decades of the twentieth century was 'principal and agent' theory, a brand of the 'rational choice' approach. It deserves a brief comment of its own, as an example of the treatment of motivation which is typical within a neo-classical economic perspective (see Box 6.1).

Box 6.1 Principal and agent theory: an economic approach to motivation within organizations

Principal and agent (P&A) theory is one element within what is often called the 'new institutional economics', or 'rational choice theory' (for a brief overview, see Peters (1999: 46–62)). Using this approach, the whole of the representative democratic process may be seen as a long, linked line of principals (those who expect something they want to be done to be done by someone else) and agents (the ones who are going to do it). Voters, as principals, want those they elect to do what they voted them into power to do (lower taxes, better health service, etc.). Parliaments are the voters' agents, but simultaneously parliaments are themselves in the position of principals *vis à vis* executive governments. In those governments ministers are (theoretically) agents of the legislature, who may be removed (by votes of no confidence, impeachment, etc.) if they are seen to veer too far off the agreed track. But ministers, like parliaments, are simultaneously both 'A' and 'P'. They are principals to all those public managers who are supposed to carry out the government's policies and programmes.

So what motivates public managers, as agents of political leaders? The economists' answer is 'self interest'. Agents will do as little as they can get away with, and they will pursue their own interests (such as higher salaries, or higher status, or more interesting work, or just an easier time) as far as the system allows them to. In so far as their interests coincide with those of the principal – fine. But, in so far as they diverge, arrangements need to be made to ensure a reasonable degree of compliance with ministers' wishes. Of course, the principal can keep a personal eye on what the agents are doing, but in a typical government context, that is not likely to be tremendously effective. There isn't enough time and there are too many agents – ministers have better things to do than look over their civil servants' shoulders all the time (that is, *monitoring costs* are high). Furthermore, in many situations it is, in practice, impossible for the minister to know the subject anywhere near as well as the agent (for example, a minister of health dealing with doctors, or a minister of defence talking to experts about the prospects and costs of a new missile). There is what P&A theorists call an *information asymmetry* between principal and agent.

One way of addressing these problems is to try to fix the relationship between P and A through a contract. The contract can specify the targets the agent must work to achieve, the information she or he must provide, and the incentives and penalties which good performance/bad performance will attract from the principal. A great deal has been written about the types of contracts that could be used in the public sector, and their strengths and weaknesses in different situations (see, particularly, Lane 2000 for a theoretical treatment and Molander, Nilsson and Schick 2002 for a sustained application of P&A ideas to government agencies). Rational choice theory has been adopted by academics in many countries but has probably achieved its greatest dominance – in academic political science and public administration – in the USA. It has also undoubtedly influenced some practitioners – most famously in the case of the radical New Zealand reforms of the 1980s and early 1990s (Molander, Nilsson and Schick 2002).

Much depends, of course, on how realistic the rational choice model of civil servant behaviour actually is. Some of the best-known early models were very simple indeed – for example the American William Niskanen proposed that civil servants just sought to maximize their budgets (Niskanen 1971). Later theorists developed more sophisticated models – Patrick Dunleavy's model of 'bureau-shaping' has already been mentioned, where clever bureaucrats opt for interesting 'policy'-type work and try to avoid highly routine, measurable tasks (Dunleavy 1991). These more ingenious developments pose many interesting questions about how to design institutions, how to draw up contracts, what kinds of incentives and penalties are likely to be most effective, and so on. However, the amount of empirical work undertaken to confirm or falsify this kind of theorizing remains limited (and the results not very convincing).

Even those who do not use or like the rational choice approach (like me!) will usually admit that its advocates have extended the agenda of questions which are asked about public sector organizational arrangements. Nevertheless, what it offers remains a singularly 'low trust' and quite narrow perspective on public life – agents, whether parliaments, ministers or civil servants cannot be trusted with much unsupervised discretion. They have to be monitored, incentivized and penalized into compliance with their principals' wishes. Furthermore, the theory admits of little possibility of underlying change. Agents cannot be educated or convinced to act in a less self-interested way, they can only be bribed or punished to keep close to the tracks laid down by the principal. Still, at the very least, all this is a useful antidote to the 'let's all pull together in an empowerment culture' kind of romanticism.

But, dear reader, you should not accept this as the final word on the matter – not least because I am not a rational choice fan. If a principal–agent approach interests you, you should try either a basic text – such as Douma and Schreuder's (1998) useful *Economic Approaches to Organizations* – or a classic article, such as Banks and Weingast 1992 or an ambitious theoretical work such as Dunleavy 1991.

By contrast with economists, psychologists, sociologists and many political scientists use rather different models of motivation. To begin with, they are less inclined than economists to *assume* that motivation is such-and-such. They are more likely to want to go out and try to check, by questioning or observing people. Furthermore, their models of motivation may be (relative to the economic models) rather complex and variable – there may be different levels of motivation which vary according to circumstances. When one kind of need is satisfied (for example, for a certain level of material wealth) the individual switches his or her target, so to speak, and is driven more by a desire for personal recognition, or aesthetic satisfaction, or love (Apter 1989). (The song *Can't buy me love* was *not* written by a pair of economists.)

One particularly important aspect of this difference between economists and 'the rest' is that many (although not all) economists are uncomfortable with notions of altruistic ('other-regarding') behaviour, whereas 'the rest' regard these other-regarding ideas as perfectly normal. This is important in the context of a discussion of civil service ethics, because many of the values under discussion – such as serving the common good or loyalty to professional colleagues – make most sense if they are regarded as wholly or at least partly altruistic. Economists, by contrast, tend to explain acts of loyalty or other collective behaviour as the result of rational individual calculation ('the smart move for me on this occasion is to appear loyal', or 'I will get the most out of this if I behave like a team player').

One analysis of motivation that focuses specifically on public servants utilizes a helpful threefold categorization (Perry and Wise 1990). It argues that motivation commonly consists of three elements:

- Rational: 'what will I get out of this?'
- Norm-based: 'what do I need to do to conform to the prevailing norms around here?'
- Affective: 'how can I support this programme that I believe in?/how can I fight this evil (hunger, crime, avoidable ill health, etc.) that I want to defeat?

Only the first of these is fully incorporated in most economic models of individual and organizational behaviour. In any particular situation, different elements may predominate. The second one (local norms) may vary a lot from one organization or role to another (for example, compare behavioural norms in a Fire Brigade with those in a nursing home for the elderly or in the Diplomatic Service). Obviously, the third also varies from individual to individual.

Finally, it is obvious that the different motives may conflict. Someone like Mary Minton may take a professional pride in her work (affective) or may have a love for her particular school (affective) which may conflict with a purely rational and self-interested calculus. Her professional pride may drive her to spend long hours working with disadvantaged children after school, even when she knows she is missing out on her social life and that it is extremely unlikely that anyone will reward her for her extra effort. Her particular fondness for Dulston Comprehensive may cause her to resist an invitation to apply for the (better-paid) headship of a larger, higher status school in the neighbouring town.

What makes public servants tick? Some empirical findings

We must begin on a warning note – an American warning note, but one which is equally true, as far as I am aware, for the UK and continental Europe:

> Systematic empirical evidence about the relationship between public service motivation and performance does not exist.
>
> (Perry and Wise 1990: 371)

The good news, however, is that there is quite a bit of empirical evidence about motivation, although it is not linked to performance (that is, we know something about the fuel that powers the daily performances of public servants, but not much about how that fuel consumption is linked to the output of the engine).

One recent survey of a matched sample of 1051 US federal government workers and 500 private sector employees arrived at the following conclusions:

> The matched sample of private employees . . . were more likely than the federal employees to have joined their organisations for the pay and security, and more likely to come to work each day for the salary, not the nature of the work or a desire to serve the public good. The private sector gives its employees three distinct advantages over government employees . . . however. First, workers in private firms are more likely than federal employees to view their senior leaders and mid-level managers as competent. Second, private employees are more likely to say that their organisations have the resources and employees to do their jobs well. And third, private employees believe their organisations are better at hiring, retaining and promoting talented employees and disciplining poor performers.
>
> (Light 2001. Mary Minton may well sympathize with the last point!)

Other evidence does tend to confirm that public sector staff have a somewhat different value mix from their private sector counterparts, although not all studies point in exactly the same direction. Boyne (2002) compared 14 studies of managerial values and found that most, but not all, pointed towards the following contrasts between public and private sector managers:

- Public sector managers tended to hold a somewhat less materialistic set of values.
- Public sector managers tended to have weaker organizational commitment.
- Public sector managers place more emphasis on the public interest (though this finding was more weakly supported than the first two).

The problem with most of these studies is that they are not strictly comparable. Different researchers have looked at values in different sets of organizations in different countries at different times. For example, the research by Paul Light referred to above focused on a large sample of federal government staff taken in the first half of 2001. It is quite possible that different results would have been obtained in a European country, or even in US state or local government (which have not been subject to quite the same long-term public criticism and negative stereotyping as their federal counterparts). So there is still plenty of room for argument – and for further research.

Last but not least, there is the question of whether the motives and ethics of public servants can be intentionally changed – re-designed by politicians and/or by management? The short answer seems to be: 'only by a considerable effort, on several fronts and using several tactics, over a sustained period of time'. Values usually do not shift overnight. Management cannot order staff to change their sometimes deeply held beliefs and feelings. Some of the management texts of the 1980s treated organizational cultures almost like furniture – if management didn't like the shape of this one it could just get another – but closer inspection of efforts at cultural change usually brought forth a more sober assessment. There is a real sense in which management, while it may be able to influence the cultural values of an organization, does not 'own' them, and cannot simply manipulate them at will. A policy briefing by the OECD reflects this more cautious assessment. Entitled *Principles for Managing Ethics in the Public Service*, it mentions that 'Increased concern about decline of confidence in government and corruption has prompted governments to review their approach to ethical conduct' (OECD 1998). This briefing paper does not suggest that government can quickly shape value change in any direction it likes. Rather it proposes a set of requirements which, taken together, stand a good chance of influencing the ethical climate in the public service. These include:

• Maintaining a clear statement of core ethical standards (for example, as a published code).
• Reflecting these standards in legislation.
• Providing sources of training and advice on ethical issues to public servants.
• Making particularly clear the rights and obligations of public servants when they discover actual or suspected wrongdoing (Mary Minton, you will recall, had access to a local authority guide to disciplinary procedure, and advice from senior officials in that authority).
• Political leaders setting an example of propriety, and of taking action where abuse is suspected.
• Managers should do likewise.
• Making decision-making processes as transparent as possible.
• In particular, maintaining clear rules for transactions between the public and private sectors.
• Maintaining mechanisms for detecting and investigating suspected unethical behaviour/wrongdoing. These mechanisms should include an independent element, that is, a body which can stand outside the current political and managerial hierarchy.
• Seeing that the conditions of employment of public servants help promote ethical conduct (in some countries public servants have very low pay, or are paid only intermittently, and in such cases the temptation to engage in corruption is increased).

Part of the message is that any one or two of these features on their own is likely to have quite a weak influence, if the other requirements are not present (see also Bovens 1998 and Goodwin 2000). Codes of ethics, for example, are useful adjuncts to other ethical practices, but by themselves are an ineffective response to corruption. Rascals will be rascals, and the existence and vigorous use of disciplinary procedures are likely to be a much more important curb on their activities than codes of ethics. Nevertheless, used in tandem with managers setting an example and with measures to ensure transparency, ethical codes can play their part in indicating, perhaps especially to newcomers, what is expected.

Incidentally, the recent work on ethics carried out by the OECD and other international bodies (such as the extensive analysis of corruption by the World Bank) was spurred not merely by the alleged threat of the NPM undermining high standards of public service, but even more by the realization that, both in the developing world, and in the 'transitional' democracies of central and eastern Europe, public policies and programmes were being repeatedly undermined and distorted by low standards of public service and, in many cases, systematic corruption (World Bank 2000).

Literature guide

The first thing to say here is that the literature about the 'human and personal side' of public management is not particularly extensive. Relative to the long lists of books and articles on the latest management reforms, on 'the new institutionalism', on organizational structures, on programme evaluation or a number of other topics, the amount of material dealing with values, motives, skills and ethics is modest (even if some of it is good). However, it has been growing – the period since the early 1990s has seen something of a minor international 'ethics boom', with many governments publishing ethical statements and codes (one of the more thoughtful examples being the Canadian *Report of the Task Force on Public Service Values and Ethics* (1996)) and academics reacting to these new developments (for example: Chapman 1993, 2000; Kernaghan 1996; Lawton 1998).

Several issues have preoccupied recent writers. One important debate has focused on the question of whether a traditional 'public service ethos' has been eroded by NPM-style reforms, which are said to have brought a flood of private sector values and practices into the public sector. Useful examples here are Berg 2001; Brereton and Temple 1999; Goodwin 2000; and, as a specimen of an enthusiastically pro-NPM 'we can re-engineer values' line of argument, van Wart 1996.

Another, more practical variant of this, has been the question of how public sector organizations can maintain and encourage what they regard as the 'right' sets of values and practices (see Light 2001 for an interesting recent US perspective on this). For example, do certain types of structure encourage or discourage ethical behaviour? For at least two centuries there has been a debate as to whether having individuals or boards at the head of public authorities promotes the greater sense of personal responsibility. There is also a long-standing argument about whether the form of the traditional bureaucratic hierarchy promotes personal responsibility or, by contrast, undermines it because it encourages individual bureaucrats always to 'pass the buck' up, down, or sideways. The question of whether codes of ethics can have much influence, or whether they are just pretty organizational wallpaper, also falls within this category. On this subject I recommend OECD 2001; Bovens 1998; and Goodwin 2000.

A third focus – one which actually goes right back to creation of the earliest bureaucratic organizations – is that of administrative discretion. Administrative (and nowadays managerial) discretion is inevitable, and, in many ways, desirable. But how can it be controlled or guided, so that discretionary authority is not abused? A classic here is Rohr's (1989) *Ethics for Bureaucrats*, and the same theme is discussed in Richard Chapman's (1993 and 2000) collections *Ethics in Public Service* and *Ethics in the Public Service for the New Millennium*.

A fourth node of debate has concerned the behaviour of politicians themselves. 'Sleaze' became a prominent issue in the mass media during the 1989–97 Conservative administrations led by John Major, and several other countries also had their ration of political scandals involving the apparent abuse of political authority to gain favours or financial rewards. In 2000, in an unprecedented move, the whole of the European Commission (or, to be more precise, all 12 Commissioners) resigned following a report into a series of doubtful practices in which at least some of them had been personally involved. For example, during the period between 1995 and 1998 the French Commissioner (and previous French Prime Minister) Madame Cresson, had employed a long-standing friend of hers, a M Berthelot, as an adviser on various issues. He was paid a total of 5.5 million Belgian francs (just over 136,000 euros) out of EU funds. When a committee of independent experts subsequently investigated this case they concluded that:

> . . . what we have here is a clear-cut case of favouritism. A person whose qualifications did not correspond to the various posts to which he was recruited was nonetheless employed. The work performed was manifestly deficient in terms of quantity, quality and relevance. The Community did not get value for money.
>
> (Committee of Independent Experts 1999: 129)

Such misbehaviour can affect public managers in a number of ways. First, ministers (or Commissioners, in the EU case) can act in a way that directly involves public managers – by requiring them to carry out their corrupt intentions (for example, by 'bending' the procedures for awarding contracts, or by pressurizing civil servants to give out seriously incomplete or misleading information). Second, there is probably an 'example' effect, that is, if public servants see their ministers regularly bending the rules they may be less inclined to keep to the straight and narrow themselves. Third, in a 'high sleaze' climate, the public may easily come to believe that the whole of the governmental apparatus – administrative as well as political – is painted with the same brush. The literature – especially, of course, the media coverage, of political scandals is vast, but serious, scholarly treatments are not so numerous. In his book on responsibility, which has already been cited on a number of occasions, Bovens (1998) does cover a number of cases of corruption, and integrates them with his general discussion of responsibility in complex organizations. The personal testimony of a civil service 'whistleblower' can be found in Clive Ponting's (1985) *The Right to Know: The Inside Story of the Belgrano Affair.* An interesting philosophical treatment of openness and secrecy is Sisella Bok's (1982) *Secrets: On the Ethics of Concealment and Revelation.* If you are interested in the downfall of the EU Commissioners, you could look at the official report which triggered their resignations – Committee of Independent Experts (1999) *First Report on Allegations Regarding Fraud, Mismanagement and Nepotism in the European Commission.* For the UK essential reading includes the reports of the Commission on Standards in Public Life (check the website at http://www.parliament.uk/guide/stan.htm). A compelling analysis of corruption in the developing world and the transitional states of central and eastern Europe can be found in the World Bank's (2000) *Anticorruption in Transition: A Contribution to the Policy Debate.*

7

Getting and giving advice on public management

The answer(s) to the key question(s)

Now, finally, I am going to address what for many practitioners is the $64,000 question (the expression is severely dated – the sum should be much larger nowadays). The question is – 'what should we do?' Surely that should be the test of all this research and scholarship – can the academics tell the managers how to manage (or, at least, how to do better what they are already doing)?

Since my response to the 'what should we do?' question may come as a disappointment (though not, I would hope, a complete surprise to those who have read what has gone before) let me get the negative moment over with as quickly as possible. First, I doubt very much whether the academics will ever be able to tell the practitioners what to do. For a number of good reasons, they can't. And, second, I do not accept that that should be the principal test of academic research into public management anyway.

That having been said, I want to argue that academic research and analysis can and does do a number of things that can help managers better understand their situation – no small benefit. Furthermore, academic work can greatly help (and has greatly helped) the rest of us (citizens) to see both the advantages and the limitations of public administration, to guard against some of its pathologies, and to foresee some of the consequences of adopting different ways of organizing the many functions of modern government. Finally, and in parenthesis (it is not the main focus of this chapter), I also want to spend a few lines defending the right of academics to 'do their thing' even if it only rarely yields practical and specific recommendations for action.

Well, what did you expect?

When practising managers start talking about academic research being 'relevant' and producing 'guidelines for action', what kind of thing do they (you?) have in mind? It could be any one or more of several different kinds of 'key' that they are hoping for. Perhaps the simplest idea would be advice as a set of instructions – do this, don't do that – ten commandments, or seven steps, or whatever, for the public manager, everywhere. After all, the gurus of generic management seem to provide such things, and, in the case of big names such as Tom Peters (*In Search of Excellence* (Peters and Waterman 1982), and other bestsellers), Michael Hammer (re-engineering), Peter Covey (personal effectiveness) and Peter Senge (the learning organization) they make a handsome living out of doing so (Jackson 2001). Through books, tapes, videos, software, personal appearances, consulting, electronic seminars and other channels they spread their universalist, improving messages to millions of managers.

One of the earliest and best-known of these recipes was Blanchard and Johnson's *The One-minute Manager* (1996 – originally published in 1983) which at one time featured on almost every airport bookstand in North America and the UK. This short tract told the (apocryphal) story of a 'bright young man' who wanted to become an effective manager. He travelled the world searching for answers to how to manage well. He spoke to many who he thought might help him, including 'government administrators' as well as managers of shops, banks and hotels, and even 'university professors', but his confusion only grew (see Blanchard and Johnson 1996: 12). Eventually he found a 'special manager' who revealed the secrets of success. These comprised a series of proverb-like statements, such as: 'people who feel good about themselves produce good results' and 'take a minute: look at your goals; look at your performance; see if your behaviour matches your goals'. The general idea was that efficiency would be increased by regular reference to a set of behaviourally-defined goals and by a brisk approach to praising and criticizing staff, in which the manager looked for positive achievements to praise but also delivered 'one-minute reprimands' when mistakes were made. According to the cover this is a 'short book that has big results'. Its limitations, however, are at least equally large (Zilbergeld 1984). One imagines it would provide little concrete guidance for the senior civil servant who is faced with a ministerial decision to downsize her department by 20 per cent, or for the ward sister who has to prepare for an external quality inspection with her understaffed team comprising a mixed group of short-term bought-in agency staff, burned-out staff nurses (who she nevertheless could not afford to lose) and green-behind-the-ears trainees. The 'one-minute manager' seems to live in a relatively simple world, free from ambiguous goals set by politicians, turf wars with rival organizations, legal procedures which are inefficient but must be adhered to, chronic staff shortages or any of the other complications which are common to the life of many public managers.

Of course, the 'one-minute manager' is among the simplest of simple prescriptions. Other gurus have longer, more complex messages to deliver. These messages have been widely received, in both private and public sectors, and on both sides of the Atlantic. The big names of generic management have certainly left their marks on the world of the public sector manager. In the UK, for example, the National Health Service launched a number of re-engineering projects modelled (at least in part) on the teachings of Hammer and Champy and their bestseller *Reengineering the Corporation: A Manifesto for Business* (see, for example: Packwood *et al.* 1998; McNulty and Ferlie 2002). Yet, on the whole, the academic community has tended to take stances of scepticism or outright hostility towards gurus and their recipes. There are a number of reasons for this. At the most straightforward level, evidence of the beneficial impact of such formulaic approaches is distinctly mixed (Jackson 2001: 13–22). To put it mildly 'there is a surprising paucity of data regarding the actual use of these management fashions' (Jackson 2001: 14). Even where we *do* have data, it doesn't point in one direction. For every case study of success there seems to be another of disillusionment and failure, or of huge efforts and only modest progress (Hackman and Wagerman 1995; Zbaraki 1998).

A second strand of criticism concerns the nature of the recipes themselves. According to a number of critics, the 'advice' tends to be both unhelpfully abstract and laced with internal contradictions. As a result the cook finds that it is often hard to relate the general recipe to the specific task at hand, and sometimes finds that sharply contrasting ingredients leave a nasty taste in the mouth. A well-known example is the way in which the dramatic productivity improvements promised by re-engineering are often achieved partly through equally dramatic 'downsizing' of the workforce. The 'human relations' side of this operation is therefore fraught with tension. Middle managers in particular are supposed to co-operate enthusiastically in sweeping changes that may well sweep away their own jobs. And even the lucky ones who survive may, in practice, be stricken with strong feelings of fear, guilt and caution – hardly the 'empowered' shock troops of future success (Wilmott 1995). Another example is the way that even those gurus who most passionately advocate 'authentic', honest behaviour actually sometimes deal with problems by defensive moves and covering up their 'real' feelings (see, for example, Argyris 2000: 15–22).

Why simple recipes are not enough

The unsatisfactory features of one-minute or seven-step solutions bring us straight back to an abiding theme of this book. *Contexts matter.* Public management is not all one thing (and neither is private sector management). Different functions, performed in different administrative cultures and circumstances, require different approaches, and different mixtures of norms and values. Therefore, it is inherently unlikely that a single set of prescriptions will work well in every – or even in most – situations. Indeed, if such a simple and effective formula existed, one imagines it would have been found long ago, and rapidly become common practice.

What is more, some public sector contexts are significantly different from most private sector contexts – as was shown in Chapter 1 and again in Chapter 6. So the guru recipes, hatched with mainly commercial situations in mind, are even less likely to give a good fit. To take one obvious example, politics – an influential feature for many public managers – is largely absent from generic recipes and their supporting analyses (Jackson 2001: 17). On the other hand, there will be *some* public sector functions where such models *might* work well. Re-engineering stock holding at a big army supply depot, or a new chief executive introducing personal effectiveness principles among a group of demoralized staff at a previously badly managed hospital – in these particular contexts good results may be obtained. Hence the mixture of success stories and dismal failures.

Even where there is some contextual fit, however, the general pronouncements of management gurus are likely to be seriously inadequate *by themselves.*
That is because of their very high level of generality. A wise manager will need to
decide about a host of more specific and detailed issues before concrete actions can
be taken. In a way this is to repeat the point about the importance of contexts.
Different theoretical perspectives have different ways of expressing this basic point.
Pragmatists point out that what appears to be the same thing evokes widely varying
responses in different organizations and countries. Take the idea of creating
semi-autonomous government agencies, for example. During the period since
the late 1980s this has been a popular sport in many countries. It was recommended
by (among others) public sector semi-gurus Osborne and Gaebler (Osborne and
Gaebler 1992). Governments should 'steer not row' they said – the tasks of rowing
should be given to professional, specialized agencies which would have the necessary managerial freedoms to seek continuous improvement. Central government
ministries would then be able to concentrate on strategic tasks. On the surface,
therefore, it sounded as though the agency form was a near-enough universal
answer to the problem of increasing managerial efficiency and customer
responsiveness. However, the moment politicians and civil servants settled down to
implement this general idea a host of differences appeared within and between
national administrations. Agencies were designed in different ways with significantly differing legal powers, budgetary arrangements, personnel authorities,
performance measurement regimes, and so on. On its own the general idea was
quite inadequate as a guideline for the specifics of what to do (Pollitt *et al.* 2001;
Pollitt and Talbot 2003).

More 'academic' theories arrive at similar conclusions to the pragmatists.
Thus contingency theorists argue that there is no 'one best way' – the most
appropriate organizational processes and structures depend on exactly what
environmental contingencies are faced by the particular organization in question:

> Contingency theory differs from all . . . universalistic theories in that it sees
> maximum performance as resulting from adopting, not the maximum, but
> rather the appropriate level of the structural variable that fits the contingency.
> (Donaldson 2001: 4)

For contingency theorists 'structural variables' include such features as the degree of
specialization, or the number of levels in the hierarchy, while 'contingencies' may
be 'internal' to the organization, or 'external'. Important internal contingencies
include the size of the organization, the amount of uncertainty in each of its
principal tasks, and the degree of interdependence between those tasks. External
contingencies include the degree of environmental uncertainty (for example, is it a
fairly stable or a rapidly changing environment?) and the degree of competition
from other organizations.

Social constructivists remind us that management problems are socially con-
structed and therefore vary from one national, institutional or local context to
another (Weick 1979; Zbaraki 1998). Weick (1979: 41, 42) for example, remarks
that:

> I think much organizational research is uninformative and pedestrian partly because people have tried to make it general and accurate and simple. In trying to accommodate all three of these aims, none have been realized vigorously; the result has been bland assertions.

Also:

> a completely general explanation . . . is hard to generate and may, in fact, be non-existent.

One might add that sometimes the result of attempts to generalize has been very un-bland: there has been a crop of quite aggressive (but still simple) assertions, as in some of the re-engineering literature.

Post-modernists – another academic grouping – insist that there 'are no metanarratives' (big stories/theories that explain and over-rule all other interpretations). They too, like the social constructivists, tend to stress contextuality (Alvesson 1995; Rhodes 1997: Chapter 9). So alternative perspectives on what may be the relevant issues and criteria are ever-present, and alternative interpretations of all texts are always available.

Meanwhile, those interested in the sociology of organizational knowledge argue that 'managerial skills differ considerably from other sorts of expertise in their limited standardization across industries, their susceptibility to change, their specificity to situations rather than problems and their diffuse, varied knowledge base' (Whitley 1989: 209). Whitley offers an interesting table of different types of skills (see Table 7.1).

Whitley argues that:

> . . . managerial skills are more focused upon particular firms or industries and less tied to specific problems. They are thus more generalizable across problems, but less generalizable across the situations where those problems occur,

and that as a result, attempts to produce

> highly general models of markets and organizations may be helpful as orienting devices since they present relatively simple ways of making sense

Table 7.1 Different types of skills (developed from Whitley 1988: Table 3, page 60)

	Generalizability across problems	
Generalizability across situations	LOW	HIGH
LOW		Managerial
HIGH	Professional (e.g. engineering)	'Political' (e.g. being diplomatic, putting people at their ease)

of complex and dynamic realities, but are scarcely directly applicable to particular managerial problems and situations.

(Whitley 1988: 60)

The aspiration to produce a general science of managing is, according to Whitley, doomed to failure.

A set of broadly parallel points is made in a different way in a lively book by a Professor of Political Science and Anthropology (an unusual and potentially fruitful combination of disciplines). In his book *Seeing Like a State*, James C. Scott (1998) charts a series of state-sponsored planning disasters, such as the Soviet collectivization of agriculture and the building of modern cities such as Brasília (Brazil) or Chandigargh (Punjab). The conclusion he draws is that 'The lack of context is not an oversight; it is the necessary first premise of any large-scale planning exercise' (Scott 1998: 346). He argues for the importance of *mētis*, a category of knowledge embedded in local experience, and to be contrasted with 'the more general, abstract knowledge deployed by the state and its technical agencies' (Scott 1998: 311). (Not only the state, one might add – with a typically American species of oversight Professor Scott appears not to have noticed that in some circumstances large private sector corporations also deploy great power and authority, combined with a determined commitment to general, abstract knowledge.) Mētis, which is contextual, experiential and sometimes implicit rather than explicit, has to be combined with technical forms of knowledge if particular applications of general ideas are to succeed.

If we now turn to 'informatics' theorists (those who study the development and application of ICTs), we find that they appear to be arriving at similar conclusions. A trio of Dutch scholars studied e-government developments in five countries. They examined the often-repeated claims that new ICTs would lead to new forms of more open and interactive government. Their conclusion was as follows:

The first question mark that can be put at the goals of a more open, client-oriented and more responsive government is that there are hardly [any] general effects. Effects are limited to the specific setting in which ICT is introduced.

(Bekkers, Homburg and Smeekes 2002: 12)

Finally, decision theorists argue that the nature of the task at hand will heavily influence the kind of analytical (or intuitive) approach which it is feasible to adopt. One kind of decision rule or decision strategy is unlikely to work equally well for many differently-structured tasks. If you would like to read a really challenging – and fascinating – book about this, try Hammond's (1996) *Human Judgement and Social Policy: Irreducible Uncertainty, Inevitable Error, Unavoidable Injustice*.

Of course, proponents of these different theoretical perspectives (contingency theory, social constructivism, post-modernism, organizational sociology, political anthropology, informatics, decision theory) would fight like cats over many other important issues, but on this one point – the possibility of universal, scientifically-based generalizations on how to manage *anything* – they tend to converge towards a position of deep scepticism. I agree!

To summarize, therefore, simple recipes for what managers should do are unlikely to help much with many of the problems which public managers face on a day-to-day basis. The reasons for this are set out in Table 7.2.

Table 7.2 Summary: some reasons why general recipes of 'what to do' for managers are so often unsatisfactory

---

- Guru prescriptions tend to be so general and abstract that they can be hard to translate into specific contexts. And contexts are frequently of large importance in determining the feasibility of a particular management 'solution'.
- On closer inspection the recipes are often found to contain internal contradictions.
- The recipes are often based on just a few cases rather than on harder, more systematic kinds of evidence. So it often turns out that there are other cases where the recipe doesn't/hasn't worked. Without a coherent analysis of contexts it is impossible to say where the recipe is likely to work and where not.
- Subsequent research sometimes shows that even the interpretation of the original cases was selective and unreliable – that there was another side to the success stories themselves. Alternatively (as happened to many of the 'excellent' companies cited in Peters and Waterman's (1982) famous *In Search of Excellence*) the 'success' proves to be quite short-lived, leaving doubts about the durability of a given set of recommended practices.
- The prescriptions, and surrounding discourse may skate over or leave out altogether crucial features of 'real life', such as 'office politics', resistance to reform or acute shortages of resources.

Beyond simple recipes: sound techniques?

Of course, the one-minute manager is an extreme. Looking out from within a European public sector, some of us may feel an easy superiority. 'How true' we may chuckle when we read that:

> given the American desire for simple solutions to complex problems, it should come as no surprise that there is a receptive audience for books claiming that difficult goals can be reached in one minute.
>
> (Zilbergeld 1984: 6)

Yet greater sophistication – if that is what we think we have – does not necessarily bring greater success. Many parts of many public sectors – European as well as North American – have invested heavily in new management techniques, such as Investors in People (IIP), Total Quality Management (TQM), the European Foundation for Quality Management (EFQM), Excellence model, ISO 9002 and benchmarking. Such techniques may appear to be much more complex, subtle, 'scientific' and 'neutral' than 'seven-steps' models. Furthermore they may not be so exclusively associated with charismatic gurus (although lesser gurus seem rapidly to spring up around each technique). Unfortunately, however, their implementation may lead to as much disappointment as do the simpler recipes. In the mid-1990s I visited an English National Health Service Hospital which was being held up for praise because it had been one of the most successful in implementing Total Quality Management. Last year I was surprised to see the same hospital appear on the national TV news because it had been strongly criticized by the Commission for Health Improvement on the grounds of poor quality care and organization. Less dramatically than this decline from grace, research has shown that many attempts to implement TQM end up falling far short of their aspirations, in both public and private sectors (Joss and Kogan 1995; Zbaraki 1998).

The application of more complex techniques, such as TQM or benchmarking, may stand a better chance of success than guru proverbs, but the (now very extensive) literature on these approaches indicates that they often fail too. It also shows that such techniques are not well-defined, 'hard' instruments that can be applied, like a torque wrench or an electric drill, in more or less any situation where a problem of type 'X' arises. Rather they are complex and frequently varying bundles of specific measurement practices, conceptual assumptions about the nature of organizational processes, and a certain amount of 'hype'. There are on-going controversies (sometimes quite vicious) among the experts and leaders as to what TQM 'really' is, and how it should be implemented. So these techniques can work out very differently in different circumstances. They, too, have to be adapted to fit particular contexts.

So what kind of advice can be given?

Have I been too pessimistic, too 'negative' thus far? It is an accusation with which I, and many other academics, am/are not entirely unfamiliar. But it is a criticism which I reject. My argument is *not* that no good advice can be given, it is that that advice can seldom take the form of universal statements of what should be done – 'do TQM', 'do re-engineering', 'create a learning organization', etc. Giving that kind of advice is like giving sweets to an unhappy child – it may produce some immediate relief, but does little to solve the underlying problem and may have unwanted effects in the longer term. (Of course, the fact that it doesn't solve underlying problems does little to reduce the abiding appeal of sweets, in one form or another – even for adults. How many of us have returned home, tired and frustrated after a hard day at the office and taken the edge off our dissatisfaction by munching through a bar of chocolate or downing a few stiff drinks?)

What *can* usefully be done is to offer help with specific problems in specific contexts. Usually this is best done not by prescribing some standard technique, seven-step programme or other 'packaged' general solution, but by listening to the practitioners and helping them clarify their own thinking about what they are aiming for, what particular problems they face, what information they need, what mixture of remedies might be applied, and with what likely consequences. In one way this is more like a kind of therapy – the adviser takes his or her cue from the manager and works to probe and clarify the manager's own thinking, rather than bringing in to play some pre-formed remedy.

At this point you may well be wanting to know more. 'OK', you say, 'academics can offer therapy and tailored advice, which Pollitt says is likely to be more useful than the generic models of some gurus, but what kind of things go into this advice – what kind of *content* does it possess?' My answer is that there are several kinds of useful advice which academics can and do commonly offer to help practising managers. These include those described in Boxes 7.1 to 7.6.

Box 7.1

Conceptual clarification: for example, what do you mean by 'public accountability'? How do you define 'quality'? These are issues where the academic is probably familiar with a wide range of literature in which such issues are discussed, which will not be known – or not in such detail – to the average manager. Academics are trained to be aware of definitional issues and their consequences, and can frequently help managers to sharpen their formulations. In particular academics can usefully insist that the problem(s) to be solved are defined as clearly as possible. This can help managers to work hard on problem identification and diagnosis *before* they reach for a solution. It is the opposite of bad consultancy, which has sometimes been characterized as 'solutions in search of problems'.

Box 7.2

Questioning false assumptions: this is a kind of therapy function. Again, academics are trained to ferret out underlying assumptions and drag them into the light of open debate. They can do this for managers as they can for students. This can prove surprisingly useful. For example, when discussing the modification of a public service better to fit the expressed wishes of users, it can be valuable to ask whether the reform is being carried out on the assumption that the modified service will still attract the same group of users? How reliable is this assumption? Are there trends which are changing the mix of users, and possibly introducing new types of user who may have different requirements (for example, more very elderly users, more users who do not have good English, more users from a particular ethnic group)? Another example would be the assumption that bonus pay will incentivize public servants to work harder. In some circumstances this may work, but in many it apparently does not. The assumptions about the beneficial effects of bonus (or 'merit') pay also tend to overlook the motivational impacts such systems have on those staff who do *not* receive a bonus.

Box 7.3

Advising on how best to collect data. Academics usually have a strong training in social science methods. When a manager needs to know something, and that something requires research in order to find it out, she or he will frequently benefit from discussing with academics the selection of methods for data collection. It may be an issue of statistical sampling, or one of how to minimize bias in interviews, or what statistical tests to carry out on an existing body of data, or what combination of methods to use when trying to establish what citizens want and expect from a particular service.

Box 7.4

Guidance on how to structure decisions: some academics are experts in decision analysis, and can advise managers on how to structure decision-making processes so as to more accurately and reliably reflect the underlying probabilities and values involved in a particular decision or series of decisions. Typically this might involve modelling the decision, making value judgements more explicit, seeking the best possible information on the probabilities of alternative outcomes, and advising on how, technically, to weight probabilities with values/utilities and to discount for effects which take place at different times in the future (Dowie 1999). Decision analysis has made considerable contributions to particular parts of the public sector (for example, health care, environmental safety issues – see the journal *Medical Decision Making*) but much less so to some others (for example, social work or management reform itself).

Box 7.5

Substantive advice based on middle-range, contextually-based generalizations: for example, that measuring the performance of professionally-delivered human services tends to be more complex and subtle than measuring the performance of standardized administrative routines such as issuing licences or checking applications for a Social Security benefit. Therefore it would be wise to use performance indicators in a more diagnostic, more cautious, less mechanical way in health care and education than in more standardized 'production' services. Or (to take another example) that contracting out has worked well for certain types of service in countries X, Y and Z, but has proved much more controversial and difficult for certain other kinds of service. This kind of advice is therefore based on substantive knowledge of what is happening in a variety of settings (and in the past). Crucial to the quality of this advice, however, is a careful discussion of the degree to which the different settings really *are* comparable – a discussion in which the manager receiving the advice would be well-advised to take an active part. For example, telling the manager of a hospital in Birmingham how TQM was successfully installed in a Toyota plant in Japan may be of limited use (there are too many glaring – and subtle – differences in context). But telling the Birmingham manager how TQM was successfully implemented in a hospital in Manchester may be more useful/transferable.

Box 7.6

Technical tips based on previous experience in other, similar contexts: for example, when measuring the time taken to deliver money benefits to claimants set the target in terms of the average time taken to complete all payments rather than the percentage of payments made within a certain time period. The former system (averaging) will oblige staff to pay attention to *all* claims, whereas the latter (completing 90 or 95 per cent of payments within x days) may tempt staff to neglect the small percentage of really complex and difficult claims (this example comes from actual experience with the UK Benefits Agency during the 1990s). Again, this is substantive, expert knowledge which comes from prolonged and focused exposure to empirical study. And, again, care is needed that lessons are being transferred across broadly comparable contexts.

Philosophically speaking, the kinds of advice listed in Boxes 7.1 to 7.6 are derived from several different intellectual bases or procedures. Some are 'best practice' types of advice, based on comparisons between cases and laying great weight on the direct reporting of experience. This has been a particularly popular type of management knowledge in business schools and at the more vocational, less academic end of the subject field. It is relatively easy to generate, and it is a type of knowledge in the creation of which the practitioner may actually have an advantage over the academic (this takes us back to that type of literature referred to earlier, in which top managers reflect on their experiences and draw out general principles).

Other types of advice, however, are drawn from theories and models of organizational behaviour, or from models of individual decision-making – they have more 'academic' or analytic foundations which involve the formulation and testing of specific propositions and models of relationships. The field of management generally, and public management in particular, have witnessed vigorous arguments between proponents of the different routes to and types of knowledge. This contest (or, at least, the American version of it) is vividly portrayed in Lynn (1996). Lynn himself comes down strongly in favour of mainstream, theory-driven, analytically sophisticated social science. He castigates enthusiasts of the 'best practice/case study' approach as follows:

> In ruling out or being dismissive of a role for instrumental or technical rationality as a dimension of effective practice, they have no where to go but towards the managerial Heart of Darkness in search of Kurtz, the legendary Public Manager cum Entrepreneur, Innovator, Risk Taker, Protector of the Constitution, and Civilizing Force, all courage and wisdom, possessing attributes that are, alas, virtually unteachable.
>
> (Lynn 1996: 105)

In a later book Lynn also develops a clear programme for the kind of research into improving governance which he prefers (Lynn, Heinrich and Hill 2001 – well worth reading). My own sympathies lie in the same direction (towards formally modelled and conceptualized social science knowledge) but I am perhaps less convinced than Lynn that the 'case study/best practice/experientially-based' tribe are fundamentally opposed to more analytic approaches. More often, I suspect, they slide towards that 'softer' type of knowledge because it is easier to produce, easier to communicate and easier to sell than more heavily theorized social science. It is less hung about with 'ifs' and 'buts' and reflections on ambiguities and insufficiencies of data. It may possess a fatal attraction for politicians, who can easily see themselves as being in the business of having to sell 'common sense' solutions to large and sceptical audiences. However, there are perhaps closer connections between the two types of knowledge than Lynn sometimes seems to allow. For example, the nostrums of 'best practice' can be and are used as a spur and target for subsequent social science research of a more analytical kind. Or, to put it more concretely, the local knowledge (mētis) of practitioners can often be used as a platform on which to pose and test more formal, abstract propositions. So in practice the line between the two types of management knowledge may not be either so clear or so heavily guarded.

It should also be noted that the kinds of advice indicated in Boxes 7.1 to 7.6 are not always popular with practitioners. They often amount to a kind of 'tough love' in which the adviser points out that the manager cannot have everything she or he wants. For example, an adviser may point out that creating autonomous management units to deliver services X and Y, while potentially increasing efficiency and initiative through specialization and de-bureaucratization, is also likely (on the basis of experience in similar contexts in other jurisdictions) to increase problems of integrating a range of related services. It may also lead to some loss of detailed political control over the two services in question. Or the decision analyst may try to persuade the politician to be clear about values that she or he would much rather remained shrouded in fine words and ambiguity – such as how many lives need to be saved before a national cancer-screening programme is deemed a worthwhile investment? Is a 17 million euro screening programme worth it if it will save on average only one life per annum? Two? Fifteen? Or, again, the adviser may warn that re-engineering a rather specialized and bureaucratic employment placement and advice agency into a 'flatter', generalist unit (in which citizens are more likely to get their advice on the first call, instead of being passed around different departments) may succeed only at the cost of losing many of its existing specialist staff, who do not wish to become generalists and will take a lot of valuable experience and expertise with them when they go (this last is a recent real-life example).

If contexts are so important, what can we say about them?

By now many of you will be getting a little bored with my reiterations of how important contexts are. Even if it is true, in some general sense, we cannot do very much *with* the warning about contexts unless we have some idea of what we are looking for. What are the features of contexts that affect attempts at better management? What kinds of technique or approach fit with (or misfit with) what kind of context?

Academics do have some ideas to offer here, although I would be the first to admit that, in total, the work on contexts is rather disappointing. There is no 'Big Guide to Contexts' to which I can point you, indeed there is not really even a good theory of contexts, just some promising ideas lying around in various parts of the public management literature. For example – to take a selective list – it does seem to matter how far a function or activity can be standardized, how far its results can be directly observed, whether it is an emergency service or a routine activity, how far users need to have a face-to-face relationship with service providers and how far it is politically sensitive. Usually, none of these factors is absolutely crucial just by itself – not in the sense that it immediately rules certain management approaches in and others out – but taken together they could be said to reduce the effectiveness and appropriateness of some approaches and increase the relative advantage of others. This assertion can be illustrated by taking a closer look at some of the 'variables' mentioned above.

Standardizability

This is important because it influences, *inter alia*, efficiency, accountability and equity. It influences efficiency because the less the outputs of a service can be standardized, the more difficult it becomes to measure efficiency (in the technical sense of an input:output ratio). If an organization is issuing licences or paying standardized benefits, then its output can be straightforwardly monitored. Unit costs can be calculated. However, if it is a school, offering lessons, or a social services department offering a wide range of clients different types of advice, then the counting of outputs becomes more problematic. Standardizability also influences accountability, because reporting unstandardized activities takes longer and tends to assume a more discursive, less quantitative format. In a way it requires more of the accountee (receiver of the account). Standardizability influences equity because, when a service cannot be measured in standard units, it is harder to be sure that users in similar circumstances are receiving similar service. For all these reasons unstandardized services are harder to contract out successfully. (Lane, generally an enthusiast for contractual forms of relationship in the public sector, acknowledges that human services pose particular problems – Lane 2000.) The contracts are incomplete, because of the difficulties of defining outputs. The monitoring of performance is also more difficult. Trust becomes correspondingly more important, long-term relational types of contracting more appropriate, and transparency more elusive.

Observability of outputs and outcomes

Outputs and outcomes which are difficult to observe generate some of the same challenges as outputs which are not standardizable. Thus, a lack of observability makes contracts more difficult to frame, accountability more precarious and trust a more precious asset. However, lack of observability is not the same as lack of standardizability – the two characteristics are analytically separate. One can have a standardized health intervention (water fluoridization, vaccination) whose outcomes are not visible for a long time. Or one can have an unstandardizable intervention which is perfectly visible, such as a policeman dealing with a fight on the street or a teacher teaching a class while parent helpers are present in the classroom.

Outputs which are difficult to observe include advice and emotional support (as a teacher may offer to a student who lacks self-confidence, or a social worker may offer to a harassed working single parent). Yet these are the things those citizens in receipt of such services may look back on as having been the most crucial aspects of the service. Outcomes may be difficult to observe because they occur over a very long time scale, or because they are multiply caused, or both. A significant reduction in environmental pollution may take many years to achieve. The success of an educational programme for young children from deprived backgrounds may not bear fruit for a decade, and then be hard to separate out from other influences. It may be a long time before the cumulative effect of planning controls become visible on the face of a crowded urban environment – and such controls will probably need to place reliability high on their agenda if they are to achieve their purpose. Low observability therefore points towards organizational forms which maximize the public service ethic, a spirit of professional commitment to clients, and good security of tenure. The application of a regime of tight, short-term performance indicators and/or contracts may, in these circumstances generate perverse incentives, as staff lower hidden aspects of quality in order to pass the measurement test.

On the other hand, governments also perform many activities of a relatively standardized nature, and where outputs can be observed and measured in reasonably convincing ways. The issue of driving licences or passports, the registration of births, marriages and deaths, the payment of fixed benefits against standard criteria of eligibility, and a variety of testing and inspection tasks all fall into this category. In these cases, *ceteris paribus*, a variety of 'at a distance' forms of organization may be both feasible and advantageous.

Political salience

Some functions tend to attract high levels of political attention, while others go on their quiet way, seldom hitting the headlines. Compare, for instance, the prison service (fairly high salience) with the meteorological office (low), or the health service (usually very high) with weights and measures (low). High political salience tends to mean a high need for transparency and accountability – a continuing readiness to satisfy various enquirers as to what has been done and why. When political salience was combined with private sector managers who had little experience of Whitehall, trouble followed for the UK prison service and Child Support Agency. When political salience was combined with a public sector manager, accustomed to the politician's insatiable desire to intervene, serious trouble was avoided (UK Benefits Agency – see Gains 2000).

So putting matters of high political salience at a great distance – at the other end of a commercial contract, or, in the case of British Rail, by privatizing and fragmenting it altogether, can easily lead to difficulties (Durman 2001). Only if there is a party political truce – a lasting agreement that some function should deliberately be put 'beyond politics – is an arm's length solution likely to be stable. The most common cases of this kind involve quasi-judicial functions, where a majority of politicians – and the general public – want party politics entirely removed from the decision-making process. The problem of achieving such a consensus may be greater in decentralized, federal states than in centralized, unitary states such as the UK, because there may be a larger number of independent political *fora* involved.

Consequentiality

Most of us can afford the tax office to make a mistake – as long as their procedures are open to complaint and correction (our 12th criterion). Most of us cannot afford for the emergency services – fire, ambulance, police – to make mistakes, at least not when they are dealing with life-threatening situations. Their actions are more immediately consequential. It is no coincidence that they tend to be the most trusted, most admired public services, and those which the public in many countries are least willing to see contracted out to commercial operators. Every time there is a major accident or calamity – recent rail crashes in Britain, the horrific terrorist attacks in New York – this public perception is reconfirmed.

Less dramatically, one may consider the case of the Canadian Food Inspection Agency (CFIA). While amalgamation of various food inspection activities within a single agency was apparently driven principally by an efficiency logic, the consequentiality of food safety meant that the positioning of the agency was also shaped by 'the pervasive belief within the food safety policy community that the federal inspection and regulation functions ought to remain within the federal government domain' (Prince 2000: 219)

Therefore high consequentiality tends to promote certain criteria to the top of the list of priorities. Effectiveness, of course, is paramount. Accessibility, speed of response and reliability are also crucial. Recent public concerns about the London ambulance service have not focused on its efficiency or transparency, or on the extent to which citizens have been able to participate in planning and decision-making. They have focused on how quickly the ambulances arrive, and whether one can always get through immediately on the telephone.

Cultural context

A mass of literature testifies to the enduring significance of cultural differences in public administration. Such differences include the contrast between centralized, majoritarian systems such as the UK and (until 1993) New Zealand, and more decentralized, multi-party consensual systems, such as usually prevail in the Nordic countries and the Netherlands. They also include the deep-rooted difference between 'public interest' states, such as the UK and the USA, and the kind of ingrainedly juridical thinking that pervades administrative life in France, Germany and most of the Mediterranean states (Pollitt and Bouckaert 2000). These differences can easily lead to misunderstandings: for example, both the UK and Germany have set up independent state telecommunications regulation bodies, which action has led some commentators to write of convergence. The convergence, however, is limited, because decision-making inside the German agency follows the classic German juridical pattern, whereas inside UK Oftel it does not (Böllhoff 2000).

> For the world is wide, with room enough for customs, tastes, principles, observances of every sort, which, once you set them in the society where they have arisen, always make sense. Observe them. Compare them, do, for your own edification. But whatever your own tastes, which you needn't renounce, please, dear master, refrain from identifying them with universal commandments.
>
> (Sontag 1993: 17)

What is the significance of such differences for the manager trying to find the optimal organizational forms for a particular public service? One message would be that choosing an organizational form that represents a big leap away from the existing cultural tradition is highly risky. Culture cannot be just 'switched off'. 'Path dependency' is a strong force – in the UK Next Steps programme it soon became clear that traditional ministerial responsibility remained the dominant rule of the game, usually trumping managerial freedoms whenever the two came into conflict (Gains 2000). The radical reforms in New Zealand have been a focus for so much international attention partly because of their very rarity – one of very few examples of a seeming 'breakthrough' from an old to a new system. Yet careful analysis shows both that this breakthrough was the product of an unusual 'window of opportunity' (of a kind not often available to reformers) and that, in the end, the brakes were applied and some edging back towards past practices began (Aberbach and Christensen 2001).

Path dependency is not a sin, but a recognition of previous investments of political capital, acquired administrative skills and trust (Pierson 2000). Occasionally reformers may be able to jump through a 'window of opportunity' (and it is part of the skill of a reform leader to recognize one) but for the most part they would be well advised to 'go with the grain'. This means, *inter alia*, that attractive foreign imports may need considerable 'editing' before they can be made minimally acceptable to the local cultural *status quo* (Pollitt *et al.* 2001).

An example may help to illustrate how some of these contextual factors can interact to constrain the types of management approach which are likely to prove effective. Let us compare the management of a local secondary school with the management of a government agency that issues car and truck driving licences. And let us also simplify the problem further by locating both organizations within the same culture, so that we don't have to worry too much about deep cultural differences of a general, national kind.

First, on standardizability, the issuing of driving licences is far more standard-izable than the teaching of children. One licence is more like another than one child is like another, and the range of ways of producing the service (issuing the licence, educating the child) is much wider for the school than for the licensing agency. So it is far easier to define and measure the process through which a licence is issued than the process through which a child is educated. The former is also simpler, meaning that the training of rank and file staff should be much shorter for licensing personnel than for schoolteachers. Teachers are professionals, who enjoy consider-able discretion in deciding how they teach and how they handle each individual child. They have a long 'learning curve' as they tackle new subjects and different types of student, and gradually amass experience and a 'feel' for the job. Those who issue licences have a shorter learning curve during which they arrive at full mastery of a much simpler and more standardized task.

Second, with respect to the observability of outputs and outcomes, roughly the same difference between the two services can be seen. To record the issuing of a licence (output) is straightforward. To record the completion of an education process is more complex – and expensive. Typically we do it mainly by examinations, but it is very hard to ensure that these are standardized and that they measure all the aspects of the educational process on which different users of the school place significant value (for example, mathematical skills, creativity, self-discipline, etc.). Culture creeps in here as well, because it may be difficult to ensure that any one exam is equally fair to students from different cultural backgrounds. So examinations themselves become an industry, with specialist supervisory bodies, elaborate arrangements for marking and standardizing marking, and a community of academic researchers investigating whether and to what extent different types of exams (in different subjects) measure what they are supposed to measure in a reliable and bias-free manner.

As for outcome measurement, this is difficult for both organizations. What are supposed to be the final outcomes of having driving licences? To prevent unskilled drivers coming onto the roads and causing accidents? To raise revenue for the state? To provide the state with systematic information about who is driving and who is not? In each of these cases the issuing of a driving licence is only one part of the equation. For example, the identification of illegal and unskilful drivers will rest more with the police than with the driving licence agency.

The difficulties are even greater for the school. What are the long-term outcomes of education supposed to be? A numerically literate and language-literate population? An adult population which knows right from wrong and possesses the self-discipline to govern their own behaviours accordingly? A 'civilized' population which understands 'civics' and is capable of enjoying the arts and crafts? A domesticated population which has acquired the basic skills of cooking and cleaning and repairing the car and looking after their own health? All of the above? But how are we to measure these long-term outcomes and, even if we can and do, to what degree can they be attributed to the influence of schools, as opposed to parental upbringing, television, the internet, the peer group, or any of the other factors which may interact to influence a young person?

If we now turn to the third issue – political salience – it is clear that driving licences are less salient politically than the media (though even this could change in the short term if the system broke down and drivers could not get their licences – as the UK Passport Office discovered to its cost during the 1990s). Education is always a salient issue, partly because it is believed to affect so many aspects of our lives – more than does the possession of a driving licence. Most parents are interested in the education of their child(ren) and that makes it an issue that politicians are obliged to take a strong interest in also. However, one local school will not always be in the headlines, so one might say that in practice the political salience of a single school is middling while that of the driving licence agency is low.

Fourth, consequentiality. Neither organization faces the same high degree of consequentiality as a fire brigade or ambulance service or air traffic control centre. Nevertheless, the consequentiality of schooling is great, albeit spread over an extended period. School success or failure definitely affects our 'life chances'. Most parents (and most children) are acutely aware of this, and therefore have an intense interest in how the school is functioning. By comparison the functioning

Table 7.3   Some contextual differences between two public sector organizations

	Driving licence agency	*Secondary school*
Standardizability	High	Low
Observability of outputs and outcomes	High (outputs) Medium (outcomes)	Medium (outputs) Low (outcomes)
Political salience	Low (usually)	Medium to high
Consequentiality	Low	Medium to high

of the licensing agency is far less consequential. Certainly it can be irritating and even highly inconvenient if someone entitled to a licence cannot get one or has to wait for a long time to receive it, but this does not normally alter the course of his or her life in the way that one's education frequently does. Nor is there any equivalence between the few minutes it takes to fill out a licence application and the years of one's life spent in school. Table 7.3 summarizes the position.

So what does all this contextual detail imply for the management of these two organizations? For the sake of brevity I will restrict these comments to the question of the suitability of an 'NPM-style' approach. Basically the argument would be that an NPM approach would probably (*ceteris paribus*) fit the licensing agency quite well, but that the school would ideally require a different approach. Consider the following: the products of the licensing agency can be easily standardized, costed and measured. Therefore it should be possible to design a system of a small number of output and cost indicators that would capture most of the important aspects of the agency's work. This system could be used both to enable top management to steer the agency and monitor developing problems, and for purposes of external accountability (to the parent ministry, parliament and the public). The 'results' would be easily understandable and – if unsatisfactory – changeable within quite a short time cycle. The process of management could be expected to proceed without much political intervention or media interest – so top management's time could be largely devoted to operational management tasks plus strategic planning for systems improvements in the future. If individual mistakes were made the consequences would be unlikely to be life-threatening or irretrievable, or even very costly.

Because outputs could be relatively easily specified and costed, it would also be possible to consider contracting out the licensing function. It could be treated as a fairly well-understood 'package' of activities.

Things would be very different in the school. Low standardizability would mean that a lot of management time would be taken up with handling unusual or unprecedented cases (what shall we do with the new girl whose parents have just arrived from Guyana and who has an acute allergy to all milk products? How shall we tackle the boy in the fourth form whose academic results are excellent but who seems to be leading a gang of bullies? Which is the best type of mathematics software to purchase now that the old system is reaching the end of its life?). These types of issue would require professional discussion with staff, and would be much more likely to be implemented effectively if some kind of consensus could be reached. Of course, a set of performance (output) indicators (exam results, truancy rates, etc.) would certainly be very useful, but it would be unlikely to capture the full range of aims and activities of the school. Therefore a number of other important factors would have to be taken into consideration alongside measured 'results'.

What is more, even the standardized results would require considerable interpretation and debate – their meaning would not necessarily be obvious, especially to parents or the media. For example, a decline in this year's maths results might be due to the sudden departure of the longstanding maths teacher after a heart attack and the difficulty in finding and appointing a suitable replacement. It could therefore be expected to be only a temporary 'blip', because now a good replacement had been found and appointed. On the other hand, signs of an increase in bullying or drug use, though not measured as part of the main school 'league table' indicators, could be a much more serious issue, requiring wide discussions with parents, students and staff. Big mistakes or omissions could have tremendously severe consequences, including the psychological or physical scarring of children or even loss of life. All these ups and downs would be played out in front of a more continuously interested audience of parents, local media, local politicians and (sometimes) national authorities than would be faced by the driving licence agency.

To manage a school, therefore, would require skills of explaining to and negotiating with not only professional colleagues but also a range of 'external' stakeholders – parents, teachers, the local media and so on. The 'diplomatic and representational' dimension of management is usually highly important for a headteacher. An acute awareness of ethical issues would also be an advantage, and discussions of what was 'fair' or 'compassionate' or 'right for the child in the long run' would no doubt feature far more prominently than in the driving licence agency. In short, decision-analysis skills would be extremely valuable to the headteacher. Operational management of standardized processes would still be important, but not as central as with the driving licence agency. Just issuing orders down the hierarchy, bureaucracy-style, would probably bring about a very unhappy school within quite a short period of time. In short, the kind of approach that would lead to success in running one of these organizations would be unlikely to fit the other.

One final reminder, before leaving this issue of the types of advice that academics can offer. The four factors discussed here and shown in Table 7.3 (five if we also include culture) is selective and illustrative, certainly not exhaustive. It is offered as a taster, not a full menu. Both the literature and the practice of advice-giving include other important contextual variables which there is no room to discuss here.

Good management: how much difference will it make?

'What should we do' (what is the key)? is one type of question. The first part of my answer (developed above) is that it depends on the context, that universalist prescriptions are likely to be of only limited help, and that a key part of the manager's craft is correctly to analyse the context before choosing the recipe. There is, however, a second type of question. Even if an appropriate recipe, technique or other course of action *is* chosen, how much difference will it make? In principle the answer could vary from everything to nothing. Will good management transform the situation, turning an expensive, ineffective public programme into a high quality, efficient service which achieves all its objectives? Or will even the best conceivable management practices only scratch the surface of a recalcitrant world, making little or no measurable difference to a programme's final outcomes?

This fundamental question about the final *potential* of good management is seldom asked or, at any rate, it is seldom explored in any explicit or systematic way. Yet it is apparent that different commentators hold very different assumptions concerning the extent of this potential.

The differences are apparent if we take a brief look at two rather polarized views on this matter. The first sees management as of huge and pervasive importance in public policy and administration. The second, by contrast, sees management as a necessary and desirable craft, but one which can seldom transform the situation. From this perspective management is an activity that helps us cope with insoluble problems, get by, stay on the road, make worthwhile improvements in how things are organized – but it does not 'outrank' or outvalue other forms of activity. It is a set of useful roles, the performance of which helps preserve some stability, encourages a little innovation, supports self-discipline, and simply gets the work done. It is not a revolutionary social force, transforming our whole society.

The manager as superman (woman)

Efficient management is a key to the (national) revival . . . And the management ethos must run right through our national life – private and public companies, civil service, nationalized industries, local government, the National Health Service.

(Michael Heseltine (1980), then Conservative Secretary of State for the Environment, later Deputy Prime Minister)

In the UK and North America, this kind of thinking became increasingly popular from the late 1970s onwards. Better management was seen as the solution to a wider and wider range of economic and social problems (Pollitt 1993: Chapter 1). In a sense it began to displace politics as the standard remedy – what we needed, even politicians themselves seemed to be saying, was less politics and more management, greater efficiency rather than new policies. This heroic – almost romantic – role for managers is already quite plain to see in Peter Drucker's writings from three decades ago (Drucker was one of the first management gurus):

> . . . it is managers and management that make institutions perform. Performing, responsible management is the alternative to tyranny and our only protection against it.
>
> (Drucker 1974: x)

'Gosh', one feels like saying, 'am I really supposed to take this seriously, or has this line somehow strayed out of a Dilbert cartoon?' (see Adams 1999). So, according to this vision, it is not democratically elected politicians, or elections themselves, or other constitutional safeguards, or an educated and aware citizenry, or a degree of social pluralism that keeps us free from tyranny, it is *managers*! Hmmm.

Frequently (though not always) the 'superman/woman' approach seduces commentators into concentrating on the more personal, psychological, idiosyncratic aspects of managing. Hence the endless autobiographies and biographies of charismatic Chief Executive Officers. Hence also the attempts of researchers in leadership studies to identify some set of special personal qualities which will explain why this group of individuals made outstanding leaders but that group did not. However, this search (which has been continuing for decades) has not come up with a nice neat list of key personal characteristics, and one reason why it has not lies – once again – in the significance of contextual differences:

> Perhaps the most resonant truth emerging from the study of effectiveness is that success is apt to reflect a good fit between individual capabilities and the demands of specific situations . . . . Individuals of widely varying skills and attributes can be effective depending on the circumstances. The proper study of public management involves the study of good fits between people and circumstances.
>
> (Lynn 1996: 92)

The manager as ordinary mortal

Management is not a solution to seemingly intractable stresses. Rather it is a means of coping with and sometimes improving only marginally tractable situations. This more modest vision of management has much to teach those in the reform business about the appropriate level of aspiration for anyone engaged in reforming complex systems. But management thinkers cannot teach others that lesson unless they give up the quasi-religious adoption of one management slogan after another as the solution to getting management right.

> (Marmor 2001. Ted Marmor is a Yale School of Management
> professor who was in the UK giving the annual Rock
> Carling lecture on health care.)

Marmor sees managers as fixers and copers, not as heroes and transformers. It can be a bit of a shock to find this more modest view of management expressed so bluntly. When I browsed through the (large) management sections of a couple of first-class bookshops recently, looking for examples of this perspective, I found very little indeed. The 'heroic' stance is now much more common – rather like those video/ DVD stores where it seems that 75 per cent of the covers show pictures of muscular men carrying weapons of one kind or another, whereas there is a total absence of covers showing men planting shrubs, making furniture or doing the washing-up. Modesty – or routinely productive activity – evidently doesn't sell.

There is, however, a longstanding perspective in the sociological and public administration research that shows senior staff – managers and mandarins – as frequently rather limited in what they can hope to achieve. They are limited by the fact that they can never hope to know much detail about the many activities which they are nominally in charge of, and can keep track of only a limited number of issues at any one time. Furthermore, there may well be incentives for staff at lower levels to 'filter' and 'slant' information about what is going on in the depths of the organization, so as to give mainly the rosy side of the picture to the bosses. As Bovens (1998: 75) puts it: 'one of the fixed themes of the literature on modern organization is precisely the restricted capability of the higher levels to control the organization.'

Perhaps the truth lies somewhere in between the manager as hero and the manager as dupe? It seems at least plausible that the influence of managers is itself something which varies according to context. In some cases circumstances are so adverse that all even a good manager can do is marginally delay or slightly ameliorate some kind of collapse or disaster. Equally, circumstances may be so easy or protected that even the most bumbling director does not do too much harm. His or her subordinates get on with the job and do their best to ignore the misguided instructions coming out of the director's office. In more mixed circumstances, however, managers may have the opportunity to make a significant difference – though it depends on their skill and powers of analysis and leadership whether or not they are able to seize that opportunity. We should avoid, however, the wholly unwarranted assumption that the solution to each and every problem facing the public sector is simply 'better management'. It would also be very nice if someone would do a bit more research on the basic question of what *sort* of differences management can make, and *when*.

Short diversion: why shouldn't we judge academic research mainly by how useful it is to practising managers?

Short answer: because some academic research is devoted simply to describing and explaining what happens in the world, which is rather different from trying to come up with recipes for improvement. To do this kind of 'basic' research academics need to be free from the constant pressure to say something which is 'useful'. Not *all* academics need to engage with such 'basic' describing and explaining, and not every academic who does that kind of research will need to be able to do it *all the time*. (In practice, in today's universities, rather few social science or management academics spend more than a small proportion of their time doing real basic research of this type.) But *some* research time and money needs to be reserved for enquiry and speculation that does not have immediate utility as its main target. This kind of research requires protection from practitioner pressures to 'give me an answer, quick'.

Furthermore, historically, we know that many of the most profound (and subsequently useful!) insights of the social sciences have derived from research in which the academic(s) concerned were wandering down their own paths of enquiry, not racing to produce a report on how to increase productivity by the end of next month.

The end is nigh

Learning about public management is not a single, straightforward process. Of course, it includes, centrally, the acquisition of well-supported knowledge about the subject, but, as I have tried to show, it entails several other processes as well. One of these processes – less often recognized – is the *dismantling* of false or oversimplified 'knowledge'. Under this heading are included some of the stereotypes (of the public and private sectors, of 'the public service ethic', of the heroic manager, etc.) which have been put up for discussion in this and earlier chapters. As the American comedian Will Rogers is reputed to have said, 'It ain't what we know that causes the problems, it's what we know that ain't so'.

Another, related, learning process is that of testing the strength of purported knowledge. Is it true that networks are becoming more numerous and important? Is it true that they bring with them greater democratic legitimacy than the 'traditional' processes of ministries consulting pressure groups and the public before announcing a new policy or programme? How would one be able to test these claims? What data would need to be collected, and how could that data be collected in a reliable way? Has anyone – particularly the speaker or writer – yet actually done this? And if they have, how large is the *domain* of that knowledge? If a study has convincingly shown that a particular management technique has born fruit in a sample of primary schools in Newcastle, how far can we generalize the finding? Does it apply just to primary schools in inner city Newcastle, to primary schools in general, to all schools throughout the UK, to schools all over the western world, or perhaps to the entire class of public sector organizations? Even if the domain is wide, is it limited in time (true only since most teachers acquired home internet connections)? or in culture (acceptable in Protestant North Western Europe, but not in Muslim Saudi Arabia or multi-religion Japan)?

A third, vital process is practice in the use of particular tools of investigation. In my opinion the best public management scholars are very seldom just armchair commentators, taking a lordly overview. They have also conducted fieldwork research in public sector organizations, and they will often have tried to give the staff of those organizations useful advice. In doing this they will have been obliged to try to use various methodologies – structured interviews, surveys, procedures for measuring inputs and outputs, techniques for measuring and weighting values, and so on. Repeated practice in the application of such techniques generates a strong craft knowledge, and a sense of the strengths and weaknesses of the types of information which each technique can yield. One can talk about these craft issues in books and articles (though I have only alluded to them occasionally in this book – one of its many limitations) but there is no real substitute for experiencing them directly, as an active fieldworker. After all, this is public management we are talking about, not metaphysics – to study the subject exclusively from the library and the internet seems almost perverse.

If you approach the study of public management in this questioning, practising way, you will probably (subjective $p = 0.9$) experience some disappointments. Visions of some breakthrough technique revolutionizing public sector management begin to fade as you realize that it isn't new, it isn't revolutionary, and the evidence for its success comes mainly from a handful of local jurisdictions in a rich part of California (and that the key book on the subject has been written by the city manager of one of these towns, or her management consultant!). On a more pedestrian level, you may look at the performance data for your local hospital more sceptically when you understand how the data is collected, by whom and under what circumstances. There may have been times during the reading of this book when you have thought that I was being too hard on the partnerships, or joined-up government, or the NPM, but my reservations about these ideas come principally from asking the kinds of fundamental questions which I hope have at least been posed, if not answered, in every chapter.

On the other hand, alongside the disappointments, you may also experience a more intriguing and durable fascination with the subject. This is because the nature of its complexity and challenge – and the scope for your personal contribution – should become clearer. Instead of waiting for the next packaged solution to come on down the line you will be armed with some sharp questions and robust tools of analysis. Together these should enable you to begin analysing management issues yourself. You will also become steadily more aware (as I certainly continue to become) how much has already been done – how much help and clarification can be derived from the research and testimony which is 'out there' waiting, if you take the time and trouble to look. And, if you are fortunate, you may eat one or other (or both) of the richest fruits which hang from the public management tree. I refer, first, to the deep satisfaction that comes from describing and explaining some aspect of management which had not been previously so well understood and, second, to offering advice to those responsible for important public functions and seeing (possibly after a considerable wait!) that it is having a beneficial effect.

ADVICE
Advice! What have they got to say?
You know how it always goes:
This one says good, that one says bad
And no one in town really knows.
It screws me up and makes me mad
Advice! Who needs advice?
(Annie Schmidt (1987)
'Raad', p. 231. Loosely
translated by the author)

References

6, P., Leat, D., Seltzer, K. and Stoker, G. (2002) *Towards Holistic Governance: The New Reform Agenda*. London: Palgrave.

Aberback, J. and Christensen, T. (2001) Radical reform in New Zealand: crisis, windows of opportunity, and rational actors, *Public Administration*, 79(2): 403–22.

Adams, S. (1999) *Don't Step in the Leadership*. London: Boxtree.

Allison, G. (1983) Public and private management: are they fundamentally alike in all unimportant respects?, in J. Perry and K. Kraemer (eds) *Public Management: Public and Private Perspectives*. California: Mayfield Publishing Co.

Allison, G. and Zelikow, P. (1999) *Essence of Decision: Explaining the Cuban Missile Crisis* (2nd edn). New York: Longman.

Alvesson, M. (1995) The meaning and meaningless of postmodernism: some ironic remarks, *Organisation Studies*, 16(6): 1047–75.

Apter, M. (1989) *Reversal Theory: Motivation, Emotion and Personality*. London: Routledge.

Argyris, C. (2000) *Flawed Advice and the Management Trap: How Managers Can Know When They're Getting Good Advice and When They're Not*. Oxford: Oxford University Press.

Ashton, T. (1999) The health reforms: to market and back, in J. Boston, P. Dalziel and S. St John (eds) *Redesigning the Welfare State in New Zealand*. Auckland: Oxford University Press.

Ascher, K. (1987) *The Politics of Privatization: Contracting Out Public Services*. Basingstoke: Macmillan.

Bache, I. (2001) Different seeds in the same plot? Competing models of capitalism and the incomplete contracts of partnership design, *Public Administration*, 79(2): 337–59.

Baldwin, R. and Cave, M. (1999) *Understanding Regulation: Theory, Strategy and Practice*. Oxford: Oxford University Press.

Banks, J. and Weingast, B. (1992) The political control of bureaucracies under asymmetric information, *American Journal of Political Science*, 36: 509–24.

Bardach, E. (1998) *Getting Agencies to Work Together: The Practice and Theory of Managerial Craftsmanship*. Washington, DC: Brookings Institution.

Behn, R. (2001) *Re-thinking Democratic Accountability*. Washington, DC: Brookings Institution.

Bekkers, V., Homburg, V. and Smeekes, M. (2002) The myths of e-government: balancing between rhetoric and reality. Paper presented to the 6th International Research Seminar on Public Management, University of Edinburgh, 8–10 April.

Bellamy, C. and Taylor, J. (1998) *Governing in the Information Age*. Buckingham: Open University Press.

Berg, A. (2001) The concept of value in public sector reform discourse, *Concepts and Transformation*, 6(1): 39–57.

Blair, T. (2002) I have learned the limits of government, *Independent*, 20 May: 15.

Blanchard, K. and Johnson, S. (1996) *The One-minute Manager*. London: HarperCollins (originally published in New York in 1983).

Bok, S. (1982) *Secrets: On the Ethics of Concealment and Revelation*. New York: Pantheon.

Böllhoff, D. (2000) The new regulatory regime: the institutional design of telecommunications regulation at the national level. Paper presented to the Conference on Common Goods and Governance across Multiple Areas, Bonn, June/July.

Borrins, S. (1998) *Innovating with Integrity: How Local Heroes are Transforming American Government*. Washington, DC: Georgetown University Press.

Bovens, M. (1998) *The Quest for Responsibility: Accountability and Citizenship in Complex Organisations*. Cambridge: Cambridge University Press.

Bovens, M. and Zouridis, S. (2002) From street-level to system-level bureaucracies: how information and communication technology is transforming administrative discretion and constitutional control, *Public Administration Review*, 62(2): 174–84.

Bower, T. (1995) *Maxwell: The Final Verdict*. London: HarperCollins.

Boyne, G. (2002) Public and private management: what's the difference?, *Journal of Management Studies*, 39(1): 97–122.

Boyne, G., Jenkins, G. and Poole, M. (1999) Human resource management in the public and private sectors: an empirical comparison, *Public Administration*, 77(2): 407–20.

Boyne, G., Farrell, C., Law, J., Powell, M. and Walker, R. (2003) *Evaluating public management reforms*, Buckingham, Open University Press.

Brereton, M. and Temple, M. (1999) The new public service ethos: an ethical environment for governance, *Public Administration*, 77(3): 455–74.

Brown, T. (2001) Modernization or failure? IT development projects in the UK public sector, *Financial Accountability and Management*, 17(4): 363–81.

Bunyan, J. (1965) (ed. R. Sharrock) *The Pilgrim's Progress*. Harmondsworth: Penguin.

Bureau of Transport and Communication Economics (1995) *Evaluation of the Black Spot Program*. Canberra: Australian Government Publishing Service.

Cabinet Office (2000) *Wiring it up: Whitehall's Management of Cross-cutting Policies*. London: Performance and Innovation Unit, January.

Castells, M. (1997) *The Power of Identity: The Information Age: Economy, Society and Culture*, Volume 2. Oxford: Blackwell.

CEAS Consultants (Wye) Ltd, Centre for European Agricultural Studies and Institute for the Management of Dairy Companies, Technische Universitat Munchen (1999) *Evaluation of the School Milk Measure: Final Report*, for DGVI, European Commission.

Centre for Management and Policy Studies (2000) Joined-up solutions to policy development. Summary of a Policy Focus Seminar on Achieving Cross-Cutting Policies, held at the Royal College of Pathologists, 24 October (http://cmps.gov.uk/whatson/cdt/sem (accessed 12 December 2001)).

Chancellor of the Duchy of Lancaster (1997) *Next Steps: Agencies in Government: Review 1996*, Cm3579. London: The Stationery Office.

Chancellor of the Exchequer (1998) *Modern Public Services for Britain: Investing in Reform*, Cm4011. London: The Stationery Office.

Chapman, R. (ed.) (1993) *Ethics in Public Service*. Edinburgh: Edinburgh University Press.

Chapman, R. (ed.) (2000) *Ethics in Public Service for the New Millennium*. Aldershot: Ashgate.

Christensen, T. and Lægreid, P. (2001) *New Public Management: The Transformation of Ideas and Practice*. Aldershot: Ashgate.

Clarke, J. and Newman, J. (1997) *The Managerial State: Power, Politics and Ideology in the Remaking of Social Welfare*. London: Sage.

Committee of Independent Experts (1999) *First Report on Allegations Regarding Fraud, Mismanagement and Nepotism in the European Commission*. Brussels: Committee of Independent Experts.

Committee of Public Accounts (1994) *The Proper Conduct of Public Business*, 8th report, session 1993–1994. London: House of Commons.

Committee of Public Accounts (2000) *Improving the Delivery of Government IT Projects*. 1st report, session 1999–2000. London: House of Commons.

Conseil Scientifique de l'Evaluation (1996) *Petit guide de l'évaluation des politiques publiques*. Paris: Conseil Scientifique de l'Evaluation.

Cracknell, B. (2000) *Evaluating Development Aid: Issues, Problems and Solutions*. London: Sage.

Crosland, A. (1970) *A Social Democratic Britain*. London: Fabian Society (Fabian Tract 404).

Cubbon, B. (1993) The duty of the professional, in R. Chapman (ed.) *Ethics in Public Service*. Edinburgh: Edinburgh University Press.

Davies, H., Nutley, S. and Smith, P. (2000) *What Works? Evidence-based Policy and Practice in Public Services*. Bristol: Policy Press.

Denman, R. (2002) *The Mandarin's Tale*. Westminster: Politico's.

DETR (Department of Environment, Transport and the Regions) (2000) Cross-cutting issues in public policy and public service. Report for the DETR, produced by a team from the School of Public Policy, University of Birmingham (http://www.local-regions.dtlr.gov.uk/cross/ccps/02.htm (accessed 15 September 2001)).

Dimock, M. (1936) The meaning and scope of public administration, in J. Gaus, L. White and M. Dimock, *The Frontiers of Public Administration*. Chicago, IL: University of Chicago Press.

Donaldson, L. (2001) *The Contingency Theory of Organizations*. Thousand Oaks, CA: Sage.

Dorrell, S. (1993) Public sector change is a world-wide movement. Speech by the Financial Secretary to the Treasury, Stephen Dorrell, to the Chartered Institute of Public Finance and Accountancy, London, 23 September.

Douma, S. and Schreuder, H. (1998) *Economic Approaches to Organizations* (2nd edn). London: Prentice Hall.

Dowding, K. (1995) Model or metaphor? A critical review of the policy network approach, *Political Studies*, XLIII: 136–58.

Dowie, J. (1999) Communication for better decisions: not about 'risk', *Health, Risk and Society*, 1(1): 41–53.

Drucker, P. (1974) *Management: Tasks, Responsibilities, Practices*. London: Heinemann.

Du Gay, P. (2000) *In Praise of Bureaucracy*. London: Sage.

Dunleavy, P. (1991) *Democracy, Bureaucracy and Public Choice*. Hemel Hempstead: Harvester Wheatsheaf.

Dunleavy, P. and Margetts, H. (2000) The advent of digital government: public bureaucracies and the state in the internet age. Paper presented at the Annual Conference of the American Political Science Association, Omni Shoreham Hotel, Washington, DC, 4 September (contacts: P.Dunleavy@lse.ac.uk and H.Margetts@ucl.ac.uk).

Dunsire, A., Hartley, K., Parker, D. and Dimitrou, B. (1988) Organizational status and performance: a conceptual framework for testing public choice theories, *Public Administration*, 66(4): 363–88.

Durman, P. (2001) A privatisation doomed from the beginning, *Sunday Times*, 14 October: 3.6.

Eccles, M. (ed. S. Hyman) (1951) *Beckoning Frontiers: Public and Personal Recollections*. New York: Knopf.

European Commission (1997) *Evaluation of EU Expenditure Programmes: A Guide* (1st edn), Brussels, DGXIX/02, January.

European Commission (1999) *Evaluating Socio-economic Programmes: The MEANS Collection* (6 volumes). Luxembourg: Office for Official Publications of the European Communities.

European Commission (2000) *Code of Good Administrative Behavior for Staff of the European Commission in their Relations with the Public* (http://www.cc.cec/guide/codepers/code_en.htm (accessed 28 October 2001)).

Fitzgibbon, C. (2000) Education: realising the potential, in H. Davies, S. Nutley and P. Smith (eds) *What works? Evidence-based Policy and Practice in Public Services*, Bristol: The Policy Press.

Flynn, N. (2002) *Public Sector Management* (4th edn). Harlow: Financial Times/Prentice Hall.

Frissen, P. (1998) Public administration in cyberspace: a postmodern perspective, in I. Snellen and W. van de Donk (eds) *Public Administration in an Information Age: A Handbook*. Amsterdam: IOS Press.

Gains, F. (2000) Understanding department–agency relationships. PhD thesis, Department of Politics, University of Sheffield.

Gaster, L. (1995) *Quality in Public Services: Managers' Choices*. Buckingham: Open University Press.

Goodwin, B. (2000) *Ethics at Work*. Dordrecht: Kluwer.

Graham, G. (1994) *Free-nets and the Politics of Community in Electronic Networks* (net-happenings@net.internic.is) (quoted in Bellamy and Taylor, 1998: 110).

Greer, J. (2001) *Partnership Governance in Northern Ireland: Improving Performance*. Aldershot: Ashgate.

Grice, A. and Russell, B. (2002) Labour to fail on public service targets, *Independent*, 14 January: 1.

Gruening, G. (2001) Origin and theoretical basis of New Public Management, *International Journal of Public Management*, 4(1): 1–25.

Hackman, R. and Wageman, R. (1995) Total Quality Management: empirical, conceptual and practical issues, *Administrative Science Quarterly*, 40: 309–42.

Hacque, M. (2001) The diminishing publicness of public service under the current mode of governance, *Public Administration Review*, 61(1) January/February: 65–82.

Hagen, M. and Kubicek, H. (2000) *One-stop Government in Europe: Results from 11 National Surveys*. Bremen: University of Bremen Press.

Hammond, K. (1996) *Human Judgement and Social Policy: Irreducible Uncertainty, Inevitable Error, Unavoidable Injustice*. New York: Oxford University Press.

Hartley, J. and Allison, M. (2000) The role of leadership in the modernization and improvement of public services, *Public Money and Management*, 20(2) April/June: 35–40.

Held, D. (1987) *Models of Democracy*. Cambridge: Polity.

Held, D. and Pollitt, C. (eds) (1986) *New Forms of Democracy*. London: Sage.

Heseltine, M. (1980) Ministers and management in Whitehall, *Management Services in Government*, 35: 5.

Heseltine, M. (1987) *Where There's a Will*. London: Hutchinson.

HM Treasury (1997) *Appraisal and Evaluation in Central Government*. London: The Stationery Office.

Hodge, G. (2000) *Privatization: An International Review of Performance*. Boulder, CO: Westview.

Homburg, V. (2000) The political economy of information exchange politics and property rights in the development and use of interorganizational systems, *Knowledge, Technology and Policy*, 13(3): 49–66.

Hood, C. (1991) A public management for all seasons, *Public Administration*, 69(1) spring: 3–19.

Hood, C. (1998) *The Art of the State: Culture, Rhetoric and Public Management*. Oxford: Oxford University Press.

Hood, C. and Jackson, M. (1991) *Administrative Argument*. Aldershot: Dartmouth.

Hood, C., James, O., Jones, G., Scott, C. and Travers, A. (1998) Regulation inside government: where the New Public Management meets the audit explosion, *Public Money and Management*, 18(2) April/June: 61–8.

Hood, C., Scott, C., James, O., Jones, G. and Travers, A. (1999) *Regulation Inside Government: Waste Watchers, Quality Police, and Sleaze-busters*. Oxford: Oxford University Press.

Hood, C., Rothstein, H. and Baldwin, R. (2001) *The Government of Risk: Understanding Risk Regulation Schemes*. Oxford: Oxford University Press.

Hunt, J. (1983) Cabinet strategy and management. Speech to the annual conference of the Chartered Institute of Public Finance and Accountancy, London.

Hupe, P. and Meijs, L. (2000) *Hybrid Governance: The Impact of the Nonprofit Sector in the Netherlands*. The Hague: Social and Cultural Planning Office.

Huxham, C. and Vangen, S. (2000a) What makes partnerships work?, in S. Osborne (ed.) *Public–Private Partnerships*. London: Routledge.

Huxham, C. and Vangen, S. (2000b) Leadership in the shaping of collaboration agendas: how things happen in a (not quite) joined-up world, *Academy of Management Journal*, 43(6): 1159–75.

IPPR (2001) *Building Better Partnerships*. London: Institute for Public Policy Research.

Jackson, B. (2001) *Management Gurus and Management Fashions*. London: Routledge.

Jackson, P. (2001) Public sector added value: can bureaucracy deliver?, *Public Administration*, 79(1): 5–28.

Joint Committee on Standards for Educational Evaluation (1994) *The Program Evaluation Standards*. London: Sage.

Jones, L. (2001) Public management reform: is the tide changing?, *IPMN Newsletter*, No. 1, (inpuman-1@lyris.unisg.ch (accessed 18 May 2001)).

Jørgensen, T. (1999) The public sector in an in-between time: searching for new public values, *Public Administration*, 77(3): 565–84.

Jørgenson, T. and Bozeman, B. (2002) Public values lost? Comparing cases on contracting out from Denmark and the United States, *Public Management Review*, 4(1): 63–81.

Joss, R. and Kogan, M. (1995) *Advancing Quality: Total Quality Management in the National Health Service*. Buckingham: Open University Press.

Kavanagh, D. and Richards, D. (2001) Departmentalism and joined-up government: back to the future?, *Parliamentary Affairs*, 54: 1–18.

Kemp, P. (1993) *Beyond Next Steps: A Civil Service for the 21st Century*. London: The Social Market Foundation.

Kernaghan, K. (1996) *The Ethics Era in Canadian Public Administration*. Ottawa: CCMD Research Paper no. 19, Minister of Supply and Services.

Kettl, D. (2000) *The Global Public Management Revolution: A Report on the Transformation of Governance*. Washington, DC: Brookings Institution.

Kickert, W., Klijn, E-H. and Koppenjan, J. (eds) (1997) *Managing Complex Networks: Strategies for the Public Sector*. London: Sage.

Kirkpatrick, I., Kitchener, M. and Whipp, R. (2001) 'Out of sight, out of mind': assessing the impact of markets for children's residential care, *Public Administration*, 79(1): 49–71.

Klijn, E-H. (2002) Governing networks in the hollow state: contracting out, process management or a combination of the two?, *Public Management Review*, 4(2): 149–65.

Klijn, E-H. and Koppenjan, J. (2000) Politicians and interactive decision making: institutional spoilsports or playmakers, *Public Administration*, 78(2): 365–87.

Kooiman J. (1993) *Modern Governance: New Government–Society Interactions*. London: Sage.

Kouwenhoven, V. (1993) The rise of the public private partnership: a model for the management of public–private co-operation, in J. Kooiman (ed.) *Modern Governance: New Government–Society Interactions*. London: Sage.

Kramer, R. (1969) *Participation of the Poor: Comparative Case Studies in the War on Poverty*. Englewood Cliffs, N.J.: Prentice-Hall.

Lane, J-E. (2000) *New Public Management*. London: Routledge.

Lawton, A. (1998) *Ethical Management for the Public Services*. Buckingham: Open University Press.

Lewis, D. (1997) *Hidden Agendas: Politics, Law and Disorder*. London: Hamish Hamilton.

Light, P. (2001) *To Restore and Renew: Now is the Time to Rebuild the Federal Public Service*. Washington, DC: Brookings Institution (http://www.brookings.edu/views/articles/light/200111ge.htm (accessed 7 November 2001)).

Linder, S. (2000) Coming to terms with the public–private partnership: a grammar of multiple meanings, in P. Rosenau (ed.) *Public–Private Policy Partnerships*. Westwood, MA: Massachusetts Institute of Technology.

Lowndes, V. and Skelcher, C. (1998) The dynamics of multi-organizational partnership: an analysis of changing modes of governance, *Public Administration*, 76(2) summer: 313–34.

Lowndes, V., Pratchett, L. and Stoker, G. (2001a) Trends in public participation; Part 1 – local government perspectives, *Public Administration* 79(1): 205–22.

Lowndes, V., Pratchett, L. and Stoker, G. (2001b) Trends in public participation: Part 2 – citizens' perspectives, *Public Administration*, 79(2): 445–55.

Lynn Jr, L. (1996) *Public Management as Art, Science and Profession*. New Jersey: Chatham House.

Lynn, L., Heinrich, C. and Hill, C. (2001) *Improving Governance: A New Logic for Empirical Research*. Washington, DC: Georgetown University Press.

Manning, N. (2001) The legacy of the New Public Management in developing countries, *International Review of Administrative Sciences*, 67: 297–312.

Margetts, H. (1998) Computerizing the tools of government, in I. Snellen and W. van de Donk (eds) *Public Administration in an Information Age: A Handbook*. Amsterdam: IOS Press.

Marmor, T. (2001) *Fads in Medical Care Policy and Politics: The Rhetoric and Reality of Managerialism*, Rock Carling Lecture. London: Nuffield Provincial Hospitals Trust.

Martin, S. and Boaz, A. (2000) Public participation and citizen-centred local government: lessons from the Best Value and Better Government for Older People pilot programmes, *Public Money and Management*, 20(2) April–June: 47–53.

Martin, S. and Parker, D. (1997) *The Impact of Privatisation: Ownership and Corporate Performance in the UK*. London: Routledge.

McCourt, W. and Minogue, M. (eds) (2001) *The Internationalization of Public Management: Reinventing the Third World State*. Cheltenham: Edward Elgar.

McNulty, T. and Ferlie, E. (2002) *Reengineering Health Care: The Complexities of Organizational Transformation*. Oxford: Oxford University Press.

Meyer, J. and Gupta, V. (1994) The performance paradox, *Research in Organizational Behavior*, 16: 309–69.

Micheletti, M. (2000) The end of big government: is it happening in the Nordic countries?, *Governance*, 13(2): 265–78.

Milner, E. (2000) *Managing Information and Knowledge in the Public Sector*. London: Routledge.

Ministry of Housing and Local Government (1969) *People and Planning: the Report of the Committee on Public Participation in Planning* (the Skeffington Report). London: HMSO.

Molander, P., Nilsson, J-E. and Schick, A. (2002) *Does Anyone Govern? The Relationship Between the Government Office and the Agencies in Sweden*. Stockholm: Report from the SNS Constitutional Project, SNS.

Mountfield, R. (2002) If the civil service is to survive, it needs the security of legislation, *Independent*, 4 March: 4.

National Audit Office (1998) *Benefits Agency: Performance Measurement*, HC952, 25 August. London: The Stationery Office.

National Audit Office (1999) *Government on the Web*, HC87. London: The Stationery Office.

Nickell, S. (1996) Competition and corporate performance, *Journal of Political Economy*, 104(4): 724–46.

Niskanen, W. (1971) *Bureaucracy and Representative Government*. Chicago, IL: Aldine/Atherton.

Noordegraaf, M. (2000) *Attention! Work and Behaviour of Public Managers Amidst Ambiguity*. Delft: Eburon.

OECD (1993) *Managing with Market-type Mechanisms*. Paris: PUMA/OECD.

OECD (1997) *In Search of Results: Performance Management Practices*. Paris: PUMA/OECD.

OECD (1998) *Principles for Managing Ethics in the Public Service: OECD Recommendation*. Paris: PUMA/OECD Policy Brief 4, May.

OECD (2001) *Managing Cross-cutting Issues*. PUMA (http://www.oecd.org/puma/strat/managing.htm (accessed 7 November 2001)).

Office of Public Services Reform (2002) *Better Government Services: Executive Agencies in the 21st Century*. London: Cabinet Office. www.civilservice.gov.uk/agencies (accessed 28 August 2002).

Osborne, S. (ed.) (2000) *Public–Private Partnerships: Theory and Practice in International Perspective*. London: Routledge.

Osborne, D. and Gaebler, T. (1992) *Reinventing Government: How the Entrepreneurial Spirit is Transforming the Public Sector*. Reading, MA: Addison-Wesley.

Owen, R. (1813) (This edition 1991) *A New View of Society and Other Writings*. London: Penguin.

Packwood, T., Pollitt, C. and Roberts, S. (1998) Good medicine? A case study of business process re-engineering in a hospital, *Policy and Politics*, 26(4) October: 401–15.

Parker, D. (1999) Regulating public utilities: what other countries can learn from the UK experience, *Public Management*, 1(1): 93–120.

Patton, M. (1997) *Utilization-focused Evaluation: The New Century Text* (edn 3). Thousand Oaks, CA: Sage.

Pawson, R. and Tilley, N. (1997) *Realistic Evaluation*. London: Sage.

Pemberton, H. (2001) Britain, governance and the 1960s. Paper presented to the European Group on Public Administration conference, Vaasa, Finland, September.

Perry, J. and Wise, L. (1990) The motivational bases of public service, *Public Administration Review*, 50(3): 367–73.

Peters, G. (1999) *Institutional Theory in Political Science: The 'New Institutionalism'*. London: Continuum.

Peters, J. and Waterman, R. (1982) *In Search of Excellence: Lessons from America's Best Run Companies*. New York: Harper and Row.

Peterson, M. (2000) The fate of 'Big Government' in the United States: not over, but undermined?, *Governance*, 13(2): 251–64.

Pierre, J. and Peters, Guy B. (2000) *Governance, Politics and the State*. Basingstoke: Macmillan.

Pierson, P. (2000) Increasing returns, path dependence and the study of politics, *Amercian Political Science Review*, 94(2): 251–67.

Pollitt, C. (1993) (2nd edn) *Managerialism and the Public Services*. Oxford: Blackwell.

Pollitt, C. (1995) Justification by works or by faith? Evaluating the new public management, *Evaluation*, 1(2) October: 133–54.

Pollitt, C. (1998) Evaluation in Europe: boom or bubble?, *Evaluation*, 4(2) April: 214–24.

Pollitt, C. (1999) Stunted by stakeholders? Limits to collaborative evaluation, *Public Policy and Administration*, 14(2): 77–90.

Pollitt, C. (2001a) Clarifying convergence: striking similarities and durable differences in public management reform, *Public Management Review*, 3(4): 1–22.

Pollitt, C. (2001b) Convergence: the useful myth?, *Public Administration*, 79(4): 933–47.

Pollitt, C. (2003) Joined-up government, *Political Studies Review* (1:1, pp 34–49).

Pollitt, C. and Bouckaert, G. (eds) (1995) *Quality Improvement in European Public Services: Concepts, Cases and Commentary*, London: Sage.

Pollitt, C. and Bouckaert, G. (2000) *Public Management Reform: A Comparative Analysis*. Oxford: Oxford University Press.

Pollitt, C. and Summa, H. (1998) Evaluation and the work of Supreme Audit Institutions: an uneasy relationship? in M-C. Kessler, P. Lascoumbes, M. Setbon and J-C. Thoenig (eds) *Evaluation des politiques publiques*, Paris: L'Harmattan.

Pollitt, C. and Talbot, C. (eds) (2003) *Unbundling Government*. London: Taylor and Francis (forthcoming).

Pollitt, C., Birchall, J. and Putman, K. (1998) *Decentralising Public Service Management*. Basingstoke: Macmillan.

Pollitt, C., Girre, X., Lonsdale, J. et al. (1999) *Performance or Compliance? Performance Audit and Public Management in Five Countries*. Oxford: Oxford University Press.

Pollitt, C., Bathgate, K., Caulfield, J., Smullen, A. and Talbot, C. (2001) Agency fever? Analysis of an international fashion, *Journal of Comparative Policy Analysis: Research and Practice*, 3: 271–90.

Ponting, C. (1985) *The Right to Know: The Inside Story of the Belgrano Affair*. London: Sphere.

Powell, W. and DiMaggio, P. (eds) (1991) *The New Institutionalism in Organizational Analysis*. Chicago, IL: University of Chicago Press.

Power, M. (1997) *The Audit Society: Rituals of Verification*. Oxford: Oxford University Press.

Power, M. (2000) The audit society – second thoughts, *International Journal of Auditing*, 4: 111–19.

Prachett, L. and Wingfield, M. (1994) *The Public Service Ethos in Local Government: A Research Report*. London: Commission for Local Democracy.

Prime Minister and Minister for the Cabinet Office (1999) *Modernising Government*, Cm4310. London: The Stationery Office.

Prince, M. (2000) Banishing bureaucracy or hatching a hybrid? The Canadian Food Inspection Agency and the politics of reinventing government, *Governance*, 13(2) April: 215–32.

Rainey, H. (1997) *Understanding and Managing Public Organizations* (2nd edn). San Francisco: Jossey-Bass.

Rainey, H. and Bozeman, B. (2000) Comparing public and privade organizations: empirical research and the power of the *a priori*, *Journal of Public Administration, Research and Theory*, J-Part 10(2): 447–69.

Rainey, H. and Steinbauer, P. (1999) Galloping elephants: developing elements of a theory of effective government organizations, *Journal of Public Administration Research and Theory*, J-Part 9: 1–32.

Rainey, H., Backoff, R. and Levine, C. (1976) Comparing public and private organizations, *Public Administration Review*, 36: 233–46.

Ranade, W. (1997) *A Future for the NHS? Health Care in the 1990s*. Basingstoke: Macmillan.

Ranson, S. and Stewart, J. (1994) *Management in the Public Domain: Enabling the Learning Society*. Basingstoke: Macmillan.

Report of the Task Force on Public Service Values and Ethics (1996) *A Strong Foundation*. Ottawa: Canadian Centre for Management Development.

Rhodes, R. (1997) (ed.) *Understanding Governance*. Buckingham: Open University Press.

Rohr, J. (1989) *Ethics for Bureaucrats* (2nd edn). New York: Dekker.

Rokeach, M. (1973) *The Nature of Human Values*. New York: Free Press.

Rosenau, P. (2000) The strengths and weaknesses of public–private policy partnerships, in P. Rosenau (ed.) *Public–Private Policy Partnerships*. Westwood, MA: Massachusetts Institute of Technology.

Rowe, M. and Devanney, C. (2002) The challenges of partnership working: a case study of a participatory regeneration project. Paper presented to the International Research Seminar in Public Management 6, Edinburgh University, April (contact: mike.rowe@ntu.ac.uk).

Sahlin-Andersson, K. (2001) National, international and transnational constructions of New Public Management, in T. Christensen and P. Lægreid (eds) *New Public Management: The Transformation of Ideas and Practice*. Aldershot: Ashgate.

Sampson, A. (1977) *The Arms Bazaar – the Companies, the Dealers, the Bribes: From Vickers to Lockheed*. London: Hodder and Stoughton.

Schmidt, A.M.G. (1987) *Tot hier toe: gedichten en liedjes voor toneel, radio en televisie, 1938–85*. Amsterdam: Em. Querido's Uitgeverij, BV.

Scott, J. (1998) *Seeing Like a State: How Certain Schemes to Improve the Human Condition have failed*. New Haven: Yale University Press.

Shadish, W., Cook, T. and Leviton, L. (1991) *Foundations of Program Evaluation: Theories of Practice*. London: Sage.

Simon, H. (2000) Public administration in today's world of organisations and markets. John Gaus Lecture to the American Political Science Association, Washington, DC, 1 September.

Simon, H., Smithburg, D. and Thompson, V. (1950) *Public Administration*. New York: Knopf.

Smith, P. (1996) On the unintended consequences of publishing performance data in the public sector, *International Journal of Public Administration*, 18(2/3): 277–305.

Smithers, R. (2002) Schools cheat to boost exam results, *Guardian*, 5 June: 1.

Smullen, A. (2002) Extract from an interview conducted in March 2002 by Amanda Smullen of Erasmus University Rotterdam as part of her doctoral research into agencies.

Smullen, A. (2003) Lost in translation? Shifting interpretations of the concept of 'agency': the Dutch case, in C. Pollitt and C. Talbot (eds) *Unbundled Government*. London: Taylor and Francis (forthcoming).

Snellen, I. and van de Donk, W. (1998) *Public Administration in an Information Age: A Handbook.* Amsterdam: IOS Press.

Sontag, S. (1993) *The Volcano Lover: A Romance.* London: Vintage.

Staats, E. (1988) Public service and the public interest, *Public Administration Review,* 48(2): 601–5.

Stewart, J. (1996) *Further Innovation in Democratic Practice.* Birmingham: School of Public Policy, University of Birmingham, Occasional Paper 3.

Summa, H. (1992) The rhetoric of efficiency: applied social science as de-politicization, in R. Harvey-Brown (ed.) *Writing the Social Text.* New York: de Gruyter.

Talbot, C. and Caulfield, J. (2002) Hard agencies in soft states: a study of agency creation programmes in Jamaica, Latvia and Tanzania. Report for the Department for International Development, UK, Pontypridd, University of Glamorgan.

Taylor, F. (1913) *The Principles of Scientific Management.* New York: Harper and Brothers.

Teisman, G. and Klijn, E-H. (2002) Partnership arrangements: governmental rhetoric or governance scheme?, *Public Administration Review,* March/April, 62(2): 197–205.

Thompson, J. (2000) Reinvention as reform: assessing the National Performance Review, *Public Administration Review,* 60(6) November/December: 508–21.

Treasury Board of Canada (1995) *Blueprint for Renewing Government Services using Information Technology.* Ottawa: Treasury Board of Canada.

UK Parliament (2002) *Standards in Public Life* (http://www.parliament/guide/stan.htm (accessed 20 February 2002)).

Usborne, D. (2002) Blomberg plots collision course with city's heroes, *Independent,* 4 January: 11.

van Gunsteren, H. (1979) Public and private, *Social Research: An International Quarterly of Political and Social Science,* 46(2): 255–71.

van Tulder, R., van den Berghe, D. and Muller, A. (2001) *The World's Largest Firms and Internationalization.* Erasmus (S)coreboard of Core Companies. Rotterdam: Rotterdam School of Management/Erasmus University Rotterdam.

van Wart, M. (1996) 'Re-inventing' the public sector: the critical role of value restructuring, *Public Administration Quarterly,* 19(4): 456–78.

Vickers G. (1973) *Making Institutions Work.* London: Associated Business Programmes Ltd.

Walker, R. (2001) Great expectations: can social science evaluate New Labour's policies?, *Evaluation,* 7(3): 305–30.

Waugh, P. (2001) Porter is ordered to repay £26.5M in votes scandal, *Independent,* 14 December: 2.

Weick, K. (1979) *The Social Psychology of Organizing* (2nd edn). Reading, MA: Addison-Wesley.

Whitley, R. (1988) The management sciences and management skills, *Organization Studies,* 9(1): 47–68.

Whitley, R. (1989) On the nature of managerial tasks and skills: their distinguishing characteristics and organization, *Journal of Management Studies,* 26(3): 209–24.

Wilmott, H. (1995) Will the turkeys vote for Christmas? The re-engineering of human resources, in G. Burke and J. Peppard (eds) *Examining Business Process Re-engineering.* London: Cranfield University School of Management.

World Bank (2000) *Anticorruption in Transition: A Contribution to the Policy Debate.* Washington, DC: World Bank.

Zbaracki, M. (1998) The rhetoric and reality of Total Quality Management, *Administrative Science Quarterly,* 43: 602–36.

Zegens, M. (1997) The dilemma of the modern public manager: satisfying the virtues of scientific and innovative management, in A. Altshuler and R. Behn (eds) *Innovation in American Government: Challenges, Opportunities, and Dilemmas*. Washington, DC: Brookings Institute.

Zilbergeld, B. (1984) A one-minute essay, more or less, on the one-minute books, *Psychology Today*, August: 6–7.

Zouridis, S. (1998) Information technology and the organization chart of public administration, in I. Snellen and W. van de Donk (eds) *Public Administration in an Information Age: A Handbook*. Amsterdam: IOS Press.

Index

PROVIDING QUALITY IN THE PUBLIC SECTOR
A PRACTICAL APPROACH TO IMPROVING PUBLIC SERVICES
Lucy Gaster and Amanda Squires

This book argues that if public services are to be 'reformed' or 'improved', achieving the best possible quality of service is essential.

It starts from the premise that citizens and users are the key 'stakeholders'. They need to be consulted and involved at every stage. Within inevitable resource constraints, it is their needs, balanced with those of society, which must be met. Service providers need to change their culture and behaviour to make this happen.

This book presents a straightforward and comprehensive model for understanding quality and putting it into practice. Existing quality philosophies and approaches are examined. Overviews of recent policy on quality in central and local government, in the health service, and in public service partnerships are included. Finally, five practitioners present practical 'vignettes' of citizen involvement, local partnerships, and quality improvement in health, housing and local government.

Providing Quality in the Public Sector is essential reading for students and practitioners in the fields of public policy, local government, health, housing and the voluntary sector.

John Crawley, Michael Greenwood, Tessa Harding, Carol Hayden and Pat Scrutton each contribute a chapter to the book.

Contents
Introduction – The public policy context – The conceptual framework: stakeholders, values, objectives and definitions – Implementing quality – Standards, monitoring and evaluation – Quality in central government – Quality in local government – Quality in health – Quality issues in partnership working – Quality from the citizen's perspective: campaigning, consultation and involvement – Partnership and participation: better government for older people in South Lanarkshire – Making it work in health: a stakeholder model for quality management – Making it work in housing: choice and need in social housing – Making it work in local government: experiences of Tameside MBC – Conclusions and reflections – Appendix: The language of quality – a glossary of terms – Bibliography – Index.

320pp   0 335 20955 6 (Paperback)   0 335 20956 4 (Hardback)

DECENTRALIZING THE CIVIL SERVICE
FROM UNITARY STATE TO DIFFERENTIATED POLITY IN THE UNITED KINGDOM

R. A. W. Rhodes, P Carmichael, J Mcmillan and A Massey (eds)

This book is concerned with the civil services of the United Kingdom, examining their characteristics and trends since 1970. It provides a map of the British civil service beyond Whitehall, giving an individual country-by-country analysis of the civil services of the UK. It considers the implications of the changing nature of the civil services for our understanding of British governance, especially in the context of the public sector management reforms of the 1980s and 1990s and the impact of constitutional change (chiefly devolution) since 1998. Given that devolution has been characterized as a process rather than an event, the book brings to bear evidence of how existing longstanding differences within some parts of British public administration may come to be replicated elsewhere in the UK.

The authors also explore two controversial propositions. First it asks whether Britain is moving from the unitory, strong executive of the "Westminster model" to a "differentiated polity" characterized by institutional fragmentation. Second, it considers whether an unintended consequence of recent changes is a "hollowing out of the state". Is the British executive losing functions downwards to devolved governments and special-purpose bodies and outwards to regional offices and agencies with a resulting loss of central capacity? Substantial empirical data (both quantitative and qualitative) has been amassed here in order to give answers to these questions.

The Devolution of the Civil Service assesses the UK's changing civil services in the wake of two decades of public sector management reforms and New Labour's constitutional reform programme, most notably devolution to Scotland, Wales and Northern Ireland. This assessment has significant implications for how we view governance in the UK.

Contents

192pp   0 335 21234 4 (Paperback)   0 335 21235 2 (Hardback)

EVALUATING PUBLIC MANAGEMENT REFORMS
PRINCIPLES AND PRACTICE

George Boyne, Catherine Farrell, Jennifer Law, Martin Powell and Richard Walker

Governments across the world are pursuing reform in an effort to improve public services. But have these reforms actually led to improvements in services? *Evaluating Public Management Reforms* develops a framework for a theory-based evaluation of reforms, and then uses this framework to assess the impact of new arrangements for public service delivery in the UK. This book:

- identifies the conceptual and practical problems of finding clear criteria for evaluating reforms
- focuses on the shifts in public management towards markets and competition, towards the publication of performance indicators, and from larger to smaller organizations
- considers what impact these reforms have had on the efficiency, responsiveness and equity of services
- comprehensively reviews the evidence on the effects of reform on health care, housing and education
- discusses the implications for public sector management.

Contents
Introduction – Criteria of evaluation – Methods of evaluation – Health reforms – Housing reforms – Education reforms – Conclusion – References – Index.

192pp   0 335 20246 2 (Paperback)   0 335 20247 0 (Hardback)